# THE WAR
# AGAINST
# THE PRESS

## Also by Peter Stoler

Decline and Fail:
The Ailing Nuclear Power Industry
The Computer Generation

# THE WAR AGAINST THE PRESS

## Politics, Pressure and Intimidation in the 80's

## Peter Stoler

Dodd, Mead & Company
New York

Published by Dodd, Mead & Company, Inc.
79 Madison Avenue, New York, N.Y. 10016
Distributed in Canada by
McClelland and Stewart Limited, Toronto
Manufactured in the United States of America
Designed by Erich Hobbing

First Edition

1   2   3   4   5   6   7   8   9   10

*Library of Congress Cataloging-in-Publication Data*

Stoler, Peter.
  The war against the press.

  Bibliography: p.
  Includes index.
  1. Press—United States—History.   2. Government and
the press—United States—History.   I. Title.
PN4855.S78   1986      071'.3      86-13469
ISBN 0-396-08757-4

*For Judith,*
*who knows why.*

# CONTENTS

*Chapter One*   The Big Chill                                         1

   The embattled press and its attackers, an introduction to the
   changing public view of the press, and a look at who is waging
   war on the media and why.

*Chapter Two*   The Necessary Evil                                    16

   The origins of the ideas of freedom of speech and the press,
   how they were embodied in the U.S. Constitution, and how
   they fostered the growth of the U.S. press.

*Chapter Three*   A New Dimension                                     37

   The advent of electronic journalism and how it changed the
   nature of the news business and America's idea of what is
   news.

*Chapter Four*   The Adversary Relationship                           57

   The press, the Vietnam War, and the growing estrangement
   between media and government.

*Chapter Five*   Watergate and the Court of Public                    70
                 Opinion

   The anatomy of an exposé; how the press helped to investigate
   a crime and oust a President.

*Chapter Six*   Winners and Sinners                                   85

   The press's success in exposing corruption and misconduct,
   its failures to spot some subtler trends; the high cost of being
   wrong.

*Chapter Seven*   The Media Held Hostage                     104

The press's role in covering terrorism. When is any coverage too much?

*Chapter Eight*   A Tilt Toward the Left or a Pull          121
                  Toward the Right?

Are the American news media dominated by liberal thinkers and does it make a difference? Are the media being pulled toward the right?

*Chapter Nine*   A Case of Libel                             135

The Westmoreland, Sharon, and Tavoulareas cases. How the threat of libel suits is intimidating the media.

*Chapter Ten*   The Perils of Polling                        155

Calling elections before all the results are in. Do polls affect election results?

*Chapter Eleven*   Shutting Off the Flow                     165

The Reagan Administration and the campaign to keep Americans uninformed; the Freedom of Information Act under attack.

*Chapter Twelve*   As Others See Us                          181

What the American public *really* thinks of the news media; the good news—and the bad.

*Chapter Thirteen*   Warding Off the Chill                   194

How the media can regain public confidence and support against its attackers.

*Chapter Fourteen*   Fighting Back                           205

How the media can assure their survival.

Source Notes                                                 209
Bibliography                                                 215
Index                                                        217

# THE WAR
# AGAINST
# THE PRESS

# Chapter One

# The Big Chill

The press is a sort of wild animal in our midst—
restless, gigantic, always seeking ways to use its
strength. The sovereign press for the most part acknowl-
edges accountability to no one except its owners and
publishers.

ZECHARIA CHAFEE, JR.,
*The Press Under Pressure,*
Nieman Reports, April 1948

They see themselves as crusaders, paladins who maintain the right with
pens instead of swords. They see themselves as keepers of a sacred tradition, started by such secular saints as Thomas Paine and John Peter Zenger,
of printing the truth without fear of the consequences. They see themselves
as heroes who, though they frequently drink too much and often seem to
have more trouble than many keeping their marriages together, can and
quite regularly do make up for the messes they have made of their own
lives by straightening out those of their readers and viewers. They see
themselves as a crucial part of the American system, watchdogs to keep
a careful eye on public and corporate officials, guardians of the rights
and liberties of the people.

Journalists, in short, tend to see themselves as the good guys, as Davids
battling the Goliaths of big business and big government, as witnesses
who risk—and occasionally lose—their lives to get to where the news is
happening and to tell their readers and viewers not only what is happening,
but what it all means. Newsmen tend to see themselves as protectors of
the weak and powerless, as righters of wrongs, as tellers of the truth. In
their mind's eyes, they are the bringers of messages that must, pleasant
or not, be heeded.

Scratch a journalist, and, as often as not, you will find someone who
considers himself at least as important to the survival of the American

republic as a congressman or senator. But scratch the man on the street and you may get a different description of journalists. For the American public does not always share journalists' idealized view of themselves. The public has always considered journalism a rather raffish trade, perceived its practitioners as being something less than gentle, perfect knights. Its opinions have been reinforced by books about the rivalry between William Randolph Hearst and Joseph Pulitzer (who cast objectivity and respect for facts to the winds in their efforts to use the Spanish-American War to sell newspapers), molded by plays like Hecht and MacArthur's *The Front Page* and films like *His Girl Friday,* and shaped by the excesses of the trade's scandal sheets. The American public thus has long thought of journalists as uncommon gossips more interested in spectacle than substance and interested only a little, if at all, in the damage their work can do to people, careers, lives. Comic Fred Allen, who tried hard and not always successfully to keep his private life truly private, spoke for people other than himself when he said acidly that "to a newspaperman a human being is an item with the skin wrapped around it."[1]

America's view of the press improved slightly during the 1970s when *The Washington Post*'s Robert Woodward and Carl Bernstein did a piece of investigative reporting that lifted the lid off the Watergate scandal and helped drive President Richard Nixon from office. The pair were hailed as heroes and lionized on college campuses, where they were regarded by students as models of what they themselves wanted to be when they grew up. So great, in fact, were the numbers of young people who dreamed of following their footsteps to fame and, yes, fortune, that top journalism schools like New York's Columbia University and the University of Missouri were overwhelmed with applicants.

But the adulation did not last. In fact, it eroded quickly once reporters began turning what James Reston of *The New York Times* once described as "the artillery of the press" on Nixon's successor, Gerald Ford. It evanesced rapidly as Americans who had once cheered as the press exposed the deceit and deception surrounding the U.S. role in Vietnam began to wonder if American troops and their leaders would have fared better on the battlefield if they had been subjected to less scrutiny in the news media. Today, neither journalism nor journalists are held in particularly high regard in the United States. "No reporter or editor needs to be told these days that the press is not a universally beloved institution," wrote columnist Anthony Lewis in *The New York Times* shortly after the 1984 presidential election.[2]

Lewis is right. Ask Americans what they think of journalists today, and they are likely to voice opinions that cannot help but make the press and its members see themselves in a different light. To a growing extent, Americans believe that journalists are rude, that they show no regard for either an individual or his office. As far as a great many Americans are concerned, journalists meddle in politics and the affairs of government; they harass businessmen, educators, and religious leaders. Nor is this all. In the view of a significant number of Americans, journalists invade the privacy of individuals, exploiting them for their own ends, then move on without so much as a thought for the pain and chaos they may leave in their wakes. Journalists, many Americans feel, are not always patriotic; they are generally cynical, arrogant, and self-righteous. They do not take well to criticism. Assuming that truth is on their side, they dismiss as uninformed cranks or unthinking ideologues those who feel, not always without cause, that journalists sometimes twist the facts to support their liberal ideas. To make matters worse, many Americans believe, journalists claim that their behavior is not only sanctioned by the Constitution of the United States, but is actually sanctified, giving them not only the right to act as they do, but the obligation.

No doubt about it: the press's status is slipping. As reporters and editors have been made increasingly—and painfully—aware, journalists, who once ranked near the top of the scale when Americans were asked whom they most admired, now rank down near the bottom, keeping company with used-car salesmen and Chicago aldermen. The National Opinion Research Center found back in 1976 that at least 29 percent of Americans had "a great deal of confidence" in the press. In 1983, it found, that figure had fallen to an all-time low of 13.7 percent.[3]

The polls showed that the press's standing had suffered. But an even more vivid indication of the press's decreasing prestige came later that year when the Reagan Administration sent U.S. troops to invade the Caribbean island of Grenada and, in an unprecedented move, excluded journalists from the operation. Journalists and their editors were outraged and argued passionately that the President was not only trampling on the press's traditional freedom, but that he was carelessly, and even possibly illegally, ignoring the public's right to know.

NBC News commentator John Chancellor, an articulate and outspoken veteran who had covered three wars and even more political battles, expressed the media view of what was happening. "The American government," said Chancellor, "is doing whatever it wants to, without any representative of the American public watching what it is doing."[4] Other reporters and editors, from *Time* and *Newsweek, The New York Times,* the wire services, and the other news networks, expressed similar views.

But their readers and viewers had few problems with the media's exclusion. Chancellor's own viewers rejected his premise that journalists stand in for, or represent, the people. In some five hundred letters and telephone calls to NBC during and immediately after the Grenada invasion, viewers supported the press ban by a striking margin of five to one. Nor did those who watched other networks take a different tack. ABC News anchorman Peter Jennings reported that 99 percent of the mail he received from his viewers supported the President. Newspaper protests against the exclusion evoked a similar response. In an informal survey of mail received by some dozen American dailies, the trade magazine *Editor and Publisher* found that letters were running three to one in favor of the Reagan Administration's decision to keep the press out of Grenada. At *Time,* which received 225 letters on the subject, the mail ran eight to one against the press.[5]

The support for the Administration's decision to exclude the press was anything but universal. But it was strong, and much of it was expressed in terms that can only be described as gleeful, or even, occasionally, vengeful. Some letter writers seemed pleased that the press had been put in its place, like the Massachusetts man who wrote to *The Boston Globe* to gloat over the fact that "the liberal media has had its day." But even many of the more thoughtful writers seemed to share some deep-seated, long-term resentment of the press. A West Hollywood, California, woman wrote to the *Los Angeles Herald Examiner* to declare that "journalists are out of touch with majority values, such as honor, duty and service to country . . . they are alienated from the very society that they purport to serve." A Colorado man told *The Denver Post* that "the media have frequently misused sensitive and explosive events as opportunities for personal glory and financial gain."[6]

Editors, few of whom were under any illusions as to the popularity of the press to begin with, were amazed by the outpouring. Admitted Max Frankel, the editorial page editor of *The New York Times,* "The most astounding thing about the Grenada situation was the quick, facile assumption by some of the public that the press wanted to get in not to witness the invasion on behalf of the people, but to sabotage it."[7]

This assumption was not, however, unique to the uninformed. Admiral Donald Metcalf, the naval officer in overall charge of the Grenada operation, quickly made it clear that he favored the idea of excluding the news media and displayed a perverse pleasure in his power to keep the press uninformed and away from the action. Under Metcalf's orders, journalists who attempted to reach Grenada by boat were turned back by the U.S. Navy, which sent destroyers racing across the bows of chartered craft and dispatched a plane to make a mock bombing run on a boat chartered by a television news crew.[8]

Nor did those journalists who did manage to reach Grenada escape being stymied by Metcalf and his minions. *Time*'s Bernard Diederich and *The Washington Post*'s Edward Cody had been hearing invasion rumors and had flown into Grenada a day before U.S. troops began landing. With what amounted to front-row seats, the two, who together had more than fifty years' experience covering Central America and the Caribbean, should have been able to scoop the world with their eyewitness accounts of U.S. Army Rangers parachuting onto Grenada's defended airfield or landing on its beaches. What they got instead was frustration as U.S. troops took them off the island "for their own safety," brought them out to ships standing offshore, and then held them there, refusing to send their reports back to their offices in New York and Washington.[9]

Reporters, noting that journalists had routinely accompanied American invasion forces in World War II, the Korean Conflict, and Vietnam, asked Metcalf why they were being treated differently now. Metcalf's reply was revealing. "Because," he said in a tone that all present found belligerent, "you guys were on our side then."[10]

Metcalf's outburst is ominous, for it reflects more than the uninformed opinion of a military man who would prefer, in the midst of an invasion, not to deal with an impatient horde of reporters, photographers, cameramen, and technicians. It is ominous because it reflects what a great many Americans believe. It is ominous because it constitutes the war cry of a campaign to discredit, to muzzle, to disarm the American news media and to trim their power to the point where they will be unable effectively to fulfill their function and keep the American public informed.

Does this mean that the First Amendment is under assault? Not directly. The language of the First Amendment remains unchanged. "Congress," it says, "shall make no law . . . abridging the freedom of the press . . ." Neither the Congress nor the President has attempted to enact such a law, at least lately. In fact, in many ways, the U.S. press has never been stronger, freer, or less constrained in the history of its existence. The obstacles that the American press must overcome to inform the people, stimulate debate and discussion, and provide its readers and viewers with the information they need if they are to judge the performance of the officials who purport to represent them are minor when compared with those encountered by journalists elsewhere around the world. The U.S. news media are and remain the world's freest. American newsmen need not be licensed, as journalists must be in some African and Asian countries. They need not get their stories past official censors, as journalists must do in the Iron Curtain countries, or as they were until recently required to do in Argentina. Nor need they put up with the minor restrictions that exist in the Scandinavian countries, or in Great Britain, from which American traditions of press freedom evolved.

Compared with the press in other countries, in fact, the American press operates unfettered. A series of U.S. Supreme Court decisions, beginning with a 1964 ruling involving an Alabama police commissioner and *The New York Times,* have all but eliminated the possibility that public officials and so-called public figures can win monetary damages for libel. Further protection has been provided by the states, several of which have enacted "shield laws" designed to safeguard practices, such as refusing to reveal confidential sources, that reporters did not claim as rights as recently as a decade ago. Still more safeguards have been set up by Congress. In an excess of apparent solicitude for the economic needs of the press, Congress has waived antitrust laws in order to preserve "failing" newspapers. Together with the Federal Communications Commission, Congress has been moving steadily toward the removal of virtually all government restrictions, including the so-called "Fairness Doctrine," on broadcasting.

The American news media are economically sound as well. A broadcast license is generally considered, and not without reason, as tantamount to a license to print money; only bad management or incredibly bad luck keep television stations out of the black. Nor are most newspapers any less well off. Daily newspapers are monopolies in all but some three dozen U.S. cities, which means that they can call their own shots on such matters as advertising rates and subscription costs.

Why, then, should the news media be worried? Why should newspaper publishers and television executives predict darkly that the days of press freedom are numbered and wonder whether the United States really wants the free press about which it has so long boasted?

The answers to these questions are obvious. They should worry because the news media are under attack. They are under attack from right-wing politicians like Senators Jesse Helms of North Carolina and Paul Laxalt of Nevada, from the preachers of the religious right, like the Reverends Jerry Falwell and Pat Robertson. They are under attack from big business, which has been using its considerable financial resources to undermine their credibility. They are, finally, under attack from President Ronald Reagan and the members of his administration, none of whom seem comfortable with the idea of a free press and all of whom would much prefer a tame press that will print what they want. They should worry, in short, because there is a war against the press and because those waging it are powerful and determined.

The war against the press is not some conflict that has just erupted, like a border dispute between countries. The war, in fact, has been going on for some time. For the fact is that American presidents and congressmen, churchmen and businessmen, average citizens, and those far above or below average, have long been uneasy about the news media. Thomas Jefferson conceded nearly two hundred years ago that the press was a necessary evil in a democratic system. Indeed, Jefferson concluded, one could not have a democratic government without a free press. "The basis of our government being the opinion of the people, the very first object should be to keep that right," Jefferson wrote a friend in 1787. "And were it left to me to decide whether we should have government without newspapers or newspapers without government, I should not hesitate a moment to prefer the latter."[11]

Other leaders also gave grudging approval to the existence of a free press. Abraham Lincoln felt that the press hindered him in his efforts to preserve the union; William McKinley regarded the press as a pack of hyenas; Woodrow Wilson complained that the press lacked the sophistication or the vision to understand his attempts to bring about world order.

Later presidents proved adept at manipulating the press. Franklin Delano Roosevelt often ignored the press and went over its head to talk directly to the people (he was beloved for his "Fireside Chats"), while Ronald Reagan is excoriated by some for adopting exactly the same approach. John F. Kennedy, who once considered journalism as a career for himself, used his not-inconsiderable charm to manipulate the media, holding frequent news conferences at which he ignored questions and gave the press, and through it, the public, just the answers he wanted.

Courted by Kennedy, the press came into the 1960s on a wave of popularity. It chauvinistically emphasized U.S. successes in space while playing down the country's failures, enthusiastically backed Kennedy's call for an exploration of America's new frontiers. But following Kennedy's assassination, the popularity of the press began to pall. It did so because the press became more probing, less likely to accept what it was told at face value. Reflecting the skepticism of many Americans, the press raised some questions about embarrassing inconsistencies in the reports of the commissions investigating Kennedy's death. Like the public, the press also began to question increasing U.S. involvement in Southeast Asia, suggesting that the administration of Lyndon Johnson was being somewhat less than honest with it and the American people. It annoyed officials and some of those who supported them by presenting them with facts that they would have preferred not to face. Newspapers and television news broadcasts described poverty in the midst of plenty, reported on government waste and inefficiency, questioned "body counts" that purported to show that the United States was winning the formless, ferocious war in Vietnam.

No one loves the bearer of unwelcome news who, as Shakespeare said, "hath but a losing office." So it was not long before politicians and those for whom they claimed to speak began confusing the medium with the message and condemning the press for telling them those things they would rather not hear. Johnson often lamented like King Lear about the problems of dealing with a press that refused to take what he said at face value. Former Vice President Spiro Agnew took matters further. Throughout his 1968 election campaign and in office afterward, he won the support of conservatives and scored points with President Richard Nixon by criticizing what he perceived as the liberal bias of the news media and attacking those whom he alliteratively described as "the nattering nabobs of negativism."

The war against the press escalated during the Nixon Administration, particularly as Nixon proceeded almost pathologically to curb leaks and control the media's access to information about what the government was doing. It slackened somewhat in the aftermath of Watergate and the administration of Jimmy Carter. But it has been escalating—and with a vengeance—since the election of Ronald Reagan, and is now more virulent than it has ever been. Clearly, what had once been a series of skirmishes has evolved into a shooting war.

The war is being waged on several fronts. It is being waged from the White House, whose current occupant has left little doubt that he regards the press as an enemy, as a force to be ignored when possible, misled when feasible, and suffered a good deal less than graciously when its attentions and demands become unavoidable. The war is being waged in the halls of Congress, where conservative senators and representatives vie with each other in criticizing the news media and in attempting to limit its access to information. The war is being waged by conservative churchmen, who have denounced the press from their pulpits and, misunderstanding what a free press is all about, called upon it to reflect the views of what they perceive to be the majority in its coverage of events. The war is being waged by businessmen, who are increasingly flexing their economic muscles in efforts, not entirely unsuccessful, to pressure the press, if not to see things their way, then at least to keep quiet about the fact that they do not. And finally, the war is being waged by the American public, a large part of which feels that the U.S. press has grown too detached from and perhaps even hostile to the government of the country. For many Americans, the press has grown too powerful, too big to control, and too willing, as well as too able, to influence what the public does, from choosing elected officials to buying consumer products.

The evidence that a war is underway is abundant. It can be seen in the conduct of Senator Jesse Helms, yapping like a mongrel at the heels of the American press, loudly impugning the patriotism of its reporters and carelessly accusing them of the kinds of slanderous activities in which he himself seems to be engaging. Let the press warn that administration policies of keeping tight curbs on any officials who would have contact with the press threatens everyone's access to information, and Helms is quick to reply. "The real threat to freedom, the real threat to freedom of speech and the real threat to our constitutional system," Helms told an audience at a Conservative Political Action Conference, "is on our TV screens every evening and on the front pages of our newspapers every day."

Nor is this all Helms, whose career has been characterized by smear tactics, has to say when it comes to criticizing the press. Helms charges that the country's leading newspapers and television news programs are "produced by men and women who, if they do not hate American virtues, then certainly have a smug contempt for American ideals and principles." The press is, in short, if not anti-American, then certainly un-American, at least in Helms's demonology.

Helms's harangues may be dismissed as nothing but billingsgate, the kinds of accusations commonly made by politicians who seek to distract critics from their records or lack of them. But Helms is not alone in attacking the press. Presidential Press Secretary Larry Speakes, whose skin seems to be as thin as his veneer of understanding, has made it clear that he considers the news media's interest in information other than that the White House cares to disseminate to be offensive and improper. Reflecting the attitudes of his employer, not to mention those of that segment of the population that supports him, Speakes has passed up few opportunities to express his contempt for the often-rowdy White House press corps or for its desire to obtain information that the Administration would rather not release.

Other administration officials reflect similar sentiments. Presidential Science Adviser Dr. George Keyworth has placed the Administration in direct opposition to the news media, saying, "We're trying to build up America and the press is trying to tear down America." One reason for this conflict, at least according to Keyworth, is that "much of the press seems to be drawn from a relatively narrow fringe element on the far left of our society." Another, he says, is that "there is an arrogance that has to do with the power of the press . . . it's easier to achieve power by being negative and tearing at foundations." Still others in the Administration see anything but unquestioning support of government actions or policies as evidence of disloyalty. A middle-ranking State Department official named John Chain posted a notice in his office waiting room accusing a *New York Times* reporter of "willingly, willfully and knowingly" publishing a story that was "harmful and damaging to the country," despite the fact that the material in the story had been openly discussed in the Canadian Parliament, not to mention other public forums.

Government officials are not the only ones after the media these days. Conservative citizens groups like Accuracy in Media have criticized the press for being too liberal, which means, in fact, for failing to reflect their views of what is best for the United States. Fundamentalist churchmen, like the Reverend Jerry Falwell, have denounced the media from their television pulpits, blasting them for failing to reflect what they see as basic Christian values and for supporting such things as the removal of government restrictions on women's access to abortion services.

Businessmen, too, have joined the hue and cry against the news media. After Massachusetts State Senator William Bulger criticized the press in a serious State House debate, Barry Gottehrer, a senior vice president of the Massachusetts Mutual Life Insurance Company, had his remarks printed in a pamphlet. He then mailed out hundreds of copies of this broadside to senators and representatives and state legislative leaders around the country. With the mailing, he included a letter in which he declared: "Elected officials and other leaders of both public and private sectors must today conduct their activities under the critical eye of journalists who frequently operate without ethical constraints or regard to factual accuracy in this area. Beyond the harm done to the reputations of our officials through faulty and misleading reporting, often it has been the long-term public interest that has suffered most severely."[12]

Challenged by *New York Times* writer Anthony Lewis, who asked him to provide a few examples to support what otherwise seems a rather sweeping charge, Gottehrer declined to respond. No matter. With proof or without, a great and growing segment of the public seems inclined to support him and to turn against the press.

Many Americans, in fact, now make no bones about their distrust of the press, noting that it has, on more than one occasion, made factual errors or allowed its own interests, political or philosophical, to undermine its objectivity on one story or another. But many Americans want to go further and, it seems, to punish the press by awarding large damages in suits brought against the media by those who feel that they have been libeled. Stanford University Law Professor Marc Franklin says that since 1976, nearly 85 percent of the 106 major libel verdicts by U.S. juries have been defeats for journalistic defendants, and that some two dozen of those verdicts awarded damages of more than $1 million. The message of his finding is clear to *St. Petersburg Times* editor Eugene Patterson, who said, "Juries are the American people. They want to punish us."[13]

Juries may not, however, be the only ones eager to punish the press. The U.S. Supreme Court seems to share some of the public's mistrust of the media. Since 1972, the nation's highest tribunal has ruled against media defendants in all four of the libel appeals it has agreed to hear.

The Supreme Court, though, is not the press's only enemy in high places these days. When it comes to communicating criticism of the news media, that Great Communicator named Ronald Reagan has shown himself to be a man of consummate skill. The President may be personally affable; the President's people, including his secretaries of state and defense, as well as other cabinet officials, seem interested in informing the public. In fact, they appear on television so often that viewers may be excused for wondering if they are public servants or paid performers. But for all its candor on those issues it hopes to publicize, the Reagan Administration has been nothing if not vigorous in its attempts to control the flow of information coming out of the government, and by so doing, to define the very nature and scope of public debate. At various times since he has taken office, the President has proposed strict regulations covering contact between government officials and employees and reporters, used the FBI to track down embarrassing leaks, and moved both to reduce the scope of the Freedom of Information Act and to impose lifetime censorship on tens of thousands of officials who have had access to classified information. Said Tom Winship, who retired recently as editor of *The Boston Globe:* "I think resentment toward the press has been stepped up by the public relations genius of the Reagan Administration."[14]

In some ways, at least, this emerging attitude is understandable. The press, by its very nature, is rarely beloved. "Nobody," wrote Sophocles, "likes the man who brings bad news." But bringing bad news is one of the primary responsibilities of the press. It has been the press, after all, that has brought its readers and viewers reports of war and disasters, of social and economic turmoil. Americans, whose tolerance for bad news increases in direct proportion to the distance that such news must travel, have long been able to tolerate news of revolutions, famines, floods, and other catastrophes if those events happened in places like Spain, China, or India. But in recent years, the bad news has come from closer to home. Since World War II, the American news media have shown Americans the turmoil of their own civil rights movement; they have shown the war in Vietnam and the protests that conflict generated at home. They have shown the collapse of a presidency and the resignation of a chief executive; they have chronicled the pain of 10 percent unemployment and brutal inflation.

What's more, the news media have brought this bad news right into the living room. In the years preceding and immediately following World War II, Americans got their news from daily newspapers, reading about events several hours, days, or even weeks after they happened, and learning only as much about what was going on as reporters and editors, working with limited space and pictures of poor quality, were able to convey. Now, Americans increasingly get their news from the volatile medium of television, which shows them events as they are happening and without editing.

The images are often overwhelming. Americans who can read about a bloody battle without flinching all too often find themselves wincing as television news broadcasts show scenes of young men maimed by bombs or bullets, of civilians slain by exploding rockets. Viewers who know that reporters regularly interview the survivors of accidents or the families of murder victims are appalled to see such interviews conducted before their very eyes. But feeling not unlike voyeurs caught in the act, they are embarrassed at watching something that they cannot, because of their own morbid curiosity, seem to shut off.

Nor are these the only new images with which television viewers—and news consumers in general—must contend. The change in the media has changed the image of the journalist himself. In the days when the term "press" referred only to that which was printed, the public tended to view reporters as friendly characters, as low-paid but good-hearted regular fellows who did their work, then stopped off to quaff a few beers with policemen or politicians while their papers went to press. Now, thanks to television, the public tends to see newsmen in a new context. It sees them as anchormen and anchorwomen, as television "personalities," rather than as journalists, as cool, comely, carefully coiffed actors who frequently make far more money than the President of the United States.

Worse than this, Americans increasingly find the press inaccessible. American newspapers used to be local industries, owned by families who lived in the communities in which they published. No longer. Mergers have consolidated those newspapers that have managed to survive into a handful of local monopolies, most of them owned by large chains that seem far less interested in local politics than they are in corporate profits. Competition, which once helped keep newspapers honest, has gone the way of the dodo and the passenger pigeon. New York City, which had no fewer than eight daily newspapers in the early 1950s, now has only three, and none really competes with the others. Instead, *The New York Times,* the New York *Daily News* and the *New York Post* confine their circulation to separate segments of the reading public. Chicago, once one of America's great newspaper towns, now has only two papers, neither of which truly compete. Other cities are in even worse shape. The *Los Angeles Times* and *Los Angeles Herald Examiner* publish in the morning and the evening; they do not go head-to-head. Dozens of other U.S. cities have morning-evening combinations that do not compete with each other. The result of this trend is not merely a reduction in the number of newspapers available to American readers; it is a reduction in the number of choices open to them as well. Once, newspaper readers, at least in America's larger cities, could count on finding a paper whose editorial voice agreed with theirs. Now, it has become difficult not only to find a paper with whose policies one can concur, but to find one that cares enough about local issues to comment upon them at all. In many larger American cities, newspaper editors and reporters are not local people with an interest in and loyalty to the communities they cover but journeymen, interested in staying only long enough to parlay their experience into better jobs. Television is subject to the same criticism. The network news broadcasts are all assembled in and originate from New York; they stress national affairs at the expense of local coverage. Local news broadcasts are all too often shoestring operations full of chatter, repartee, and "happy talk" and short on the kind of substance that was once the lifeblood of the medium-sized or small-town daily.

But worst of all, Americans complain that the press is unreliable and say that they cannot believe what they read in print or see on the screen. Journalists, they complain, make up facts, or twist them to prove whatever points they are trying to make. They concoct anonymous sources to support their conclusions; they alter quotes. After all, critics point out, *Washington Post* reporter Janet Cooke *was* caught and forced to admit that she had invented the eight-year-old heroin addict around whom she built a 1981 Pulitzer Prize-winning story; other reporters have also been caught stretching the truth to make their stories read better.

But what bothers people more than things like the Cooke affair, which was an anomaly, are the dozens of cases, cases that occur every day, in which the media miss the point of a story or treat it in such a way as to make things seem worse than they are. What bothers them, too, are the inquisitorial attitudes displayed by many reporters, who, they complain, demonstrate a deep mistrust of any authority and always tend to assume the worst about anyone in any official position. "The press," says one longtime "news consumer" who speaks for thousands, perhaps millions, of fellow readers and viewers, "always seems to be out for blood . . . anyone's blood."

Finally, many Americans feel, the press is no respecter of privacy, but regards everyone and everyone's life as grist for its mills, pursuing and badgering people in the often-abused idea that it is somehow safeguarding the public's "right to know." Americans resent the spectacle of reporters camping on someone's front lawn in the hope of catching him or a member of his family on camera as he emerges from his house. They resent it when public officials and private citizens are forced to disclose details of their financial situations or medical histories for reasons that often seem considerably less than compelling.

Americans, in a word, are angry at the press, and many, in high places and low, are determined that, like the broadcaster in the film *Network,* they are "not going to take it any more." Their attitude is understandable. Americans have always been uneasy about any institution that grows so large as to appear unmanageable, and the news media certainly conform to this criterion. Americans, too, have always resented bad news, whether it comes from politicians or the press, and punished its bringers with disapproval.

Americans, it seems, now want to punish the press for its power and for its pervasive influence on their lives. Within the past year, they have supported proposals to penalize reporters for publishing information leaked by government officials, endorsed ideas for legislation that would restrict editors and publishers from commenting upon the conduct of elected and other officials, backed bills that would require licensing of journalists, and endorsed efforts to make the press reflect majority attitudes rather than express itself independently.

Such measures would certainly penalize the press and trim its power considerably. But in imposing such restrictions, the public would not only punish the press; it would punish itself. Restricting the press might keep it from reminding people that they are less than perfect. Weakening the press would strengthen the hand of government and allow it and its officials to conduct their business free from the scrutiny they so frequently find embarrassing.

But weakening the press would not strengthen the United States. Quite the contrary, weakening the press would weaken democracy and undermine the ability of the American public to exercise the rights it holds so dear. For, as political philosophers from Thomas Jefferson on have recognized, the press, a free press, is a crucial element in a democracy. The press, in fact, plays one of the key roles in a democracy, providing a common ground of knowledge and analysis, a meeting place for national debate. The press is the link between the people and their institutions. Without the information provided by newspapers and television, Americans would have little information and no basis for deciding what to believe and whom to trust and support. Just as a growing mistrust of government could cause a breakdown of order, so could a growing hostility to the press sever the ligaments of a workable society.

Without a strong and trusted press, the public would have almost no way to keep its government and other institutions honest. For government, and particularly the federal government, has vast power to mislead the people and manage the news. Officials can conceal impending actions until their effects are irreversible. Other large institutions—corporations, unions, hospitals, police forces, banks—can operate with impunity, making decisions that affect the lives and welfare of millions if their activities are not subject to scrutiny. Without a strong press to protect it, freedom itself can disappear.

This is what makes the war on the press so frightening. One can easily understand the attitude of officials toward an institution that serves as a watchdog, questioning their conduct and informing the public what they are doing in its name. One can understand the attitudes of others—business executives, religious leaders, as well as less respectable individuals— toward an institution that informs the public as to the implications of their actions, points out when they have been disingenuous, and compares what they say with what can be determined to be the truth. Government, big business, big labor, big religion all have reason to resent the press.

But the American public has nothing to gain from crippling its news media. And, it has a great deal to lose. The scary thing is that it does not seem to realize this . . . or worse, that it does not seem to care.

# Chapter Two
# The Necessary Evil

In order to enjoy the inestimable benefits the liberty of the press ensures, it is necessary to submit to the inevitable evils that it creates.

ALEXIS DE TOCQUEVILLE,
*Democracy in America,* 1835

It is dropped on the doorstep each morning, purchased from a sidewalk vendor, delivered after school by a youngster from the neighborhood. It tells what is happening in Washington, in Paris, or in such exotic and out-of-the-way places as Kathmandu and Kabul. It tells which teams won and lost the previous night's baseball games, takes note of births, deaths, and weddings, regales the children with the continuing trials and tribulations of good ol' Charlie Brown, and lets their mothers know which items are on sale at the local supermarket. Priced at anywhere from twenty to fifty cents, it remains one of the world's best bargains, a printed package that informs, entertains, and, more than just occasionally, infuriates, and that can be used afterward to light a fire, stuff a package, and even wrap up the garbage.

Flashy or sedate, well-written and edited or fairly tossed together, responsible or exactly the opposite, the newspaper is a fact of American life. Most Americans at least glance at one every day, just skimming the headlines or reading each and every word as if their lives depended on the information these words contained. Many Americans, particularly those in government and politics, big business and communications, read several, finding themselves feeling strangely out of touch unless they have seen, say, *The Washington Post, The New York Times*, and *The Wall Street Journal*. Some Americans start their days by reading the editorials and the political columns, others by turning first to the sports pages. An elderly reader may turn first to the death notices to see if a friend is among those listed; a teenager may purchase a paper for the sole purpose of finding out what is playing at the movies; a commuter, heading for the office, may open his paper directly to the crossword puzzle. But everyone, or almost everyone, at least looks at a newspaper every day.

Even more people watch television. Millions of Americans begin their days by watching programs like NBC's "Today" and ABC's "Good Morning America," catching up on at least some of the news as they dress or bolt their breakfasts. Millions more sit down to supper with Dan Rather and the "CBS Evening News" or Tom Brokaw and the "NBC Nightly News." Millions refuse to switch off their lights and go to sleep until they have seen the eleven o'clock news broadcasts on their local stations. In between, millions more watch television news programs like CBS's "60 Minutes" or ABC's "20/20" or view network news specials on such things as airplane hijackings in progress. In fact, studies show, the majority of Americans get their news not from newspapers, but from television, that all-seeing but frequently jaundiced electronic eye that brings people and events from around the corner or around the world directly into their living rooms and provides its viewers with an immediacy and a presence that can be every bit as terrifying as it is titillating.

Uncounted millions, too, supplement their newspaper reading and television viewing with radio listening. Teenagers and subteens may regard radio as little more than a source of background noise, a device to bring the thumping music that saves them from the silence they seem to dread. But their elders regard radio as a ready source of information. Countless Americans listen to the "CBS World News Roundup" each morning at their breakfast tables or as they drive to work, as much to be reassured about what has not happened overnight as to learn what has. Millions tune in to the all-news stations that have taken to the airways in every major American city to offer their listeners a twenty-four-hour-a-day diet of information. Many Americans learn of events first by hearing about them on the radio, then run to switch on their television sets for pictures before finally reading about them the following morning in their newspapers.

Americans, in fact, are addicted to information. The country's two major weekly newsmagazines, *Time* and *Newsweek,* boast of circulations of 4.5 and 3 million respectively, and claim that four to five times that number actually read each copy. *U.S. News and World Report* has a circulation of more than a million. *The Wall Street Journal,* the closest thing the United States has to a national newspaper, circulates more than two million copies each business day, far exceeding the 850,000 copies circulated by *The New York Times,* the nation's newspaper of record. *The Boston Globe,* New England's most influential newspaper, sells a quarter of a million copies a day. And even smaller papers do well in their coverage areas. *The Manchester Evening Herald* may be published in a community with a population of only 18,000. But it sells 12,500 copies a day, or one to nearly every household in the area just north and east of the Connecticut state capital at Hartford.

"We are," said Michael O'Neill, former editor of the New York *Daily News,* "a nation of news junkies. Whether we recognize it or not, we are 'hooked' on news."[1] Why do people listen for hours to an all-news radio station? Why do people sit for hours in front of their television sets to watch news conferences that they can read about in minutes in their newspapers the next day? Why do people who have seen an actual news event unfolding before their eyes on live television still buy a newspaper and read about it the following day? Because information, news, has become our life's blood, because we've grown accustomed to knowing what's going on, and because we're all secretly afraid that we'll miss something.

It was not always like this, of course, even in America. It is not like this today in most countries of the world. In most nations, information is hard to come by, while that which is available is generally distrusted. Russians are great readers, devouring volumes of poetry and fiction like starving men devouring bread. But if the Soviet citizens spotted traveling to and from work on Leningrad's streetcars or Moscow's modern, art-deco subway are any indication, they do not read newspapers. Citizens of the Soviet Union look at the copies of *Pravda* and *Izvestia* posted on bulletin boards in factories and throughout the cities, but the sight of someone actually reading his own copy of either of these semiofficial newspapers on a subway train or a park bench is a relative rarity, and for reasons that should be obvious. Russians do not really trust their news media, and while they will quote either *Pravda* or *Izvestia* to foreigners with the certainty of a religious zealot citing Scripture, they betray their attitudes toward both by losing themselves in literature.

Things are no different in much of the rest of the world. In many Central and South American countries, the press is subject to official censorship, which manifests itself in the blank spaces that stand out starkly on the pages of many newspapers. In the Middle East, newspapers can print material that the government does not wish published only at the risk of being closed down. Even Israel, the only democracy in that region, has laws that allow censorship.

In most countries, censorship stems from the same basic belief—that criticism of the government is seditious at best and tantamount to treason at worst. Even in England, from which American traditions of press freedom evolved, the idea of press freedom is relatively recent. There, the phrase "freedom of speech" originated during the struggle of Parliament to achieve the privilege of free debate; the history of this right thus proceeded separately from that of free speech as a civil liberty. In fact, the phrase "freedom of speech" itself first appeared in a proclamation issued by King James in 1620. The proclamation did not seek to guarantee this right, but rather to restrict it. The king had relatively few objections to the free discussion of many subjects. But he inveighed against what he termed the "excess of Lavish and Licentious Speech in matters of State." His message was clear. People might discuss other matters freely. But the right to free speech did not extend to matters of state, which the king said were "no Theames or Subjects fit for vulgar persons or common meetings."[2] It was not, in fact, until the last quarter of the eighteenth century that "freedom of speech" was anything but a parliamentary right. Until then, it guaranteed no more than a legislator's immunity from punishment for anything said by him in his official capacity during a legislative session.

What led to the change? Niccolò Machiavelli recommended in *The Prince* that people, meaning everyone but the Crown, speak with "reserve and respect." But speaking with reserve and respect is not the same as speaking freely. Freedom of speech as we know it today had, of course, some basis in everyday experience; people spoke freely among friends and trusted associates. But freedom of speech as a right remained unknown to both legal and constitutional history on either side of the Atlantic before 1776, when it was elevated to constitutional status by the Pennsylvania Declaration of Rights.

What led to its recognition as a right was the growing recognition by the people, from the Crown on down, that the truth of their opinions, especially regarding religion, was relative rather than absolute. Moreover, there was the growing confidence of governments that they could withstand criticism. Freedom of speech could never be recognized as a right as long as governments felt insecure and considered dissent, whether religious, political, or philosophical, as treasonous. Only when governments felt strong enough to survive criticism could they recognize the rights of people to say what they wished. King George could not grant his unruly American colonists the right to freedom of speech as long as their freedom and the exercise thereof challenged his sovereignty. It remained for the colonists, who had seen enough of controlled presses and laws aimed at stifling dissent, to grant it to themselves.[3]

This, of course, is exactly what they did. George Mason recognized that "the freedom of the press is one of the great bulwarks of liberty and can never be restrained but by despotic governments,'' as he penned the Virginia Bill of Rights a full month before his colleagues completed the Declaration of Independence.[4] James Madison recognized the importance of a free flow of information in a democracy. He wrote that "a popular government without popular information or the means of acquiring it, is but a prologue to a Farce or a Tragedy; or perhaps both. Knowledge will forever govern ignorance; and a people who mean to be their own governors must arm themselves with the power, which knowledge gives."[5]

The new nation's founding fathers recognized this several years later when they sat down to draft the constitution by which the country would be governed. For the import of the First Amendment to the Constitution is nothing if not clear. It says that Congress shall make no law abridging either freedom of speech or of the press or of the free exercise of religion or of the right of the people to assemble peaceably.

The new law provided official protection to religious and political dissidents and assured journalists that they could print what they chose. But even before that law was enacted, a tradition of press freedom was developing in what would eventually become the United States of America. The man who gave birth to this tradition was a printer named John Peter Zenger.

He was an unlikely hero. Born in Germany in 1697, he came to America in 1710 and spent the next sixteen years working, first as an apprentice, then as an employee of printers in and around Baltimore. In 1726, he established his own printing business in Chestertown, Maryland; a couple of years later, he moved to New York.

It was there that his problems began. On November 5, 1733, Zenger published the first issue of the *New York Weekly Journal*, the official organ of a group opposed to the policies of colonial Governor William Crosby, an imperious individual who was involved in the kinds of land deals that would today get any office holder indicted. Crosby did not take kindly to criticism. A year after the original issue of the paper appeared, he issued a proclamation condemning its "scandalous, virulent, false and seditious reflections" and offering a reward for the apprehension of those responsible for the publication. A few days later, Zenger was arrested and charged with libel.

Zenger remained in jail for nearly a year, editing the *Journal* from his prison cell. His case did not come to court until August 4, 1735. But once it did, it did more than a pack of professors to secure press freedom in America. Zenger's judge wanted the jury hearing the case merely to consider whether the statements to which Crosby objected had been made; he proposed leaving the question of whether or not they were true to the court itself to decide. Zenger's lawyer, Andrew Hamilton, objected. He said that the jury was competent to consider the truth of the statements themselves, and the jury agreed. Deciding that the statements were true, it acquitted Zenger of libel, handing Crosby a defeat and taking a giant step toward establishing the right of the press to print what it wished.[6]

The adoption of the First Amendment in 1791 did not, however, end efforts by either the U.S. government or the states to curb the press. The adoption of the First Amendment was an epochal advance in civil and political liberty. It established that the people, as sovereign, had the right to say what they pleased about the government, which was their servant, and which governed with their permission. It reversed the historic notion that the government, as embodied by the Crown, could punish the people for speaking out against it. It forbade the government from cutting off the hands of pamphleteers or from drawing and quartering printers who published material it considered seditious, as the government of England did well into the eighteenth century.

But it did not prevent the U.S. government from trying to limit criticism of its officials and performance. Only seven years after the First Amendment was adopted, Congress violated its guarantees by enacting the Alien and Sedition Acts. Written while Europe was shaken by the French Revolution, these laws promised severe sanctions against anyone who wrote, printed, or uttered words that would bring the President, the Congress, the government, or the military into "contempt or disrepute."[7]

The first indictment under this act was handed up against Congressman Matthew Lyon of Vermont for writing an article attacking President John Adams. Lyon's article was nothing if not accusatory. Criticizing the government, he wrote that "every consideration of the public welfare was swallowed up in a continual grasp for power, in an unbounded thirst for ridiculous pomp, foolish adulation and selfish avarice." And he published a letter from an American living in France who suggested that Congress commit the President to a madhouse. Lyon was convicted under the shameful law, sentenced to four months in prison, and fined $1,000. His constituents clearly regarded his conviction as a badge of honor. They reelected him to Congress while he was still in jail.

Public displeasure over the Alien and Sedition Acts helped defeat Adams's Federalist Party in the next election and to bring Thomas Jefferson into the presidency. Jefferson won further public support by pardoning those convicted under the acts, while Congress went so far as to repay most of their fines. Jefferson suffered, as all presidents before and since have, from criticism at the hands of the press, and often expressed the feeling that the press was, at best, a necessary evil in a democracy. But despite his displeasure, Jefferson stuck to his principles and left the press alone.

So, for the most part, did his successors. Presidents and the Congress made no laws limiting freedom of expression. But the First Amendment did not forbid states from doing so, and some did. Throughout the South, for example, it was illegal to advocate, either in print or by utterance, the abolition of slavery, and those who did so faced not only the law but those who took it upon themselves to act outside it. In Alton, Illinois, an angry mob attacked the religious journal, *The Observer,* an antislavery paper published by the Reverend Elijah Lovejoy. On no fewer than three separate occasions, in fact, Lovejoy's presses were dragged from his shop and dumped into a nearby river. On each occasion, he brought in new equipment, insisting on his right to publish his views. At one time, he told a threatening crowd that "the present excitement will soon be over; the voice of conscience will at last be heard." Lovejoy predicted that people would eventually realize that he was right. But he himself did not live to see such recognition. In 1837, a mob dragged him from his house and killed him.

Freedom of speech and freedom of the press did not disappear during those turbulent years. But they did not flourish more than sporadically as circumstances and the government's ability to weather dissent waxed and waned. Abraham Lincoln took steps to stifle dissent during the Civil War, suspending the right of habeas corpus and permitting the arrest of nearly 40,000 suspected of being disloyal to the union. But criticism of the government was uncurbed during the unpopular war with Mexico, and rose to a crescendo during the Spanish-American War, when those elements of the press that were not competing with each other to push the country into the conflict, or to score often spurious scoops, vied with each other to criticize the government for getting involved.

World War I saw the government actively involved in a campaign to curb free expression. In 1917, Congress passed the Espionage Act, making it illegal to obstruct recruiting by the military or to impair the war effort. A year later, it enacted a second piece of legislation, sometimes known as the Sedition Act, that made it unlawful to express opinions contrary to government policy, especially where the war or conscription were concerned. Under this law, some two thousand people faced prosecution, one of them a woman named Rose Stokes. She was sentenced to ten years in prison for a letter in which she stated: "I am for the people and the government is for the profiteers." A Vermont minister, the Reverend Clarence Waldron, drew a fifteen-year sentence for distributing a leaflet urging that Christians not enter the armed forces.

The actions were unfortunate. But their effect was not, for it was during this period that the U.S. Supreme Court began, for the first time, to formulate a First Amendment doctrine. The doctrine was best stated in the 1919 case involving Charles Schenck, who appealed to the High Court to overturn his conviction for distributing circulars opposing the draft. The case did not turn out well for Schenck; the Court upheld his conviction. But the case did turn out well for the cause of free expression, for it led to the first statement of how far one could go in stating his views. The statement was written by Justice Oliver Wendell Holmes, who said:

> The most stringent protection of free speech would not protect a man in falsely shouting fire in a theater and causing panic . . . The question in every case is whether the words are used in such circumstances and are of such a nature as to create a clear and present danger that they will bring about the substantive evils that Congress has a right to prevent. It is a question of proximity and degree.[8]

A 1925 case provided another landmark decision. Deciding on the appeal of Benjamin Gitlow, who had published a Socialist manifesto in a left-wing New York newspaper, the Court held that the Fourteenth Amendment to the Constitution protected those freedoms guaranteed in the First Amendment. The Court did not, however, uphold Gitlow's appeal, finding that his advocacy of "revolutionary mass action" could incite readers to overthrow the government.

The Gitlow decision turned the Fourteenth Amendment into a means of forcing state and local governments to respect the First Amendment's guarantees of free speech and a free press, and assured that any law that denied such rights could be successfully challenged. It was not long before one was. In 1931, the Supreme Court struck down a Minnesota law that permitted authorities to shut down offensive publications. The Court made it clear in *Near* v. *Minnesota* that it had nothing but contempt for the Minneapolis *Saturday Press,* a blatantly racist publication that had printed a series of articles charging, in the most scurrilous terms, that a gang of Jewish criminals was behind the rackets that then flourished in Minneapolis. But the Court made it equally clear that even offensive publications and offensive utterances were entitled to the protection of the Constitution. Quoting James Madison, the Court declared that "some degree of abuse is inseparable from the proper use of everything, and in no instance is this more true than that of the press . . . It is better to leave a few of its noxious branches to their luxuriant growth, than, by pruning them away, to injure the vigor of those yielding the proper fruits."[9]

With government protection or without it, though, the U.S. press grew.

The American press was little more than a collection of pamphleteers, publishers of broadsides, and a handful of single-page newspapers back in colonial times. But it did not take long for it to mature into a healthy and powerful industry.

The American press, in fact, grew like a colony of mushrooms after a rainstorm. Early colonial papers were essentially newsletters, single-sheet affairs modeled on English publications and run off on flat-bed presses. Later publications followed the form of the London *Gazette,* which was founded in 1665 and which had the distinction of being the first English news publication to be issued in what is now recognized as the traditional newspaper format. Packets of *Gazettes* were shipped to the American colonies from England; files of the paper were maintained in many colonial coffeehouses and taverns, which served as local centers for exchanging information and gossip; at least two copies of the *Gazette* were reprinted on American presses for distribution in the colonies. The *Gazette* also served as the model for a 1689 publication called *The Present State of New-English Affairs.* Authorized by the Massachusetts legislature, this could hardly be considered a newspaper because it did not appear regularly. But it did at least look like one and it did at least try to fulfill one of the functions of one. Its subhead read: "This is Published to Prevent False Reports."

The first truly American newspaper was published a year later, in 1690, by Boston's Benjamin Harris, who intended his *Publick Occurrences Both Foreign and Domestick* to be published monthly unless "any Glut of Occurrences" made its more frequent publication necessary. The glut never materialized, at least in time to save the paper. Only four days after its first issue appeared, the colony's governor and council noted that it had been published without the least "Countenance of Authority" and ordered it suppressed. Their action was unfortunate. Measuring only six by nine and a half inches and containing only three pages (the fourth was left blank so that readers could add items of their own before passing the paper along to friends), *Publick Occurrences* may not have looked much like a modern newspaper. But the paper, which contained some gossip about the scandalous conduct of the King of France and some reports on battles in the ongoing French and Indian War, was decently written.

So was the first continuously published American newspaper. The Boston *News-Letter* was launched in 1704 by the city's postmaster, John Campbell. A single sheet that was only slightly larger than *Publick Occurrences,* the *News-Letter* was published weekly and was filled with items rewritten or copied from London journals, notices of meetings or religious gatherings, Indian depradations, and shipping news. It also contained some pretty sensational stuff, including an account of how the pirate Edward Teach, better known as Blackbeard, was slain during a battle at sea. But despite ambitious efforts, the *News-Letter* did not do well. Its publication was suspended twice during its first six years; even after it had been in business for seven years, Campbell complained that he could not sell 250 copies per issue.

Still, Campbell and his family managed to keep the *News-Letter* going. The paper, which was determinedly Royalist, folded during the Revolution, ending a lifespan of seventy-two years that made it one of the longest-lived American newspapers of that period. That it managed to survive that long was more than a minor accomplishment; the *News-Letter* had stiff competition from a weekly known as the *Boston Gazette*. Launched in 1719 by William Brooker, who had succeeded Campbell as Boston's postmaster, the *Boston Gazette* resembled its competitor in both appearance and editorial policies.

But the *Gazette*, too, had some competition. It was originally printed by James Franklin, who put it to press with the help of his thirteen-year-old brother, Benjamin. When Brooker's successor took the paper to another printer, the angry Franklin needed little encouragement from a group opposed to both the civil and religious authorities that ruled the colony to bring out a paper of his own. The result was the *New England Courant,* which made its first appearance in 1721 and which made a radical departure from the kind of newspaper that then prevailed in the colony. The *Courant* gave scant space to news, but much to essays that were entertaining, informative, or just plain provocative. It published attacks on the stern Mather brothers, Cotton and Increase, aired unpopular religious views, offended the authorities, and ultimately won James Franklin a month in jail. James eventually made Benjamin the paper's publisher— forbidden by the authorities to publish a paper, he canceled his brother's apprenticeship and substituted Benjamin's name for his own on the paper's masthead. The move, coupled with a secret document renewing Benjamin's indenture, was patently illegal. But the ploy was successful; the authorities left the paper alone for the next three years.

The success of Boston's earliest newspapers inspired others. By 1735, the town, which still had a population of less than 20,000, boasted five newspapers. Other colonial cities were not far behind. Philadelphia had the *American Weekly Mercury* and eventually Benjamin Franklin's *Pennsylvania Gazette*. New York had Zenger's *New York Weekly Journal*. New Haven had the *Connecticut Gazette*. Maryland, meanwhile, had a *Gazette* of its own, this one founded in Annapolis in 1727. South Carolina had the *South Carolina Gazette,* which made its debut in Charleston in

1731. A Scottish printer named James Johnston established the *Georgia Gazette* at Savannah in 1763.

Predictably, these papers played an important part in the American Revolution. They started doing so with the passage of the Stamp Act in 1765, which imposed a tax of a half-penny on each copy of a two-page newspaper, a penny on each copy of a four-page publication, and a tax of two shillings on each advertisement. That the tax was high goes without saying; on some papers, it amounted to an impost of fully 50 percent of the price of the publication. The English had accepted such taxes with barely a murmur, but colonials, who had no representation in Parliament, objected. Writers in the *Boston Gazette* and *Evening Post* and the *Pennsylvania Journal* printed articles protesting the tax, while their papers carried stories commenting favorably on the mobs that intimidated tax collectors and destroyed shipments of stamped paper. Forbidden to publish without the stamps, many papers simply defied the ban, while others evaded it by changing their names and appearing as broadsides and hand-bills rather than newspapers. No colonial paper appeared with the hated stamp.

Most of the papers were outspoken in their opposition to the Crown and its impositions on the colonies and the colonists. But perhaps none was as outspoken as the *Boston Gazette,* whose circulation reached a record-breaking two thousand as revolutionary fervor mounted. Only Isaiah Thomas's *Massachusetts Spy,* which made its first appearance in 1770, rivaled the *Gazette* when it came to patriotism. Though both papers were driven out of Boston by the authorities, both continued to publish and to influence events. So did *Pennsylvania Magazine,* one of whose contributors was none other than Thomas Paine. Paine published everywhere he could. He suggested in a letter to the *Pennsylvania Journal* that colonial independence from England might be necessary to secure an end to the slave trade. And he suggested more in his well-known pamphlet *Common Sense,* which appeared in January 1776, selling more than 120,000 copies and forcing colonials to confront the idea of separation from Great Britain.

Paine's pamphlet paved the way for the Declaration of Independence, which was carried in full in the last issue of *Pennsylvania Magazine.* His first "crisis paper," published in the December 1776, issue of the *Pennsylvania Journal,* helped stiffen the spines of the colonials, who were then in open rebellion. That paper, quoted so often that it is familiar to every American schoolchild, began:

> These are the times that try men's souls. The Summer soldier and
> the sunshine Patriot will, in this crisis, shrink from the service of their

country; but he that stands it now deserves the love and thanks of man and woman.[10]

There were no fewer than thirty-seven newspapers in publication in the American colonies at the time the Revolution began on April 19, 1775, and most of them fared well during the conflict. But those in areas captured by the British sometimes did not. Solomon Southwick, publisher of the *Mercury,* buried his press and went into hiding when the British took Newport, Rhode Island. Peter Timothy, editor of the *South Carolina Gazette,* was made a prisoner of war when the British took Charleston, South Carolina, in 1780. But most publications had more trouble with the paper supply than they did with the British, for the war meant that paper could no longer be imported and placed a heavier burden on colonial paper mills than most could bear. But despite these setbacks, and despite the fact that colonial newspapers had no organized system for covering the war but rather relied on private letters and semiofficial messages, the papers managed, after a fashion, to report the Revolution.

They did this despite a good deal of official harassment. Royal governors and judges tried their best to curb colonial newspapers' growing boldness, only to find their attempts stymied by the unwillingness of grand juries to indict. But mobs often succeeded where officials failed when it came to dictating what a paper might—or might not—publish. The patriotic Sons of Liberty successfully exerted pressure on Tory newspapers, forcing them either to see things their way or not to see them at all.

But the colonial papers also functioned with considerable support. George Washington repeatedly encouraged the patriotic press; he even helped establish the New Jersey *Gazette* so his troops would have a newspaper to read while they were encamped in the state during the winter of 1777. He also gave a local paper mill some worn-out tenting so that it could be made into newsprint. The result was that American newspapers emerged from the War for Independence with the gratitude of those who had helped fight the war—and considerable prestige as well.

The American press enjoyed more freedom than that of any other country in the world. As states adopted their own constitutions, nine of the original thirteen included provisions protecting freedom of the press.* Alexander Hamilton saw no need to include guarantees of press freedom in the U.S. Constitution, questioning whether it was possible to include a definition of this freedom that did not leave ''the utmost latitude for evasion.'' But Jefferson and his supporters prevailed; Jefferson actually

*Such protection was omitted by the legislatures of Connecticut, New York, New Jersey, and Rhode Island.

wanted Virginia to withhold its approval of the Constitution until both freedom of the press and religion were assured.

This does not mean, however, that everyone loved the press. Alexander Hamilton and Thomas Jefferson both had reason to resent the new nation's newspapers, almost all of which attacked one or the other during their political careers. Local politicians had even more reason for rancor, as the papers tended to aim their most scurrilous sallies at them.

But still, the U.S. newspaper industry grew, expanding with the nation itself. By 1830, there were some 1,200 dailies in simultaneous publication in the country. Many of them were as highly partisan as their editors, some of whom felt no need to rely on facts when it came to criticizing those with whom they disagreed. Nor were their readers any less eager when it came to responding to articles to which they objected. Early American editors, in fact, needed to be as skilled with pistols as they were with pencils, for they were often called out and required to defend their honor and that of their papers in duels, especially in the South. Editors also spent a good deal of their time and space attacking each other. The editor of the New York *Argus* used his pages to call competing *Minerva* editor Noah Webster an "impious disorganizing wretch."

In between attacks, they also managed to cover some news. Though still lacking any organized system for disseminating information, American papers managed to cover the War of 1812, discuss the implications of the U.S. decision to pick up what later became known as the Louisiana Purchase from France, let the public know what its elected officials were up to in Washington, and help influence the outcome of national elections.

What turned the American press from a collection of small, limited-circulation newspapers into a major force in the country's intellectual, social, and political life, however, was the advent, in the period between 1833 and the beginning of the Civil War, of the penny paper. The penny paper was made possible by the Industrial Revolution and the invention that year of the steam-driven printing press. Until its invention, printing was a slow process, carried out largely on awkward, flat-bed presses that limited both the quality and the numbers of papers that could be printed. The development of powered presses revolutionized the newspaper business, allowing publishers to run off thousands of copies of each edition and to sell them cheaply. It not only changed the nature of American newspaper publishing; it changed the nature of the American newspaper's reader, bringing daily newspapers to millions who might not otherwise have read them at all. Between 1833 and 1869, the number of newspapers published in the United States more than doubled, rising from 1,200 to about 3,000. By 1833, there were three times as many newspapers being published in the United States as there were in France or England.

The penny papers made newspaper reading affordable. Before 1830, a subscriber to a mercantile paid eight to ten dollars a year for a four-page paper that appeared six times a week. But the publishing revolution soon saw such prices slashed. The Boston *Transcript,* founded in 1830, was a modest, well-written paper that sold for the then-unheard-of price of four dollars a year; it was also strong enough to defend the Irish immigrants against the prejudice that was then keeping them out of work and housing in the city. A year later, the Boston *Morning Post* made its appearance; a third four-dollar daily, the *Mercantile Journal,* came on the scene in 1833.

What most changed the nature of American newspapering, though, was the publishing revolution that took place in New York. The man who began it was a tall, gawky Yankee named Horace Greeley, who arrived in New York in 1828 with ten dollars in his pocket and the idea of parlaying his experience as a printer into a venture to publish a penny paper. Greeley, who made a living by printing a small triweekly with a partner named Francis Story, lacked the capital to launch a larger paper. But he managed to persuade the owner of the New York *Morning Post* to sell his paper at the dramatically low price of two cents a copy. Greeley and Story then bought out an entire press run and tried to sell the paper on the streets, something that had not been done before (many newspapers, in fact, refused to sell single copies but sold only to long-term subscribers or to distributors who bought in bulk). Weather conspired against their plan, and the new paper never achieved popularity. But the seed that Greeley had sown germinated. In 1833, Benjamin Day brought out the New York *Sun,* which sold for a penny, had a fresh, flippant style, and carried a feature that assured that the masses would like it— a police-court report whose writers set the tough, humorous tone that police reporters have followed ever since. The *Sun* succeeded; in fact, it succeeded brilliantly. Within two months of its debut, the *Sun* had a circulation of two thousand; within four months, its circulation had climbed to five thousand. By 1834, it reached ten thousand.

With its penchant for printing whatever was interesting and readable and its tendency to give weightier subjects considerably less space than the country's six-cent papers, the *Sun* attracted wide readership. But this was not the only reason for its circulation success. Borrowing from the example set by English publishers, Day sent newsboys out into the streets to hawk his papers. Selling the newsboys the *Sun* for sixty-seven cents a hundred if they paid cash and seventy-five cents a hundred if they bought on credit, Day soon built up an aggressive sales force.

Once Day showed that it could be done, other publishers followed his example. The New York *Transcript* tried to go the *Sun* one better by specializing in coverage of illicit sexual affairs, prizefights, and criminal trials. *Man,* an ancestor of the modern labor daily, appeared in 1834 to appeal to the interests of the unionized worker; the *Ladies' Morning Star* came on the scene in 1836, primarily as a protest against what its publisher, William Newell, considered the immorality of the *Sun* and similar papers.

But the paper that turned American newspapering on its ear was New York's *Herald,* which was launched in 1835 by the redoubtable James Gordon Bennett. A brilliant, though occasionally florid, writer with an apparent talent for personal controversy, the Scots-born Bennett intended from the start to be to journalism what Shakespeare was to drama. After trying unsuccessfully to start a paper called the *Globe* and to purchase the *Pennsylvanian,* Bennett took the $500 that represented the sum of his assets and started the *Morning Herald.* Initially, the *Herald* looked no different from the other penny papers. But under Bennett's leadership, it quickly took on a character of its own, with better local and foreign coverage than any of its competitors and first-rate financial coverage that made it must reading on Wall Street. Within six months, the *Morning Herald* was on the verge of overtaking the *Sun* and might have had not a fire destroyed the paper's printing plant and forced it to suspend publication for nineteen days.

Bennett, however, used the hiatus well. When the *Herald* reappeared, it was a new newspaper, a freewheeling journal in which writers were encouraged to express their opinions in news columns and from which all trace of stuffiness had been expunged to turn it into a paper that thought of itself as "spicy." Even those who found the *Herald* irresponsible admitted that it was the most readable newspaper they had ever seen.

Bennett's success infuriated his rivals and triggered one of New York's first newspaper wars. Other papers attacked not only the *Herald,* which they considered scandalous, but Bennett himself, whom they considered even more so. The war hurt the *Herald,* which found its circulation suffering, and forced Bennett to curb at least some of his journalistic and personal excesses. But the war did not hurt the development of American journalism; instead, it helped improve it. The need to keep up with Bennett, who established a Washington bureau, kept correspondents in major European capitals, and sent fleets of boats out to meet incoming ships in order to get a first look at overseas dispatches, forced his rivals to take similar steps and to make their own papers newsier and more readable. The rivalry also led to the development of modern war correspondence as the papers of the penny press went head-to-head in covering the war with Mexico. All the major papers sent their correspondents to cover the conflict, which broke out in 1846. Most set up elaborate systems for getting the news back, employing relays of riders to carry dispatches from the field to the telegraph lines that could transmit copy back to New York, Boston, and Baltimore. Eventually, most got together to form the country's first wire service. Staggered by the high telegraph bills they had amassed and dissatisfied with the amount of news they had been able to get, editors of New York's major dailies met a year after the war and formed an organization whose members would receive, in one telegraphic transmission, all the foreign news from ships arriving at Boston. The name of the new organization: The New York Associated Press.

American newspapers made their share of waves during the Mexican War, criticizing the government for its role in a conflict many considered unnecessary. But these were only wavelets compared to those they would make in the years that followed over the issue of slavery. Papers in the Northeast, particularly in Boston, New York, and Philadelphia, railed against slavery; papers in the South, predictably, defended it; the papers being launched in cities like Chicago, St. Louis, and San Francisco split on the issue, some defending the South's "peculiar institution" as a matter of states' rights, others finding the possession of one human being by another both immoral and indefensible.

Abolitionists who aired their views in print faced little, if any, harassment from the government. But they did face considerable opposition from those who upheld the idea of slavery. Kentucky's politician/editor/soldier, Cassius Clay, angered people so with his antislavery editorials in his *True American* that a mob attacked his plant, took possession of his press, and shipped it north to Cincinnati. A mob attacked the offices of the *Liberator* and manhandled editor William Lloyd Garrison. Philadelphia's *Pennsylvania Freeman* was sacked and burned three times. But despite these assaults and the refusal of some postmasters to handle abolitionist literature, the tradition of press freedom managed to survive.

Vigorous, often to a fault, American newspapers might have remained much as they had been after Reconstruction had they not been literally forced to change. The man who forced them to change and, in the process, helped usher in a whole new era in journalism was Joseph Pulitzer. Mustered out of the Union Army at the end of the Civil War, Pulitzer managed, after working as a mule skinner and as a hand on riverboats, to find himself a job as a reporter for a German-language paper in St. Louis. He quickly expanded his area of operations, acquiring the worthless St. Louis *Dispatch* and combining it with the *Post*. Under Pulitzer's hard-driving management, the new paper succeeded and the *Post-Dispatch* soon became the leading evening paper in St. Louis.

Its success, though, did not satisfy Pulitzer, whose brother Albert, with whom he did not get along, had just established the New York *Morning Journal*. In 1882, Joseph Pulitzer, too, went into business in New York, acquiring the failing *World* from the shady financier Jay Gould for $346,000 and vowing to turn it into a crusading newspaper. Brightening up the paper's look with neater, cleaner typography and improving its appearance with the use of woodcuts to illustrate items, Pulitzer made other changes as well. He lifted the *World*'s circulation from 20,000 to 40,000 in four months and put rival newspapers on notice that they had better work hard if they expected to compete with him. They did, but despite their efforts, the *World* continued to grow. By 1884, its circulation was up to 100,000, so satisfying Pulitzer that he had one hundred guns fired off in City Hall Park and gave every one of the paper's employees a high silk hat. When the paper's circulation topped 250,000 later that year, Pulitzer had a silver medal struck.

Building circulation was not Pulitzer's main accomplishment, though. Creating a modern newspaper was. More than any editor before him, Pulitzer professionalized the news business, hiring a staff of alert and persistent reporters who scoured the city for interesting news and wrote about it entertainingly. More than any editor before him, too, he promoted the paper, touting its successes on his masthead and encouraging others to pay attention by staging such stunts as sending reporter Nellie Bly (born Elizabeth Cochran) around the world to retrace the fictional voyage of Jules Verne's Phileas Fogg. And more than any other editor, Pulitzer innovated, conducting various censuses to determine such things as the number of churchgoers in the city, as well as running public opinion polls to learn and report how people, from senators and congressmen to the man in the street, felt about various issues and events. Most of all, though, Pulitzer crusaded. He took on such corporate giants as Standard Oil and the New York Central Railroad; he exposed and brought about improvements in the conditions confronting immigrants at Ellis Island; he engineered the resignations of public officials suspected of graft and corruption. He also got deeply involved in politics, building up Grover Cleveland for the presidency. He ran contests. He offered *World* readers more for their money, expanding the paper's size and giving them twelve, fourteen, sometimes sixteen pages for the same two-cent price they would have had to pay for smaller packages. He did, in short, everything modern-day newspaper publishers do to promote their papers, and not only did he do it well; he did it first.

Pulitzer's *World* dominated New York and thus the national newspaper scene from the time of its founding. Others challenged the *World*'s dominance and failed. But one bumptious westerner did not. Californian William Randolph Hearst admired the *World,* but he thought he could do what Pulitzer did even better. So, in 1895, he bought the troubled *Morning-Journal,* dropped the word "Morning" from its masthead, and declared war on the *World*. It was a conflict in which no quarter was sought or offered. In San Francisco, Hearst had outflanked the opposition by hiring the best journalists available at whatever salary he had to pay; in New York, he did the same thing, signing up such stars as Stephen Crane and Alfred Henry Lewis. He poured money into his paper, taking ads in rival papers to promote his own and spending a fortune on illustrations for the sensational crime, disaster, and scandal stories he knew readers would relish. He made the *Journal* into New York's great Democratic paper, espousing William Jennings Bryan and his free-silver cause. And he did what he started out to do. By the end of its second year, the *Journal* had overtaken the *World* in circulation.

The war between the *Journal* and the *World,* both of which were nothing if not sensational and both of which carried cartoons printed in the color yellow, gave currency to the phrase "yellow journalism." It also helped to get the United States into a war. Both newspapers paraded their patriotism, competing with each other to demonstrate which was the most ardently American. So it was only natural that both should see an opportunity to prove their points, while boosting their circulation, in the appointment by Spain of Valeriano Weyler as Captain-General of the troubled island of Cuba. Both papers sent correspondents to Cuba to report on the activities of the man they had already nicknamed "the Butcher." And both went well beyond the bounds of traditional journalism to scoop each other on additional stories. Hearst sent correspondent Karl Decker to Havana to rescue a beautiful Cuban girl, Evangelina Cisneros, from prison. He pulled out all the stops when the American battleship *Maine* exploded and sank in Havana Harbor, offering a $50,000 reward for information on the person or persons who had sunk it. Ultimately, he forced Pulitzer to support a war for which he had little taste. Seeing what jingoism had done for the *Journal*'s circulation and anxious lest the *World* fall behind, Pulitzer dove into the fray, sending reporters of his own to Cuba and ignoring the facts whenever they got in the way of a good story.

Both papers covered the eventual war extensively, reporting voluminously and enthusiastically as American armed forces defeated a weak and disorganized Spanish army in Cuba and routed the Spanish navy in the battle of Manila Bay in the Philippines.[11]

The *World Journal* rivalry, characterized by angry accusations, fraudulent dispatches, and planted stories, calmed down slightly after the Spanish-American War. But the kind of journalism the papers had created persisted. Yellow journalism, with its shrill, scare headlines, its lavish use of pictures of dubious significance, its frauds and faked interviews, and its ostentatious sympathy with the underdog, had spread far beyond New York, cropping up in, among other places, Cincinnati, St. Louis, and San Francisco. *The Denver Post* was a deep shade of yellow; so was the *Boston Post*. Both papers regularly ran headlines that promised far more than the stories beneath them could deliver; both traded heavily in sex and sensationalism; both seemed, at least, to have scant respect for the facts.

Yellow journalism eventually died of its own excesses. Shortly before the assassin Leon F. Czolgosz murdered President McKinley, the *Journal* carried an editorial suggesting that leaders as contemptible as the paper obviously found the chief executive should be killed. When the assassination actually occurred, the public reacted with outrage; Hearst was hanged in effigy, which did not hurt him at all, and the *Journal*'s circulation dropped off, which did. Hearst, saying that he was only fighting for the people, changed his paper's name to the *American and Journal*. The *Journal*'s imitators changed their tactics and toned down their papers. Within a few years, true yellow journalism had ceased to exist; it flared up briefly during the New York tabloid wars of the 1920s before dying out almost entirely. Today, only the name and the sensational *New York Post,* published by the Australian-born Rupert Murdock, remain to bedevil newspaper editors.

Yellow journalism was often shameful. But it also made some positive contributions. The yellow press's passion for investigative stories and exposés gave rise to a whole new "literature of exposure" and led to the evolution of a group of journalists known as "muckrakers." The name, first applied to them in 1906 by an angry President Theodore Roosevelt, was not intended to be complimentary; Roosevelt borrowed it from a passage in John Bunyan's *Pilgrim's Progress* that denounced "the Man with the Muckrake . . . who could look no way but down." But those dubbed with the term wore the name with pride, for they felt that they were performing a social service by exposing such things as the manipulations of the nation's large corporate trusts and the deals in which many politicians engaged, or by describing conditions in American factories, mines, and farms.

The muckrakers, who had their heyday in the period between the end of the Spanish-American War and the beginning of World War I, got their start in the January 1903, issue of *McClure's Magazine,* which carried articles on municipal government, labor, and trusts by such deeply probing journalists as Lincoln Steffens, Ray Stannard Baker, and Ida Tarbell. And these articles, combined with other writings, had their effect. Edward Markham's novel *Children in Bondage* helped bring about the passage of laws limiting child labor. Upton Sinclair's *The Jungle* led almost directly to enactment of the Pure Food Act. David Graham Phillips's series "Treason of the Senate," which ran in *Cosmopolitan* during 1906, and which inspired the President's epithet, was a major factor in the passage of the Seventeenth Amendment to the Constitution, which provided for the popular election of senators and which helped turn Congress's upper house into a responsible legislative body.[12]

The American press redeemed itself to a great extent in the new century. The press did a commendable job covering the events leading up to World War I and reporting on the war itself. It did a fine job covering the stock market crash of 1929 and the Depression that followed it, letting Americans know that they were not the only ones thrown out of work or rendered penniless by the economic upheaval, and investigating and outlining the steps that had to be taken if the United States was to lift itself out of the morass into which it had sunk.

But the press's finest achievement during the first half of the century was its reporting of World War II to the American people. The scope of this task, which was truly global, the censorship hurdles that had to be overcome, the problems of communication and the personal dangers faced by the newsmen who covered the war were all staggering. But from the time that Pearl Harbor was attacked until the moment the Japanese signed the surrender documents aboard the battleship *Missouri,* American journalism distinguished itself. Some 1,600 newsmen, from newspaper reporters through magazine writers to filmmakers and radio broadcasters, were accredited to cover the war. In addition to the nation's major press associations like the Associated Press, United Press, and the International News Service, thirty individual newspapers and twelve magazines, including *Time, Life,* and *Newsweek,* had reporters on the war fronts. Newsmen flew in B-17 bombers as they dropped their loads of explosives on Germany's industrial centers, accompanied U.S. invasion forces as they went ashore at Normandy, in France, and at hitherto unknown islets in the Pacific. Reporters like Ernie Pyle passed up the opportunity to hang around headquarters and wrote about the war from the private soldier's point of view. Edward R. Murrow let his listeners know what it was like to live through the blitz that came close to destroying London. Thirty-seven journalists died while covering the story of their lives.

The war's end saw American newspapers riding, like skillful surfers, the crest of a wave of popularity and respect. In the late forties, Americans tended to believe what they read in their papers, or heard over that new medium, radio, where news broadcasts often ended with the words, "for further details, consult your local newspaper." The approbation was understandable. The American press had covered the biggest stories of the century completely and, given the limitations from which no institution run by humans can escape, accurately as well. And it continued to cover the news, reporting the war crimes trials at Nuremberg, the death of Babe Ruth, the Berlin Air Lift, the bloody birth of the state of Israel, and, on a pleasanter note, the marriage of England's Princess Elizabeth.

The press made mistakes, to be sure. It waited far too long before subjecting Wisconsin's Red-baiting Senator Joseph McCarthy to the kind of scrutiny that eventually made his quest for political power crumble. The *Chicago Tribune* erred memorably when it came out with a headline announcing Thomas Dewey's defeat of incumbent Harry Truman in the 1948 presidential election.

But, as the decade of the forties came to a close, the nation's newspapers began looking warily over their shoulders, for some new competitors were entering the news business and challenging print's long-held dominion. The new competitors were electronic. Radio, which was just beginning to come into its own, offered listeners a sense of immediacy that newspapers and other print media could not provide, even though it relied heavily upon the printed word to provide the material that its announcers read over the air. Television offered its viewers even more. It offered them a chance to be there and see news as it was happening and it would, as it came into its own, change the face of the news business completely.

# Chapter Three

# A New Dimension

Electronic media are received media. Print is a perceived medium . . . perceived media require time to be understood. Received media are instantaneous. As a result, people react to received media, whereas they interact with perceived media.

Tony Schwartz,
*Media: The Second God,* 1981

It is all-knowing, all-powerful. It has no corporeal form, but exists all around us, in the ether. It is inescapable, always there. Its ways are mysterious, beyond our comprehension.

This may sound, at least to some, like the description of a deity, an omniscient god. In a way, it is. But it is not a god that existed before man, or that came into being from nothing. Rather, it is a man-made deity. It is the electronic media, which man created. It is what adman/polymath Tony Schwartz calls, and with good reason, "the second god."

Schwartz's term may strike some as irreverent, even blasphemous. But it is, on the contrary, merely accurate. For few things, from religion itself to the exhortations of religious, political, and economic prophets, influence our lives as much. The electronic media, radio and television, have become the world's most powerful means of communication. They enable people to see and hear events as they happen. They bring the world and the events that occur in it, from fun and games to full-scale war, right into our living rooms and our consciousness. They, more than any other institution, be it church, school, or government, determine what every American knows, thinks, and wants.

They began as playthings. Radio, at least in its infant days, was viewed mainly as a means of enabling ships to communicate or to permit someone to hear the scratchy voice of a comic as he told his jokes or to listen to the tinny sound of a band playing in a studio or hotel ballroom in a distant city. Except for shippers, who communicated with their craft by means of a mysterious system of dots and dashes known as the Morse code, few people saw radio in its earliest days as much more than a toy.

Nor did people see television, which was actually invented in the thirties but not developed commercially until after World War II, as much more. Science-fiction films featured such devices as telescreens and videophones that enabled viewer/listeners to see the faces of those with whom they were speaking, but few seriously envisioned a day when the blue-gray glow of the television screen would light the eager faces of the inhabitants of nearly every home in the nation.

Certainly, the newspapers did not initially see the electronic media as competitors. Even after radio had graduated from a plaything to which one could listen a few hours a day to a gaggle of national broadcast networks, news programming occupied only a fraction of the time any station spent on the air. The earliest news broadcasts, in fact, were little more than interruptions. A staff announcer, chosen for his orotund, sonorous tones rather than for any demonstrable journalistic skills, read a tightly written digest of the day's newspaper headlines. Later, once broadcasters recognized the advantage of being tied in to the news services such as the Associated Press, United Press, or the International News Service, the announcer tore the latest news summary off the teletypewriter and read it on the air, often with the noise of the machine in the background to convey a sense of excitement and add a touch of newsroom verisimilitude.

As the twenties gave way to the thirties, radio stations began to expand their news programs, some of them offering several "major" broadcasts of fifteen minutes each daily. But not even the broadcasters themselves felt that they were competing with the print media as purveyors of information. As late as the beginning of World War II, in fact, announcers on the CBS network used to sign off with the suggestion that listeners who wished details on the news items just aired read their local papers.

The thirties did, however, see a new development—the advent of the news commentator. With their unique speaking styles and trademarked sign-ons and sign-offs, not to mention their strong, freely expressed views, radio commentators like H. V. Kaltenborn, Gabriel Heatter, Fulton Lewis, and Walter Winchell became media stars. As the thirties gave way to the forties and the war in Europe and Asia began to dominate America's thoughts, growing numbers of Americans began to tune in to these news commentators regularly in the hope of learning how the conflict was progressing. In millions of homes around the country, Americans sat down every evening at 7:00 P.M. to listen as Winchell opened his program by saying: "Good evening, Mr. and Mrs. America and all the ships at sea . . ." It mattered little that Winchell and his counterparts told their listeners nothing that had not already been made available to the newspapers; what mattered was that these oracles of the airwaves would tell their listeners first. The evening papers, which ran off their last editions minutes after the stock markets closed at 3:00 P.M., were printed, read, and in the waste basket by the time the beeping of a key sending Morse code announced that Winchell was ready to broadcast. The morning papers, most of which went to bed around midnight, would not be on the streets or on people's doorsteps for nearly twelve hours. But Winchell, Kaltenborn, Lewis, and a host of others were there with the news.

What turned radio news into a serious threat to newspaper hegemony was a combination of two things: World War II and CBS. Up to the war, radio news was essentially print news read aloud; it was news that had originally been prepared by newspapers or for them by the wire services, rewritten into a five- or ten- or fifteen-minute package and read aloud on the air. But shortly after the beginning of the war, this changed. CBS's William Paley had sent the brilliant Edward R. Murrow to Europe, charging him with the task of "covering" the Continent and arranging special broadcasts. CBS was willing to broadcast *some* news. But it was not eager to originate this news itself. Hiring newspapermen to discuss developments was all right, Paley felt, but for CBS personnel to do the reporting themselves would commit the network editorially.

Faced with Paley's reluctance to put his network actively into the news-gathering business, Murrow persisted. He hired William L. Shirer, a journalist with extensive newspaper and wire service experience, and arranged for him to cover Hitler's great party rally in Nuremberg. Overcoming resistance, Shirer and Murrow continued to broadcast the news; Shirer, who had been in Vienna at the time of the Anschluss, raced to London to broadcast that story only twenty-four hours after it happened. A week later, Murrow and Shirer arranged and aired the first world news roundup ever broadcast, cueing in reports from correspondents around the globe in a manner little different from that followed today by radio and television producers. It was not, Shirer later conceded, the best roundup he had ever heard. But it was the first, and it started something. "From that hasty development sprang the principal format of broadcast news—first over the radio, then over television—as we have known it ever since," Shirer wrote in his autobiography.[1]

It did indeed. With its reports relayed into the CBS studios in London by short wave, the program lacked the smoothly professional quality of those broadcasts that CBS now airs as a matter of routine. But it worked.

New York asked its European correspondents to set up another the next day.

Writing about the experience years later, Shirer, who later went on to write the best-selling *Rise and Fall of the Third Reich,* could still recall the thrill of knowing that his words were going out over the airwaves to millions of listeners in the United States. He was, he recalled, impressed by radio's reach. But what impressed him even more was the medium's immediacy. Newspapers took time to produce. But radio was—or could be—instantaneous. The moment something happened, Shirer realized, he, or Murrow, or any other witness, could be on the air, letting listeners know what was going on.[2]

As it turned out, Murrow and Shirer were more impressed with radio's potential than their employers back in New York. Shirer, who covered England's shameful sellout of Czechoslovakia at Munich, was delighted when CBS approved the idea of his doing a five-minute daily report from the city where the future of Europe was being decided. But he was annoyed that New York wanted him to cable his reports beforehand if he felt the news did not warrant his using so much valuable time. "My God," he wrote. "Here was the old continent on the brink of war—Hitler might start it within twenty-four hours, Prague might be wiped off the map overnight by the big bombers—and the network was most reluctant to provide five minutes a day to report it."[3]

The network, of course, did spare the time. It also spared some cash, allowing Murrow to assemble a team of first-rate newsmen who also happened to have good radio voices, men like Robert Trout and Charles Collingwood, to name just two. Working together, these men added a whole new dimension to the news. Murrow, for example, did more than merely report on the number of bombs dropped on London during a typical day of the Battle of Britain. He originated his report from the roof of a building from which he could see and describe the searchlight beams probing the night sky like scalpels, the flashes of the antiaircraft batteries, the bursting of bombs. Listeners could not see these things, except as Murrow described them. But they could hear the "orchestrated hell" of which he spoke, and they knew that when Murrow opened his broadcasts with the words "This is London . . ." they would feel as if they, too, were there.

The combination of commentators and the growing professionalism of the newsmen employed at least by the major networks helped bring radio into its own during World War II, and assured that the medium would remain an important part of the nation's news business in the years that followed. For by the time the war ended, it was clear that a new kind of newsman had arrived on the scene, a man who could think—and talk—on his feet, and one who could manage to convey, if not the whole story, then certainly enough to satisfy most listeners, in the incredibly short space of sixty seconds. Many radio stations, to be sure, still considered news programming to be a matter of "rip and read," of tearing the latest news summary off the wire service teletypewriter and having it read, often by a staff announcer who, whatever his other qualifications, frequently had no understanding whatever of the stories he was broadcasting. Some stations still follow this practice, in fact. But a growing number of radio stations began to hire newsmen themselves and to broadcast news more regularly. By the late forties, every radio station in the United States included some news in its programming; many carried three major news broadcasts of ten or fifteen minutes duration early in the morning, at midday, and in the early evening; a few pioneers offered the news, or at least the headlines, every hour.

The networks and local broadcasters, however, were not the only ones to realize the potential of radio. Politicians were even quicker to seize upon it as a way of reaching large audiences and, more important, for achieving an intimacy with them that they could never achieve from the podium. Franklin Delano Roosevelt understood intuitively that radio was an intimate medium, and one that was ill-suited to the formal style of speaking to which most politicians were addicted. One could not, he realized, orate over the air. But one could talk to people conversationally.

Which is precisely what Roosevelt did in his broadcast "Fireside Chats." FDR used these weekly broadcasts to speak directly to the American people, using the fact that he was speaking from his living room to establish contact with people who were listening to him in theirs. Listeners heard him pause and ask for and drink a glass of water, heard him refer to his little dog Fala, knew and could recognize the sound of their president's voice and feel that they knew him.

Roosevelt was not, of course, either the only politician—or the first—to use radio to speak directly to the American people. Others, including the troubled, proto-Fascist Father Coughlin, who took to the airwaves to denounce Jews, immigrants, and a host of other so-called "enemies" of his kind of America, found radio better than any soap box. So did advertisers, who used radio to sell Americans everything from soap to breakfast cereals. All took to it for the same reasons: more than newspapers ever could, radio allowed them to reach their constituencies, their audiences, their markets, directly.

But even as radio came to permeate American life, even as Americans began to listen to their radios constantly in their homes, cars, and offices, a more powerful rival was developing. Throughout its gestation period in the twenties and thirties, television had been seen by at least some visionaries as the medium that would not only entertain, but inform mass society and improve the popular mind. The end of World War II found mass society ready. The decades of development had prepared the public for the idea of television; the years of work to produce transmission equipment and television receivers had been well spent. In the late forties, when television was becoming available and increasingly affordable, most Americans could not wait to welcome the new medium. Those who could not afford their own sets took trips downtown so the whole family could stand in front of a department or appliance store window to watch programs being transmitted from New York or Hollywood.

In a practical manner of speaking, television came of age in 1948, the year that stars like Milton Berle and Ed Sullivan booked scores of celebrities onto their shows. Four networks, NBC, CBS, ABC, and Dumont, offered a staggering variety of programs from puppet shows to prizefights. But the programming that had the most profound effect on the American viewer was the news.

And a different kind of news, to boot. Radio, like newspapers, after all, required only words. Television demanded pictures, and television news meant the kind of reporting that offered visual images as well as spoken words.[4]

Early television news met its visual requirements simply. Basically, television news programs followed the "talking head" format, showing an announcer sitting at a desk while reading copy that had been rewritten from wire service material, plus some still pictures, charts, maps, and film footage of recent events. Not only did the networks have trouble blending aural and visual materials; they had trouble getting, processing, and distributing film of current events.

Small wonder, then, that television news failed to impress most viewers. A 1948 survey showed that better than 46 percent of television owners preferred comedy and variety shows to news and public affairs programs. Nor did the majority of television viewers see much need for better news programming; when asked what they would like to see more of on television, 22.7 percent chose new and better movies. Only 1.2 percent said they wanted more news.

TV news did not progress rapidly. In 1953, *Variety* reported the industry's view that "television, in the news field, is not providing enough variety or depth of understanding in its coverage of world events." Four years later, *Variety* noted that while methods for gathering news and getting it on the air were improving, the actual visualization process was at a standstill.[5]

But despite its problems, television news began to acquire a following. In 1948, news and news-related broadcasts accounted for about 15 percent of NBC's program schedule. By the middle of the following year, that network's nightly "Camel News Caravan," with John Cameron Swayze, which remained on the network until it was replaced in 1956 by "The Huntley-Brinkley Report," held the distinction of being the highest rated multiweekly show on television. By the late fifties, television was on its way to replacing both newspapers and radio as Americans' primary source of news. By the end of 1957, for example, CBS's "Douglas Edwards and the News" was reaching 14.1 million viewers daily and some 34 million at least once a week. Huntley and Brinkley were viewed in 7.6 million homes each night. The numbers are impressive by themselves. They become even more so when compared with what the print media were doing. At that time, *Time* magazine was reaching 8.1 million readers each week; *Life* was reaching 30.4 million.[6]

The problems faced by the networks, though, were minor when compared with those of the local stations. The networks at least had money to spend and reached audiences large enough to win commercial sponsorship for their news programs. But local broadcasters had neither the skill nor the resources to do first-rate news programs. Videotape, which can be easily and inexpensively edited, did not replace film until the late fifties. Lacking film-processing facilities, local stations either purchased film from the networks or bought it from commercial film producers and newsreel companies like United Press-Fox Movietone. Nor could local television outlets afford to produce first-rate programming. Local stations lacked the money to afford mobile units that could get out to the scene of a story and transmit it back to the station; local advertisers had neither the money nor the interest to fund top-quality news programs.

But despite these problems, there were still things that television could do well, and one of them was to broadcast self-contained events, panel discussions, and documentaries. As early as 1948, the networks carried live coverage of the Republican and Democratic party nominating conventions. In 1949, CBS carried live coverage of United Nations debates. In 1951, no fewer than 94 of the 108 television stations in the United States joined together to carry live coverage of the signing of the peace treaty between the United States and Japan, sending the program from San Francisco to the entire country by means of a coaxial cable/microwave link set up for the occasion.

Nor did television lag when it came to informing the public about government activities. In 1951, television moved into a Senate hearing room for live coverage as the Senate Crime Investigating Committee, chaired by Tennessee's Estes Kefauver, questioned top underworld figures, including Frank Costello, about their activities. The impact of these broadcasts, which preempted other morning and afternoon programming, was enormous. A March 1951, audience survey found that every television set turned on in New York was tuned in to the hearings.[7]

Television also pioneered the panel discussion program, in which newsmakers and journalists sat down before the cameras to discuss national or world affairs. Discussion programs were not new, of course; radio had carried them for years, without managing to attract an audience of any but the most dedicated listeners. But television panel discussions thrived from their very beginning because they enabled viewers to see as well as hear the senators and congressmen, diplomats, political candidates, and businessmen whose ambitions and activities shaped their lives. Originally, programs like NBC's "Meet the Press" and ABC's "Town Meeting of the Air" were aired simultaneously on radio and television. But a new crop of programs originated especially for television soon joined them. CBS came up with "Face the Nation"; ABC offered "Press Conference" and "Open Hearing."

The other type of program at which television excelled was the documentary. CBS's Fred W. Friendly, one of the pioneers of that type of programming, said in 1959 that the documentary promised not only to be a key part of the television anatomy, "but its very backbone." Nor was this all Friendly had to say. In a statement that proved prophetic, Friendly predicted that television would command the biggest audiences in the history of communication, and, depending upon how well or badly those in control used it, make Americans either the best- or worst-informed people in the world. Friendly, in fact, warned the industry that it must use the evolving medium wisely, and, in a message that many feel may well have gone unheard, urged the television industry to use television's enormous power responsibly. His argument was evangelical. ". . . If we are to hold up a mirror to the world with one hand and a microphone with the other," said Friendly, "we must be worthy of conducting the greatest mass information gazette in the history of man. To use it simply as another method of peddling soup and peanut butter will be to destroy a reporting and, therefore, selling, opportunity never handed to any race of men."[8]

Friendly had ambitious plans for using the medium for documentaries. But before he could implement these plans, a more pressing news event intervened—the Korean Conflict. The war, which broke out in June 1950, and to which President Truman promptly dispatched U.S. forces, was the first major international test for television news. But it was not, like the war in Southeast Asia a decade later, a television war. Television simply was neither technically nor professionally ready to report the Korean War thoroughly.

In fact, the networks were not prepared to cover the Korean Conflict on television at all. CBS and NBC were equipped to cover the war on radio only; they still were not prepared to coordinate words and pictures. For its film, television relied, as it had been doing for the past several years, on newsreel producers; they and the U.S. Army Signal Corps provided most of the film American television viewers saw of the war.

Covering the war forced the television networks to rely upon the armed forces for more than film, too. Like all other journalists, television reporters depended upon the military for access to headquarters and battle areas, for transportation, for housing, and, in some cases, for the transmission facilities necessary to get their reports back to their studios.

Understandably, early coverage of the war was disappointing. Limited by technical difficulties and military censorship from showing anything the U.S. military did not want shown, television news operations showed what was available. Sessions of the U.N. Security Council were frequently aired less than two hours after they occurred. The networks also made up for their inability to cover the day-to-day fighting adequately by presenting special reports that relied less heavily on up-to-date film than the daily news. CBS aired a four-part series titled "Crisis in Korea," using film spliced together from network footage, newsreels, and Signal Corps material. Coverage could have improved even further when Murrow, still an innovator, produced a thoughtful, perceptive program on the history and significance of the Korean War. But the program was never aired. Network executives, feeling that parts of it went against orders from General Douglas MacArthur forbidding news personnel from criticizing command decisions, censored it themselves.

But CBS did air other programs Murrow produced on the war. It broadcast his look at a day in the life of an infantry platoon; it aired another show tracing the experiences of three GIs who were wounded in the fighting and evacuated to hospitals. It let the soldiers speak for themselves in a poignant program titled "Christmas in Korea."[9]

Most important, it allowed Murrow and Friendly to create a journalistic tradition, and to show that television journalists need not take a back seat to the high standards set by the newspapers. The programs the pair produced were noted for the care with which they were assembled and the balance with which they were presented. Patriotic without being jingoistic, notably free of rhetoric and filler, the programs showed that television could contribute to understanding of and debate on important issues.

The end of the Korean War found television news stronger and more respected than it had ever been. But the years after the war presented the medium with a new challenge. The war had intensified America's long-standing fear of communism, which few understood, but for which many held an almost primitive hatred. An ambitious, unscrupulous politician, Senator Joseph McCarthy, decided to exploit this fear. Other senators had warned during the war of the dangers of Communist subversion and of Soviet plots for world domination. Some, like Chairman of the House Committee on Un-American Activities Harold Velde, announced campaigns to weed Communists out of government.

But no one captured the public's attention or imagination like McCarthy. And no one did a better job of using the new medium of television for his purposes. McCarthy seemed to know instinctively what would make good television; he seemed to know that what television news producers needed were short, dramatic statements that could be easily inserted in nightly news broadcasts. He also knew that television increasingly made news in other media, and, appearing regularly on news panel shows, he delivered himself of statements that were picked up by radio and incorporated into the headlines of the following day's newspapers.

Hardly a day went by, it seemed, when McCarthy was not on television. Whether dominating Senate hearings with his cries of "Point of Order," or waving a sheaf of documents and announcing that he held in his hand a list of the names of ten, twenty, thirty, fifty Communists in the State Department, McCarthy commanded both the video screen and the national consciousness for nearly two years. He silenced opponents by shouting them down or impugning their patriotism. He all but accused 1952 Democratic presidential candidate Adlai Stevenson of working for Moscow.

Television, which accepted and reported McCarthy's accusations uncritically, making little effort to ascertain whether they were accurate or to put them into perspective, was the key to McCarthy's success. But it was also the key to his destruction. The men who turned that key were Murrow and Friendly, who examined McCarthy and his tactics, showed how he defamed and browbeat witnesses. Their "See It Now" segment, aired in 1954, revealed McCarthy for the bully he was, depicting him as an unscrupulous, mannerless boor who could conduct his attacks secure in the belief that his congressional immunity would protect him from legal responsibility for his actions.

Murrow did not attack McCarthy for his abuses. Instead, he lay the blame for his rise on the acquiescense of the American people, who had let their fear of communism blind them to an equally dangerous menace, the abuse of anticommunism. In the coda with which he closed his program, Murrow eloquently blamed a nation for having created the monster before which it now cowered. In words that those who viewed the original program can still remember, he said:

> This is no time for men who oppose Senator McCarthy's methods to keep silent, or for those who approve. We can deny our heritage and our history, but we cannot escape responsibility for the result. There is no way for a citizen of a republic to abdicate his responsibilities. As a nation, we have come into our full inheritance at a tender age. We proclaim ourselves—as indeed we are—the defenders of freedom, wherever it continues to exist in the world. But we cannot defend freedom abroad by deserting it at home. The actions of the junior senator from Wisconsin have caused alarm and dismay amongst our allies abroad and given considerable comfort to our enemies. And whose fault is that? Not really his; he didn't create this situation of fear, he merely exploited it—and rather successfully. Cassius was right: "The fault, dear Brutus, is not in the stars, but in ourselves." [10]

Murrow's criticism stung McCarthy, who demanded and was given air time to rebut the program. He did not use it well. The half-hour rebuttal spent more time questioning Murrow's loyalty than it did explaining the senator's actions, and made many viewers realize the aptness of Murrow's evaluation.

McCarthy's conduct thereafter continued the process. When McCarthy's Senate committee voted to permit television coverage of its probe of possible Communist infiltration of the U.S. Army, the senator thought that the medium that had helped him rise to power would continue to work for him. Instead, it helped undo him. The hearings, in fact, proved a devastating experience for McCarthy. Its previously supple spine apparently stiffened by Murrow's program and growing public disillusionment with the senator, the Republican administration refused to cooperate with McCarthy. The senator's sullen, belligerent attitude cost him further friends. Americans resented it when McCarthy attempted to humiliate the Secretary of the Army. The senator himself was stunned when attorney Joseph Welch, whose aide the senator viciously attacked, turned on him and asked, before a national television audience, "Have you no sense of decency?" Viewers were upset, then angry, as television coverage of the hearings made it clear that McCarthy had no evidence to support the charges of disloyalty that he made so casually. Before the year ended, McCarthy's rise to power was over. The Senate voted 67 to 22 to censure him for his abusive conduct toward his fellow senators; his supporters increasingly saw him as an embarrassment. When the Democrats gained control of the Senate in the 1954 elections, they stripped him of his committee chairmanship. Two years later, his career in ruins, the drinking problem that had long plagued him getting worse, McCarthy died, and, as H. G. Wells noted in another context, "his world with him."

Television changed the way politicians communicated with the people. Office holders, from the president on down, realized that they could reach more potential voters in a minute on television than they could in a month of campaign stumping, and, starting with President Eisenhower, began pouring the lion's share of their campaign budgets into television advertising. They also began meeting with the people via television. Eisenhower opened the presidential news conference to television, trusting that the medium's ability to convey his affability and homespun sincerity would more than make up for his tortured syntax. President Kennedy and his successors followed suit. Richard Nixon used television to appeal directly to Republican voters when Eisenhower talked of dropping him from the GOP ticket. Nixon's 1952 "Checkers Speech" may have been maudlin, but it tugged at the heartstrings of millions of Americans and forced Eisenhower to retain him as running mate.

But while television was changing the way politicians communicated with the people, it also changed the way in which the people saw politicians. Back when people had to rely on newspapers for their information, they were forced to accept the reporters' impressions of those about whom they were writing. Now, seeing those who sought their votes for office or their consent for actions they were about to take, they could form their impressions for themselves.

Which was exactly what they did in 1960, when the three television networks, for the first time in history, brought them a live debate between the two candidates for the presidency. An estimated 75 million Americans either watched or listened to the first of the "Great Debates."[11] And most found that they liked John Kennedy more than Richard Nixon.

It is not difficult to understand why. Young, vigorous, dramatic, Kennedy was nothing if not appealing. Dark and saturnine, his famous and unfortunate "five o'clock shadow" accentuating his jowls, Nixon looked as shifty as his political rivals had long tried to portray him. Never mind that Nixon was politically the more experienced of the two men. Never mind that he had more facts and figures at his fingertips. Never mind that he simply knew more about government, about international affairs, than Kennedy. Analysts of the debates have since suggested that, had they been carried only on radio, the overwhelming majority would have considered Nixon the clear winner. But the fact is that the debates were carried on television and that Kennedy was clearly the more telegenic of the two.

Kennedy knew this. He knew that television would work for him. And he made it do just that. He was the first president to meet regularly with the press, appearing before newsmen and, even more important, television cameras, and he was the first president who actually seemed to enjoy the exercise, to relish the opportunity to exchange quips with newsmen, whom he both liked and respected. He established a precedent that his successors were expected to follow. Presidents since JFK have been praised—and criticized—for the number of times they have met with the press.

Television's ability to cover the news has improved enormously since the Korean War and the static, studio-bound "Camel News Caravan." Local television stations have acquired both the equipment and the skill to do the kinds of things that once only the networks could dream of doing, such as sending camera crews to cover ongoing events and airing them simultaneously. The television networks have achieved a level of professionalism that continues to amaze even the medium's critics. The major network news broadcasts today are as slickly professional as technology and a sense of stagecraft can make them. Communications satellites enable correspondents in places like, say, Lebanon, to let viewers see fighting that may have occurred only a matter of hours earlier. Fed back to network news headquarters in New York from around the globe, this videotape can be quickly edited into usable footage, which is often shown in a corner of the screen while an anchorman like CBS's Dan Rather or ABC's Peter Jennings narrates the story from behind his desk. Computerized graphics provide visual images for stories that, unlike fighting, fires, or other disasters, do not make for good pictures.

Television also attempts to cover more. The networks, at least, maintain news bureaus in Washington and other world capitals. They do not stint when it comes to spending money and sending people to where news is being made. The networks spent millions covering the war in Vietnam, providing gavel-to-gavel coverage of the Republican and Democratic conventions, getting crews in to cover the bloody, often confusing guerrilla war in Central America, showing the unfolding tragedy of South Africa.

Television, indeed, has made news, and not just because the comments of a cabinet officer on "Meet the Press" are picked up by the wire services and run in newspapers the following day. The 1984–85 famine that gripped Ethiopia, the Sudan, and other African countries, produced little more than yawns when newspapers carried stories on the subject. But once television picked up the stories and brought the specter of starvation into the living rooms of its viewers, public interest picked up and people began demanding that something be done to alleviate the problem.

Television, in fact, has changed the public's perception of just what constitutes news. Newspapers may still deal with fairly abstract stories like those on taxes, the economy, or efforts to amend the U.S. Constitution. But television tends to avoid anything that is not visual, which means that given a choice between drama and substance, it tends to choose the former. American television crews, for example, stayed in Central America while the fighting in El Salvador escalated, but once the guerrillas' efforts to overthrow the country's U.S.-backed government slacked off, most of the network crews went home. "My editors want war," said NBC's Fred Francis by way of explanation. "If there's no shooting, they think there's no story."[12]

Francis's complaint is not unique. Even print journalists, including those employed by such prestigious publications as *The New York Times, The Washington Post, Time,* and *Newsweek,* lament that their editors show little interest in stories from which action is missing. "New York wants bang-bang," complained one newsmagazine writer who spent a month in Central America without managing to get a story into print.

The problem, however, is more acute on television, where audiences, too, want action, and where the ability to build and hold an audience determines such things as ratings, and thus the amount that a television station can charge advertisers for the time to peddle their products. Which means that, to viewers, critics, and participants alike, television news often seems superficial.

For the most part, it is. There simply is not that much to most television news programs, and not because television is not interested in doing better. Television operates under limits that do not plague the print media; time and space are both in short supply on a television news program. The typical half-hour news program, for instance, really amounts to only twenty-four or twenty-five minutes once time for the commercials that make it possible is deducted. It does not take a great many words to fill this time. In fact, since most broadcasters read at the rate of about 15 typewritten lines a minute, it takes no more than 375 lines—about 15 double-spaced pages worth of material—less copy than it takes to fill two columns of *The New York Times*—to fill up a television news program.

Dividing this among the eighteen or more stories that comprise the average news broadcast, this factors out to very little time indeed. Most television stories are covered in sixty seconds or less, or perhaps a single page of typewritten copy. Some stories can be covered in this amount of space; many stories, like a report, say, on the discovery of a body and the suspicions of law enforcement authorities that murder was committed, can be covered, to the extent that the average viewer needs to know about them, in well under a minute. But many require more time if they are to tell viewers any more than they would get from examining the headlines of a newspaper.

Which explains why so many stories get short shrift, or why less important stories with good visual possibilities often get more airtime than important items that cannot be covered visually. Congress, for example, gets relatively little time on television for the simple reason that complicated pieces of legislation cannot be easily explained in sixty or even ninety seconds. Indeed, coverage of Congress has declined dramatically in the last decade. According to an article in the *Washington Journalism Review,* in fact, the number of stories on Congress carried by the three networks during the period between 1980 and 1984 was only half that carried by the nation's major television broadcasters in the five years that preceded this period. Newsmen from the networks go to Congress to get reaction to decisions or actions by the President and members of his cabinet. But they rarely cover Congress itself. The reason is readily apparent. "Television news requires a steady diet of pictures, color, personalities, and stories that can be told in a minute and a half," says Greg Schneiders, a former Carter White House aide who now works for a political consulting and research firm. "Legislating is not only dry; it is non-visual. There are few good pictures."[13]

Similar stories are also shortchanged. Many broadcasters confine their business news to a few lines on such economic indicators as the Dow-Jones averages. Many eschew the issues involved in political campaigns and concentrate instead on the personalities of the candidates involved.

Many television newsmen acknowledge the problem and concede that television alone does not provide viewers with all the news and information they need in order to exercise their rights and fulfill their duties as citizens. As NBC's John Dancy has conceded: "We will never replace newspapers in the amount of content or interpretation that we're able to give a news event. People will just have to read if they want to be informed."[14]

Most Americans seem to realize this; most know that television is both qualitatively and quantitatively different from the print media. The differences are not always matters connected with the media; they include the people who "perform" on it as well. Those differences, in fact, can be dramatic. Most of the people who work in print are, after all, journalists first and foremost; with few exceptions, they are hired for and hold their

jobs through their ability to ferret out and write up the stories to which
they are assigned, not for their on-camera appearances or the mellifluous
tone of their voices. Television broadcasters, whatever their journalistic
skills, are also performers. Some are as good at reporting as they are at
performing before television cameras; most network correspondents, for
example, need lessons from no one when it comes to identifying, reporting, and presenting a news story; some display a doggedness that does
credit to the entire tradition of journalism. Rivals may have made some
snide comments when CBS's Dan Rather donned native garb and slipped
across the border to meet and report on the Afghan guerrillas resisting
the Soviet occupation of their country. But not even the most jealous of
Rather's critics denied that ''Gunga Dan,'' as they dubbed him, had
managed to get himself a good story. Critics may charge ABC's Barbara
Walters with asking an occasional inane question as she uses her own
celebrity to land interviews with world leaders and Hollywood stars. But
none of those who snipe at her would turn down the chances she has had
to interview such figures as Egypt's Anwar Sadat or Britain's Margaret
Thatcher, or deny that she has turned her tête-à-têtes with them into full-
scale news breaks.

The television networks, in fact, generally bring a high level of professionalism to their programming, finding stories and presenting them as
well as their medium permits. But the same, unfortunately, cannot always
be said for local news operations. Some, indeed many, local newsmen
and women are little more than good sight readers, able to take copy they
have only seen once and read it convincingly. Many, perhaps most, were
chosen for their jobs as anchormen and women more for their on-camera
presence than for any understanding of news and what makes it important.
Some display their ignorance of journalism inadvertently, like the New
York anchorman who insisted on covering the Israeli invasion of Lebanon
and made it clear in his first report that he probably could not cover a
news story if it happened to him. Others display it accidentally, by asking
questions that show they have little understanding of the stories they are
covering. One television newsman generated first amusement, then anger,
when, sent by his station to cover the 1979 nuclear power plant accident
at Pennsylvania's Three Mile Island, he dominated press briefings with
his stentorian voice and his habit of asking questions that demonstrated
that he did not know the difference between a nuclear plant and a nuclear
bomb. Some of his embarrassed colleagues finally took him aside and
explained, not without some asperity, that whatever the plant at Three
Mile Island might do as a result of the accident, it would not blow up
like the bomb that leveled Hiroshima.

Television has changed the American public's view of the news, turning many Americans from readers to "consumers" of information. It has also forced viewers to rely heavily on news editors' and producers' views of just what is worth knowing. Newspaper readers, after all, in effect construct their own newspapers, selecting both the items they wish to read in any day's edition and the order in which they read them. Television viewers can make no such selections. They must view what the editors select for them in the order they select it—or view nothing at all.

More important, television news has changed the public's view of those who gather and present the news. Managed out of New York and clearly more attuned to Eastern interests than to those of, say, Iowa or Kansas, the television networks seem awfully remote and distant to a viewer in Peoria, whose town makes the national news only when a politician deigns to visit it or when the corn crop fails. This distance disturbs many Americans, who tend to add television in general and the news business in particular to the list of institutions that they distrust simply because of their power, their size, and their remoteness.

Television has changed the image of the newsman himself. In the days when print was the principal means of disseminating the news, Americans could look at the often seedy, frequently ill-dressed, generally underpaid people who wrote, edited, and printed their newspapers and feel that they were at least cut from the same cloth as they themselves were. Television has given Americans a whole new image of the newsman, showing them a well-paid, well-dressed fellow who is often only too well aware of his own importance.

Television has hurt the image of the newsman in other ways, too. It has done this by showing the newsman, particularly the television newsman, at work, and what it shows is not always pleasant. At presidential news conferences, the public sees television newsmen like ABC's Sam Donaldson, whose booming baritone can and occasionally does drown out a whole roomful of reporters, asking what seem to be rudely phrased questions of the only official in the United States elected by all of the people. In the wake of the car bombing of the U.S. Marine barracks in Beirut, it saw something even worse. Newsmen, mainly television newsmen, camped outside the homes of those awaiting word on whether their husbands or sons were among those killed in the blast; they then showed the anguished faces of those getting the dreaded news on national television.

What has happened is obvious. Television has changed the journalist from a witness to happenings to a participant. It has enabled people who would not otherwise do so to see journalists at work, to examine the attitudes they bring to a story, to study the methods they use to get it. As *Washington Post* Editor Ben Bradlee has put it: "Television has changed the public's vision of the reporter into someone who is petty and disagreeable, who has taken cynicism an unnecessary extra step." Oakland *Tribune* editor Robert Maynard agrees. "When people see a TV person shoving a mike in front of a grieving relative," says he, "all of us in the press appear to be boorish and ghoulish."[15]

Television executives note in their defense that print reporters can be just as obnoxious as those who work for the electronic media. Their point is well taken. Reporters for the tabloid press in particular were noted for slipping into the homes of the families of accident or murder victims to obtain recent photographs; bad manners are bad manners whether exhibited by a newspaper reporter or a television journalist. But television's self-defense ignores the reality of the situation. Print reporters can get away with egregiously aggressive behavior because print itself is abstract rather than immediate. "The printed press does not show the reporter asking the question," says NBC News editorial adviser Reuven Frank. "What is peculiar to television is that the intrusiveness is part of the story."[16]

It is unfortunate that this is so. But some other aspects of television are equally unfortunate, and perhaps none more so than the fact that television is a business in which journalism is a sideline. For unlike newspapers, television networks were not formed for the purpose of providing news and information. They were formed for the purpose of making money for their owners and stockholders. They do this by selling air time, and they do this, in turn, by offering the kind of programming that attracts audiences. For the more people who watch a television station or a given program, the more that station can charge for those thirty- or sixty-second spots that advertisers hope will persuade people to buy their products. This means, then, that even news must pay its way and attract viewers. A television anchorperson who fails to attract a following will be replaced just as readily as a comic whose jokes fall flat. This means that television cannot afford to take the news *too* seriously. For, as Tony Schwartz puts it, television is a two-sided coin: "The positive side to electronic media news broadcasts is their ability to inform the world instantaneously about developments that affect all the people of the world. The negative side is the determination to please commercial time buyers by keeping the news 'entertaining' at any cost, resulting in a tendency to make the size of the audience more important than the significance of the news."

Schwartz's point is well made. The rise of television has created as many problems as it has solved. It has solved, at least to a great extent, the problem of getting information to large, indeed, often astronomically large, numbers of people quickly. But it has created a problem arising out of how the news is recognized, perceived, and presented. For on television, the news exists in a medium in which facts are not necessarily sacred. With the exceptions of the comic strips, the astrology column, and, possibly, the advertisements, a newspaper can, despite frequent criticism of some papers, still be seen as a collection of facts, a publication put together for the sole purpose of presenting information.

But on television, this is not possible. News, which accounts for an average of 15 percent of any station's total programming, is clearly not the predominant product of the medium. It exists in a blurred context where fact and fiction coexist. For some, behind the cameras or in front of them, the difference can be hard to distinguish. Viewers often become so wrapped up in such things as soap operas that they speak about the characters in "All My Children" as if they were neighbors, rather than roles played by actors and actresses on a show whose only purpose is to be sufficiently entertaining to enable the sponsor to buy himself an audience for his commercials. Television executives and producers often find it equally difficult to make the distinction. They sometimes forget that in life, unlike television, all problems do not get solved before the last commercial, or that in life, problems often do not get solved at all. What they do know is that all television tends toward drama. So they go for the dramatic in news as well as entertainment, stressing conflict over substance and opting, when possible, for the entertaining story over the items that inform.

Television's ability to influence the public's perception of the news is enormous. A camera that shows one hundred demonstrators gathered in front of a courthouse can, unless it shows that neighboring streets are either empty or populated with people going about their business normally, convey the impression that insurrection is imminent. A television news editor who continually selects footage of a telegenic but otherwise unimportant official can foster the view that the subject is far more influential than he really is.

For television has, in a way, become the tabloid press of the eighties, the medium that attracts and keeps its following by selecting the sensational, that finds major conflict in honest disagreement, that sees doom where there is only disaster—and not always very great disaster at that. Viewers watching New York television stations at the end of the summer of 1985 could easily be understood to be on the verge of hysteria about the spread of the disease known as acquired immune deficiency syndrome, or AIDS; reporting on these stations made it sound as if something as catastrophic and contagious as the Black Plague were about to erupt in the United States. Nor could television viewers be condemned for seeming unconcerned about presidential proposals to increase their tax burdens; the same stations barely covered these stories at all.

Television's influence would be unfortunate if it affected television viewers alone. But it does not. For television, with its vast power, now influences the print press, too, and helps to determine what it publishes. Many newspaper and magazine editors order their staffs to produce stories that they have seen on television. *The New York Times,* to be sure, is not likely to carry a major story on a French train accident on page one simply because a television station, which was able to obtain film footage of railroad cars strewn across the countryside, led its news broadcast with the item the previous evening. Nor is *The Washington Post* likely to run a major story on a Vancouver man's holding his two-year-old-son hostage merely because television stations, which had pictures of the distraught man holding his child out the window by an ankle, gave the story big play. Both publications know that such stories rightly belong inside the paper and recognize that their front pages should be devoted to more important items.

But other newspapers are not quite as confident, and many know that the trick to attracting readers is to offer an arresting headline. No newspaper in the United States, in fact, seems to do this more regularly than the *New York Post,* which has tried consistently to go television and its visual approach to the news one better. New York television stations once led their evening broadcasts with a story describing how an air conditioner had fallen from the window of a Manhattan apartment building to smash to the sidewalk several floors below. The story, with footage of the window from which the air conditioner fell and shots of pedestrians looking at the crushed machine on the pavement, received about ninety seconds worth of play on local television news programs. It got the whole front page of the next day's *Post,* which carried the hyped-up headline, "Terror From the Skies." Fortunately for those who might have wondered just what was really going on, the paper refrained from going too much further with its hyperbole. There are, after all, more than eight million people in New York. If the *Post* had really wanted to show up television in the handling of its own story on the falling air conditioner, which injured no one, it could have run a subhead announcing, "Millions Escape Death."

# Chapter Four

# The Adversary Relationship

Cameras. That's all I see wherever I look. Sometimes, I'm not sure whether I'm a soldier or an extra in a bad movie.

American infantryman
in Vietnam, 1965

Michael Arlen of *The New Yorker* named it "The Living Room War." Others, depending upon where they stood—and still stand—politically, called it a noble crusade or a national tragedy. But everyone agrees that the formless, ferocious war that raged in the small southeast Asian country of Vietnam for nearly a decade became part of the national consciousness as no other conflict before it had managed to do. For no war in American history—or that of any other country, for that matter—was covered like the war in Vietnam.

From the time American advisers first went to that troubled land in the early 1960s until the moment that the city of Saigon fell and the last Americans were airlifted off the roof of the U.S. Embassy by helicopter, the war was covered by the American news media with an intensity that defied belief. Few aspects of the war, from the fighting in the towns, hills, and jungles of Vietnam, to the protests against American involvement in the conflict at home and abroad, went unreported in the newspapers, on radio, on television. Few aspects of the war went unanalyzed or escaped comment. World War II and Korea had been covered by reporters whose access to the action and ability to report was tightly controlled. In Vietnam, the press had virtually complete freedom to go anywhere and report anything. The result was to give the American people, and especially American television viewers, the most complete closeup ever provided of a war in the process of being fought and to turn the press from observers into kibitzers, ready, willing, and able, like the old men who hang around in parks and watch chess games, to comment on the contest in progress and to offer their own suggestions as to what the players should be doing. "This war," lamented U.S. Ambassador Ellsworth Bunker at one point, "was fought in a fishbowl. Everybody saw what was going on. Every American, from the GI on the battlefield to those who stayed at home, was involved in it."

Bunker's evaluation is accurate. The press in general and television in particular helped to make the conflict in Vietnam into a war with no fronts. It turned every American into a witness to the war. It made most Americans, willingly or not, participants. The press did not do any of these things casually. It did not do all of them deliberately. Nor, as some have since charged, did the American news media set out from the start to hamper first one administration, then another, in its conduct of the war or to pressure the United States to withdraw from the field. The press, at least initially, supported U.S. involvement.

Large-scale American involvement in Vietnam can be said to have begun with the so-called Tonkin Gulf incidents, which occurred on the evenings of August 2 and 4, 1964. The United States had, of course, been involved in Vietnam before those dates. The country had, in fact, been involved in Vietnam since 1956, when together with the South Vietnamese, it refused to honor a commitment to support elections aimed at unifying the land, which had been partitioned into North and South Vietnam following the French defeat at Dienbienphu. That refusal bound the United States to assist a country that controlled less than half of its forty-three provinces and which, since the 1963 murder of the corrupt, dictatorial Ngo Dinh Diem, had been plagued by instability and threatened by coups.

The choices that faced President Lyndon Johnson as he ran for reelection in 1964 were not unlimited; he had, really, only three options. He could withdraw U.S. military and technical advisers from South Vietnam, leaving the unpopular government to sink or swim on its own. He could accept the suggestion of French President Charles de Gaulle and attempt to create a unified Vietnam that would be politically neutral in the contest between East and West. Or he could remain in Vietnam, increasing both the size and the scope of the U.S. commitment.

Determined, among other things, not to go down in history as the president who had "lost" Vietnam, Johnson chose the latter course. But in making his choice, he realized that he needed substantial support for his actions at home. To get it, Johnson, who was hardly the first American president to do so, decided to manipulate the media.

The means he chose to do this was the Tonkin Gulf Incident. The incident was a two-part affair. The first part took place on the evening of August 2, when the U.S. Destroyer *Maddox* was fired upon by North Vietnamese patrol boats while cruising in the Gulf of Tonkin. The second part took place two days later when the *Maddox,* accompanied now by the destroyer *C. Turner Joy,* reported that it had again come under fire from North Vietnamese patrol craft, which this time launched torpedoes against the American vessels.

The years since then have produced strong evidence to suggest that the second attack never took place and that reports to the effect that it had were, to put it kindly, somewhat exaggerated. The destroyers were steaming through rain squalls and high seas and having trouble interpreting the signals on their sonar equipment; their commanders, aware of what had actually happened two days earlier, were nervous and worried lest they become targets.

The accuracy of the reports, however, seemed unimportant to the President and his aides. Determined not only to get tough with the North Vietnamese, but to show the public that he was getting tough, Johnson went on television almost immediately after the initial reports of the second incident were received to announce that he had ordered air strikes against four ports and an oil storage facility in North Vietnam. What he did not announce was that the captain of the *Maddox,* questioning his own initial reports, had sent the Pentagon a message urging a more complete evaluation of the "incident" before any action was taken.

What Johnson did reveal, though, was his desire for a congressional resolution supporting his action, a statement making it clear that the United States was "united in its determination to take all necessary measures in support of freedom and in defense of peace in Southeast Asia."[1] He had no trouble getting it. Three days later, the House of Representatives passed the Tonkin Gulf Resolution by a vote of 414 to 0, while the Senate approved it by a margin of 88 to 2. From then until the end of the conflict, it would be the closest the United States would come to issuing a formal declaration of war.

What helped the American public to accept this, and the inevitable escalation of the war, was television. Other presidents had, of course, committed American troops to combat without declarations of war; Truman had done so in Korea and Kennedy had done so when he sent American combat advisers to Vietnam. The Constitution gave the president power to protect U.S. security. But, as communications historian J. Fred

MacDonald has noted, "it was TV that made protracted, undeclared war acceptable."[2]

Television did not do this deliberately. In many respects, it did this unthinkingly. It did it, in part, because the Tonkin Gulf Incident made good television. Following the August 2 attack, television gave Senator Hubert Humphrey the opportunity to appear on "Face the Nation" and praise the U.S. Navy for reacting in an "admirable" manner to the provocation.[3] The medium gave other national figures, senators, congressmen, and other political figures the opportunity to appear before the cameras— and the nation—to express their outrage.

Johnson, it must be said, used the medium masterfully. On August 4, he requested television time from the networks, which not only granted it but interrupted their programming throughout the evening to announce that he would be delivering an important message later that night. When the President finished making his announcement, the networks switched to the Pentagon, where Secretary of Defense Robert McNamara stood ready with maps and pointer to explain what the United States had done and why.

Neither the television networks nor, for that matter, the newspapers, raised many questions about the incident; in fact, they tended to accept the Administration's announcements and explanations without question. Few asked what U.S. warships were doing in what were, after all, North Vietnamese territorial waters. Fewer still asked for solid evidence to establish that the attacks that led to the U.S. action had actually occurred. Only ABC's Howard K. Smith seemed bothered by the incidents, wondering aloud why a "peanut-sized sea power" like North Vietnam would attack the world's strongest nation "on an element where U.S. power is almost unanswerable." Others, it seemed, operated on the assumption that if the government said something, it must be true.[4]

Johnson kept U.S. efforts in Vietnam confined largely to air attacks until after the election that gave him the presidency in his own right; he could not, after all, give the American people reason to be as "trigger happy" as he accused his rival, Republican Senator Barry Goldwater, of being. But after his inauguration, Johnson began to escalate U.S. efforts dramatically. The United States had only 21,000 troops in South Vietnam at the time Johnson was elected in November. By June 1965, that number had risen to 75,000 and two months later, it had climbed to 125,000. By the time Richard Nixon replaced Johnson in the Oval Office in January 1969, there were more than half a million American troops in Vietnam.

The military effort was not the only one escalated. The number of journalists in Vietnam also increased. By the end of 1965, each of the three major television networks had a bureau in the South Vietnamese capital of Saigon, as did such networks as Metromedia, Mutual, and Storer Broadcasting. The Associated Press and United Press International served most of the country's smaller newspapers and provided audio material for a large number of radio stations. But most large newspapers and magazines, including *The New York Times,* the *Los Angeles Times, The Washington Post,* the *Chicago Tribune* and *Daily News, The Boston Globe,* and *Time* and *Newsweek,* had their own bureaus in Vietnam, while many smaller and medium-sized papers sent reporters into the country from time to time to at least do stories with a hometown angle. Between them, they managed, as *Time*'s former Saigon bureau chief, the late Marsh Clark, once put it, "to cover the holy hell out of the war."[5]

They certainly did. Much of the early coverage of the war centered on the now-famous "Five O'Clock Follies," the late-afternoon briefings at which top U.S. military spokesmen summed up the day's actions in the field and attempted to bring the press up to date on the "body count," or the numbers of Vietcong and North Vietnamese troops killed by American and South Vietnamese forces. It did not take too long for the coverage to become critical. Reporters who went out on operations with American forces knew that they counted any Vietnamese killed as enemies and routinely exaggerated the numbers killed in any action. So they soon began to suspect the figures that were being released in Saigon, particularly as they began to add up the numbers and reach an unpleasant conclusion: that North Vietnamese forces were so numerous that they were able to withstand the tremendous losses they were taking without any diminution of their fighting capacity, or that the American authorities were lying about the numbers of enemy troops killed.

Some newsmen tried taking a humorous approach. One television reporter, in a tone that at least initially suggested innocence, elicited surprise when he asked one briefing officer if Vietcong reproduced and grew to maturity faster than other Asians. When the officer, too slow to see that he was being set up, asked the reason for such a strange question, the reporter was ready with a reply. After adding up the body counts released over the previous year, he said, he had reached the inescapable conclusion that either the figures being put out by the American authorities were inflated, which would be unthinkable, or that the Vietcong were able to replace their losses as fast as they incurred them.[6]

Others were more serious in their efforts to learn exactly what was happening. Many went into print or on the air with stories pointing out the discrepancies between the reports from combat areas and those released by U.S. military headquarters in Saigon. More began to question the military's pursuit of a policy that equated success with killing Vietcong rather than winning the support of the South Vietnamese themselves for an effort to keep their country from falling to the Communists. The "Five O'Clock Follies" soon became a scene of acrimony as journalists, almost all of whom now felt that they were being told considerably less than the truth, took out their frustration on the lower-level officials who were left to run the briefings after their superiors, realizing that such exposure was unlikely to advance their careers, abandoned this arena.

Working in the streets of Saigon and Hue, and accompanying the troops on missions, the media brought the war home to the American public. Television crews filmed the maimed bodies of Vietnamese killed and wounded by the bombs the Vietcong were fond of setting off in crowded urban streets. They showed young Americans fighting and being afraid, using their cameras to catch the combination of bravado and boredom, of fecklessness and fear that characterizes war and those who fight it. Night after night, television news broadcasts carried footage showing what had once been villages pocked by bomb and shell craters; they showed people being evacuated from their homes and sent to live in supposedly "safe" areas; they showed American men killing and they showed some of these same American men dying. Night after night, Americans who were just about to sit down to dinner or who had just risen from the table got a look at what was being done in the name of their country by their countrymen.

The pictures were nothing if not disturbing. Americans were shocked when the television networks showed pictures of U.S. soldiers, their sons and brothers, using their trusty Zippo lighters to fire the thatched roofs of Vietnamese houses. They wept as they saw pictures of young soldiers or marines writhing in agony from wounds.

On television, over the radio, in the newspapers, certain images burned themselves into the American mind. A naked Vietnamese girl, her clothes burned off by napalm dropped from an American plane, running screaming down a dusty dirt road. A South Vietnamese general raising a revolver and blowing out the brains of a Vietcong who, it was later revealed, had been responsible for the deaths of several members of his family. The bodies of South Vietnamese villagers massacred by U.S. troops at My Lai. The young face, too young, really, considering his responsibilities, of the lieutenant court-martialed for the massacre. The hollow-eyed faces of soldiers, looking far older than their nineteen or twenty years, who had endured too much tension and had had too little sleep.

The words accompanying the images provided no more comfort than the pictures. The press dutifully reported when first one Secretary of

Defense, then his successor, said that he could see the proverbial "light at the end of the tunnel" and claimed that North Vietnam was reeling from the punishment being meted out by the United States and its bombing raids on Hanoi. But these reports conflicted with the disturbing fact that the United States seemed no closer to victory while the North Vietnamese seemed no closer to defeat.

Other reports were equally disturbing. Journalists noted that many American units were plagued by disciplinary problems. They reported instances in which enlisted men had refused to follow or obey commands issued by officers they considered too eager to take risks, cases in which overambitious officers had been "fragged"—killed or injured when their own men tossed fragmentation grenades into their tents. The press reported on the growing availability and use of drugs, particularly marijuana, among American troops, some of whom "toked up," or got high, before going into battle.

Their reports contrasted radically with those that had been filed during World War II and the Korean Conflict. Then, everyone supported the war effort and few soldiers questioned the reasons for their being at war. Now, few soldiers felt any ideological interest in their efforts; to most, Vietnam was a place where the best they could do was survive until their tours were over.

Both the Johnson and Nixon Administrations, as well as U.S. military authorities in Vietnam, resented this reporting and tried to do what they could to tone it down. Both Johnson and Nixon, as well as their aides, complained to newspaper editors and television network executives about their negative attitudes. Johnson and Nixon both accused the American press of playing into the hands of the enemy and slowing down efforts to attain a negotiated end to the conflict. The Nixon Administration went into a security frenzy when *The New York Times* obtained and printed Pentagon documents contradicting official statements about what the United States was and was not doing in Vietnam. Nixon was livid when the press revealed that the United States was secretly widening the war by bombing suspected Vietcong sanctuaries and North Vietnamese supply routes in Laos and Cambodia.

Nor was the news from the home front any better. Antiwar activists, quiescent during the earliest years of the war, began to escalate their protests as the conflict continued. Thousands of young people, most of them there because they opposed the war, clashed with police during the 1968 Democratic National Convention in Chicago. The protests, covered live by the television networks and reported in detail by the print media, showed Americans an ugly picture of their nation. Anyone with access to a television set could see Chicago's Mayor Richard Daley shouting epithets at Democratic Senator Abraham Ribicoff or watch club-wielding Chicago police wading into crowds of antiwar protesters with a zeal that would have done credit to a regiment of Nicholas Romanov's cossacks. As the war went on, newspapers and television stations showed their readers and viewers the spectacle of thousands of Americans marching on the Pentagon to protest the war and the tragedy of young men and women shot and killed by panicky National Guardsmen during a protest at Ohio's Kent State University. The press portrayed a country divided, a country in which, while a majority still supported the war and what they, at least, understood as an American effort to contain communism in Asia, a great and growing minority felt that the country had made a mistake getting involved and was making a worse error by continuing the conflict.

Like the fictional picture of Dorian Gray, the portrait painted by the press was prophetic. Americans may not have liked what they saw on television or read in their papers. But, like bystanders at an accident, they could not turn away. They could only watch in horror as some of their sons foreswore their American citizenship and emigrated to Canada or to Sweden to avoid going into the army, or as others burned their draft cards and risked jail for refusing to be inducted. They could only watch with a fearful fascination as the death toll from the conflict continued to mount. And, watching the actions of first Lyndon Johnson, then Richard Nixon, as they increased the tempo of a war it was becoming increasingly clear they could not win, they could only wonder if the philosopher George Santayana was not correct when he described a fanatic as one "who increases his effort when he has lost sight of his goal."

The Vietnam war was a first for the American press. Other wars, the War with Mexico, the Spanish-American War, had been unpopular, either with the public or the press. But no conflict in American history proved as unpopular as the war in Vietnam. And none radicalized the press as much, either. By the end of the sixties, many of America's major publications had either begun to editorialize against the war or to make it clear that they wanted it brought to a quick end. Much of the U.S. press applauded when Vermont's Senator George Aiken offered his simple formula for a U.S. exit from Southeast Asia: "Declare victory and go home." More urged the United States to enter into negotiations with the government of North Vietnam and expressed approval when Secretary of State Henry Kissinger began the talks that would eventually bring the United States and North Vietnam to a negotiating table in Paris.

Nor was this the only area in which the news media, to a greater or lesser extent, began to question their government. Reports from South Vietnam increasingly depicted the country as corrupt and its leaders, Nguyen Van Thieu and Nguyen Cao Ky, as venal. Television reporters and print newsmen reported that South Vietnamese youth were avoiding service in a war in which American boys were dying.

More significantly, the press began to question U.S. presidents and their aides. The media stopped short, for example, of accusing President Nixon of lying to them about the U.S. bombing of Cambodia. But they did make it perfectly clear that they felt that he and his administration had been considerably less than ingenuous about American actions and intentions. Gradually, the press took an adversary role where the war was concerned, questioning the government at every turn, comparing officials' new statements to their earlier utterances, letting them know in no uncertain terms that their credibility was crumbling.

The war, in fact, made the press in general and television in particular come of age. American editors and television producers had always tended to support national leaders. *The New York Times,* after all, had acceeded to John F. Kennedy's request that it kill a story that could have given away U.S. intentions to invade Cuba and "blown" what turned out to be a disastrous landing at the Bay of Pigs. The press had always had a tendency to close ranks whenever Americans were at war. It followed this tendency at the beginning of the Vietnam War. But not for long. The war touched off a professional debate, especially within television, partly because its stations were federally licensed, partly because television hated to make anyone unhappy. Former CBS correspondent David Schoenbrun discussed the debate in a 1966 article in *Variety,* reminding his colleagues that they were covering a war that had not been officially declared. He asserted that in covering such a war there should be "no rules other than the conscience of each reporter and editor and the fortitude with which he can resist pressure to accept wartime rules without a war officially existing." Schoenbrun understood that Americans wanted to and should join hands when their nation was at war. But this did not mean, he said, that Americans should shut off their minds. "Close ranks, yes," wrote Schoenbrun. "But to close ranks does not mean to close our minds."[7]

For television, the tension between patriotism and professionalism was terrible. The newsmen who worked in Vietnam, where they befriended and got to know American command personnel at headquarters and came to like and admire American soldiers in the field, found themselves under pressure to report the story as the government wanted it told and to have their stories reflect favorably on the American fighting man.

Reporting the Vietnam War was not easy. To begin with, it was, as wars tend to be, risky, and several reporters were killed, wounded, or captured. Many more suffered from the climate and the ailments endemic to it. And all, whether they worked for newspapers or radio or television stations, had to face and overcome the logistical problems of covering a war that was being fought thousands of miles and several time zones away from their broadcast studios or presses. Journalists had to get to and from the battlefield, meet flight schedules for getting their film back to the United States, file in time to get their stories into the morning papers.

They also had to deal with a U.S. military establishment determined to put the best face possible on the war. For, if there was a large press contingent in Vietnam, there was an enormous military publicity machine, too. This machine was run out of the U.S. Army's Hometown News Center in Kansas City, as well as out of Vietnam, and it operated, like most public relations operations, on the principle that the only news worth putting out was good news.

That the military would try to manage and control the flow of news about the war did not seriously bother most of the journalists assigned to cover the conflict; they at least half expected it. What did bother those assigned to cover the conflict was the military's tendency to get nasty about reports that the White House and Pentagon did not like. The Pentagon compiled tapes of television coverage and sent them to Vietnam so that field commanders could be aware of what the networks were saying about them. And this was not all the Pentagon did. In 1966, government spokesmen publicly chided CBS reporters Martin Agronsky and Peter Fromson for airing reports that were accurate but unpleasant to hear. The Pentagon objected even more strongly when another CBS correspondent, Morley Safer, aired his report showing U.S. Marines torching a Vietnamese village. The image of Americans forcing Vietnamese farmers out of their homes, coupled with Safer's ironic commentary that the operation represented "the frustration of Vietnam in miniature," provided a sharp counterpoint to the official releases designed to portray the war as a noble effort to help a grateful ally.

The government's response was equally sharp. President Johnson ordered a check of Safer's background and learned, possibly to his surprise, that the reporter was not a Communist, merely a Canadian. To some officials, that was worse. Arthur Sylvester, assistant secretary of defense for public affairs, branded Safer "a cheap Canadian" and charged him with being inimical to U.S. efforts in Vietnam.[8]

The combination of Pentagon reaction and growing confidence helped to stiffen the spines of Vietnam War correspondents, particularly those who represented television stations, and to lead to more independent reporting. This does not mean, though, that TV reporting suddenly began to hit as hard as that appearing in print. Many print reporters admired their television colleagues for the courage they displayed when it came to getting good film footage. But they—and a great many television journalists, too—felt that television reporting generally lacked depth.

Others charged that television reporting lacked guts. *Life*'s Brock Brower complained that television correspondents seemed unwilling to look behind the official statements, rosy predictions, and plain lies being put out first by Johnson's administration, then by Nixon's. John Gregory Dunne took to the pages of *The New Republic* in 1966 to write off television documentaries on Vietnam as "a puff of nothing."[9]

Their charges were not without validity. Early television documentaries did tend to be superficial, showing bewildered GIs coping with the climate, the confusion, and the 'Cong, but determined to get the job, whatever that might be, done. Some of these documentaries were, in fact, little more than puff pieces, in which Hollywood actors who had either served in the armed forces or spent a good part of their careers playing soldiers, or both, narrated programs that presented the war strictly from the government's point of view and avoided asking even the most obvious of questions as to why the United States was involved in the conflict.[10]

But gradually, the electronic media's acquiescence in the government's public relations efforts changed, giving way to a willingness to face—and ask—tough questions. Eric Sevareid, one of television's most thoughtful reporters, took to the air in 1966 to present a discouraging view of Johnson's predicament in Vietnam in his "Viet Nam Perspective." Sevareid noted that the war was spreading into Laos and Cambodia, accused the Administration of wishful thinking in its reports on American progress, and noted that even if the United States managed to "win" the war, it would not be able to get out of Southeast Asia, for then it would be faced with the task of supporting a poor, war-ravaged nation.

Still, when it came to expressing their reservations about the U.S. role in Vietnam, many television reporters felt compelled to publish in print rather than air their views electronically. In 1967, CBS reporter Mike Wallace confessed in *The Nation* that he could not talk about certain things on television, could not compare, for example, the unpatriotic attitude of the South Vietnamese army with the morale and dedication displayed by the Vietcong. NBC's acerbic David Brinkley, whose on-the-air partner Chet Huntley supported the Administration's policies, also went into print to declare his opposition. In 1967, he told *TV Guide* that the United States should stop the bombing of North Vietnam, which was not as effective as the Air Force claimed it was. Furthermore, he expressed the view that the United States should "take the first settlement that is even remotely decent and get out, without insisting on any kind of 'victory.' "[11]

Others soon joined the chorus of opposition. CBS's Walter Cronkite and NBC's Edwin Newman both blasted the bombing of North Vietnam. Cronkite went even further, and in a February 1967, speech at Johns Hopkins University, blasted the American political right as know-nothing and assailed the government for being dishonest about U.S. aims and actions in Vietnam. The King Broadcasting Company, which owned stations in major markets around the country, began editorializing against escalation of the war and questioning the political premises that had led to U.S. involvement.[12]

The Administration's insistence on bombing the north, in fact, came under increasing criticism from many quarters. The print press had opposed it almost from the start, and major newspapers like *The New York Times*, *The Washington Post* and the *Los Angeles Times* had editorialized against it. Nor were the news magazines any less eager to end an exercise they considered ineffective; by 1969, both *Time* and *Newsweek* had made it clear that they believed the bombing should be banned. Now broadcasters, too, began to raise their voices against the air war, particularly on radio, which had always been ahead of television when it came to carrying informed commentary. NBC's Howard Tuckner, who covered the war for twenty months, returned home to declare quite flatly that the war was not going well for the United States and to note that American military officials were beginning to believe that the United States could come out the loser if the conflict continued. Brinkley was even more discouraging, noting that despite U.S. efforts, North Vietnam and the Vietcong were stronger than ever and even more determined to carry on the fight. "It is clear to all, or should be," said Brinkley, "that fighting the war at the present level is accomplishing nothing."[13]

By the end of the Vietcong's famed Tet Offensive of 1968, the great majority of journalists, in both the print media and the electronic, agreed. For, although the combined forces of North Vietnam and the Vietcong failed in their bid to destroy U.S. military power in South Vietnam, their attacks, in which they even managed to get some guerrillas into the grounds of the American embassy in Saigon, did demonstrate that administration assertions that the war was near an end were, to put it mildly, overly optimistic. One administration spokesman after another had been insisting that the United States was "winning" and would soon be able to bring its boys home. All had, to repeat the cliché that became common during this period, been seeing "light at the end of the tunnel." The Tet Offensive showed the whole country that such light, if visible at all, could only be the headlamp of an incoming express train.

The United States did not lose Tet; American troops inflicted enormous losses on both North Vietnam and the Vietcong. But Tet, and the American public's understanding of what it meant, did mark a turning point in the conflict. For from that moment on, only the most unreconstructed of optimists was willing to believe administration officials when they maintained that the war was going well or to grant the government's request for more troops, planes, money, to fight a war that the majority already felt was costing the United States too dearly in lives and resources. Even Henry Kissinger, who had been as hawkish on Vietnam as others in the Nixon Administration, acknowledged that Tet turned things around. "Henceforth," said Kissinger, "no matter how effective our actions, the prevalent strategy could no longer achieve its objectives within a period or within force levels politically acceptable to the American people."[14]

The press did not, as some have subsequently charged, make it impossible for the United States to win the war, for it was not the press that turned up the pressure on President Nixon and prevailed upon him politically to enter into the negotiations that at least allowed the United States to withdraw from Vietnam. The press, after all, only told the American people what was happening in Vietnam. It told Americans who was doing what in their name, and noted the discrepancies between what it was being told by officials and what its reporters could see and its cameramen photograph. In Vietnam, at least, the press, sometimes skillfully, sometimes less so, only did its job. The press provided the American public with information. It was the public, not the press, that made the Administration withdraw from a war it could not—at least at a price Americans were willing to pay—win.

## Chapter Five

# Watergate and the Court of Public Opinion

The two young reporters at *The Washington Post* . . . became popular heroes for a time after their work helped keep the pressure of public scrutiny on the unanswered questions in the Watergate case . . . But as important as the *Post* and its officers and reporters were, what is more important is that the *Post* is part of a free press, protected by the Constitution.

JUDGE JOHN J. SIRICA,
*To Set the Record Straight,* 1979

It began as a third-rate burglary. It started on June 17, 1972, when five men, including four strongly anti-Castro Cubans, broke into Democratic party headquarters in Washington's fashionable Watergate hotel and office building and installed electronic bugs in the telephones belonging to two aides to Democratic National Chairman Larry O'Brien. It developed into much more, a farce that made people shake their heads in wonderment that smart people could behave so stupidly, an outrageous assault on the Constitution of the United States, a tragedy that shook the whole government and undermined a nation's faith in itself and its institutions. It ended in a moment of high drama when President Richard Nixon, rueful but unrepentant as he faced the prospect of being impeached, convicted, and removed from office, sent his secretary of state a one-line letter resigning the presidency.

Considered coolly, the Watergate story was not one of those things that announce themselves as a major development. When five men who had been caught inside Democratic headquarters were arraigned in a Washington courtroom later that day, both *The Washington Post*'s police reporter and other observers were willing to write them off as "a bunch of crazy Cubans." Even when one of them, James McCord, who was clearly not a Cuban, revealed that he had once worked for the Central Intelligence Agency, few saw the significance of the story. Nor did the story itself, which ran in the following day's editions of the *Post,* suggest that there was much more to the break-in than met the eye. The lead of that story said simply: "Five men, one of whom said he is a former employee of the Central Intelligence Agency, were arrested at 2:30 A.M. yesterday in what authorities described as an elaborate plot to bug the offices of the Democratic National Committee here." Another paragraph went on to note: "There was no immediate explanation as to why the five suspects would want to bug the Democratic National Committee offices, or whether or not they were working for any other individuals or organizations."[1]

It was not, in fact, until the next day that either of the two *Post* reporters whose names would become so strongly identified with the case began to realize that they might have something more than mere breaking and entering on their hands. One of the things that made them realize this was a story on the Associated Press wire identifying McCord as security coordinator for the DNC's rival Committee for the Reelection of the President (CRP). Something else that set off signals in the minds of the two reporters was the fact that address books belonging to two of the Cubans arrested for the break-in contained the name and telephone number of a man named Howard Hunt and notations suggested that he was some-how connected with the White House.[2]

The two reporters had not originally set out to cover the story together. Their pairing was an accident, a by-product of the way newspaper assign-ments are handed out. Certainly, the two never thought of themselves as a team. In fact, if they thought of each other at all, it was as rivals. Robert Woodward, twenty-nine, was a handsome WASP, a Yale graduate with a reputation as one of the *Post*'s office politicians. He was not considered a particularly good writer. Carl Bernstein, twenty-eight, was almost the exact opposite. A college dropout, he had been in the newspaper business since age sixteen, when he had worked as a copy boy at the *Post*'s rival, *The Washington Star*. He had longish hair. He was a tough reporter. And he could write.

The two had regarded themselves as competitors the day after the first story when they were called in to work on a follow-up. They got together because a *Post* editor asked Bernstein to rewrite Woodward's story. They were paired because, as Woodward himself conceded, Bernstein made the story read better.[3]

The *Post*'s second-day story, which identified McCord as an official of CRP, took another step toward showing that the Watergate break-in might be something more than a third-rate burglary. The paper's reporters, who would later be lumped together under the single name "Woodstein," took a bigger step the following day when Woodward dialed the White House and asked for Howard Hunt. The operator who answered rang for him in the office of Charles W. Colson, a special counsel to the President. Hunt was not there, but his whereabouts were hardly a secret. The White House told Woodward that Hunt worked as a writer for a Washington public relations firm, and it confirmed that he also worked for Colson as a consultant. Learning this, Woodward moved quickly. He called Hunt at his office and asked why his name and telephone number were in the address books of two of the men arrested at the Watergate. His question came as a shock. Hunt reacted strongly, then quickly calmed down. "In view that the matter is under adjudication," he said, "I have no comment." Then he hung up.

Woodward and his editors debated what to do with the information they had just obtained. The debate resolved itself when one of Woodward's sources told him that the Federal Bureau of Investigation regarded Hunt as a suspect in its investigation of the incident and when a *Post* editor uncovered an earlier story identifying Colson as one of the top men in the White House's department of dirty tricks. The result was a story headlined "White House Consultant Linked to Bugging Suspects."[4]

Slowly, other pieces of the puzzle began to fall into place. Woodward, Bernstein, and other reporters and editors at the *Post* began to accumulate bits and pieces of information suggesting that the Watergate break-in may have been part of a well-organized effort to spy on and disrupt the Democrats. Other newspapers, *The New York Times* and *The Boston Globe* in particular, and CBS News began to look more deeply at the story, particularly after President Nixon, whom the press had long distrusted, responded to questions at a June 22 news conference by issuing a carefully worded statement that said, "The White House has had no involvement whatever in this particular incident."

But it was the *Post* that pursued the story most diligently. Woodward and Bernstein learned, despite White House denials, that Hunt had been assigned to look into Senator Edward Kennedy's private life. But once they reported this, the story stalled. Sources dried up; people refused to talk. Over his objections, Bernstein was taken off the story and sent off to cover Virginia politics; Woodward went on vacation.

Then, however, the story came back to life. The Long Island, New York, afternoon newspaper *Newsday* introduced a new actor into the unfolding drama by reporting that a former FBI agent and former White House aide named G. Gordon Liddy had been fired by Attorney General John Mitchell, former head of CRP, for refusing to answer investigators' questions about Watergate. A few days later, Bernstein was called back from Virginia; the *Times* had just carried a front-page story reporting that some fifteen telephone calls had been made from the Miami home of one of the Watergate burglars to CRP offices in Washington and that more than half these calls had been made to an office occupied by none other than Liddy.

Checking out the story, Bernstein picked up other tidbits. He learned that more than $89,000 had been deposited and withdrawn from the Miami man's bank account that spring. He learned, too, that the money had come from Mexico. Working with Woodward, he also learned that a $25,000 check, raised by a midwestern businessman for Nixon's campaign chest and turned over to CRP Finance Chairman Maurice Stans, had been deposited directly into Bernard Barker's bank account. The discovery firmly connected CRP to the burglary.[5]

Other discoveries tended to confirm the connection. On August 22, the second day of the Republican National Convention in Miami, the *Post* gave front-page placement to a story reporting that the Government Accounting Office had been auditing CRP and had concluded that the committee had mishandled more than half a million dollars in campaign funds. CRP, understandably, denied that it had done anything wrong. But its denial proved revealing, for in the course of claiming that CRP was innocent of wrongdoing, spokesman Van Shumway confirmed the existence of CRP's so-called "security fund."

Encouraged by the fact that their efforts were producing stories, *Post* editor Ben Bradlee kept Woodward and Bernstein on the Watergate case. Realizing that their task was not going to be easy, the two reporters began to devote themselves to nothing else. Each man kept separate lists of telephone numbers, which were to be called at least twice a week to make sure that no possible source went uncontacted. The two also kept every scrap of paper relating to Watergate, saving all their notes, all drafts of their stories. Tentatively at first, then with less hesitation, the two began to work as a team. As a rule, Woodward, the faster of the two, wrote the first draft of their stories, which carried both their bylines; Bernstein, the better writer, rewrote them, tightening them and honing their language. City editor Barry Sussman, thirty-eight, who had been detached from his other duties and assigned to Watergate, then went over them, looking for gaps to be filled, inconsistencies to be reconciled, problems to be avoided.[6]

The system worked. On August 26, Bernstein's digging uncovered the first references to CRP's Mexican money-laundering operation, an elaborate scheme set up by some high Republican officials to encourage Democrats, large corporations, and others to give money to the GOP but to assure that their contributions could not be traced. Under it, money given to GOP fund-raisers was deposited in Mexican banks, then transferred to American accounts from which it made its way to CRP in flagrant violation of both the letter and the spirit of the laws covering campaign contributions. That same day, the *Post* and other publications were able to report even more about CRP; the GAO released a report listing eleven "apparent and possible" violations of the election laws and referring the matter of the committee's monetary manipulations to the U.S. Department of Justice for investigation.

Nor were these the only developments in the story as the 1972 election campaign moved out of the convention halls and onto the hustings. Reporters' diggings began to produce bits and pieces of information that pointed to an inescapable conclusion—that the roof was about to fall in at CRP. Worried sources, most of whom seemed understandably fearful about being quoted in the *Post* or other publications, told frightening stories about what was going on at the President's reelection committee, stories about wholesale destruction of documents, of high-level paranoia, of people wondering when their names would suddenly surface in print. The worries were not unfounded. On September 15, Hunt, Liddy, and the five Watergate arrestees were indicted for conspiracy, burglary, and wiretapping.

The indictments, however, raised more concern than complacency on the part of Woodward and Bernstein, for, like CRP and the people around the President, the Justice Department seemed to dismiss the crime as the "third-rate burglary" that high Republican officials had claimed it to be. The indictment had barely been announced before Bernstein, in a fit of frustration, telephoned the Justice Department to ask why the charges were so limited. After all, he asked, did not the Justice Department have the same information as *The Washington Post*?[7]

Bernstein's question went unanswered—at least initially. But the lack of an answer added substance to what the two reporters, not to mention other Washington newsmen and their editors, had increasingly suspected—that a massive coverup was under way to protect those who might have known about, or even ordered, the Watergate burglary. The suspicions were soon confirmed when Woodward began meeting with a secret source. Woodward had known the man, a member of the executive branch, for years and trusted him implicitly. He also understood early in their renewed relationship that his source would leak no new information. What he would do, though, was confirm any information that Woodward obtained elsewhere and let him know when his inquiries were heading off the track. Woodward also understood that his source had to be careful; he could not, for a variety of reasons, meet openly with a reporter, especially with one from a paper the White House considered the enemy. Woodward could not call his source at his office. Instead, as they arranged, he would signal him by placing the potted plant on his apartment's balcony in a certain place. His source would then mark Woodward's newspaper, indicating what time he would meet with him in an underground parking garage.

Woodward told his editors about his informant, whom he identified to them only as a "deep source." His editors gave the man a more colorful name. They dubbed him "Deep Throat," the title of a pornographic movie that was then big on the X-rated circuit.

Woodward's meetings with his source were the stuff of which spy thrillers are made. Whenever a meeting was scheduled, Woodward would leave his apartment late at night and take a taxi, or sometimes two, to a point within walking distance of their rendezvous. He would then walk the rest of the way, taking a circuitous route to make sure that he was not being followed. The cloak-and-dagger precautions seemed worth the effort. From the time they began talking until the Watergate story was wrapped up, Deep Throat proved himself a fount of information.[8]

On September 16, for example, Woodward contacted Deep Throat to read him a draft of a story reporting that federal investigators had learned from Nixon campaign workers that high CRP officials were involved in funding the Watergate break-in. Woodward was concerned as to whether the story could go that far. Deep Throat assured him that he could go even further. The result was a story that strengthened the link between CRP and the burglary. Said the story's lead: "Funds for the Watergate espionage operation were controlled by several principal assistants of John N. Mitchell, former manager of President Nixon's campaign, and were kept in a special account of CRP, *The Washington Post* has learned."[9]

The value of Deep Throat's guidance was established when Woodward called spokesman Van Shumway for CRP's response to the story. Shumway issued a general statement denying that CRP was guilty of any improprieties. What he did not deny was the substance of the *Post*'s story.

Further confirmation of Woodward and Bernstein's suspicions came when the pair called on Hugh Sloan, a former CRP official who had resigned from the committee because he could no longer condone some of the practices to which he was privy. A decent man whose conscience clearly bothered him, Sloan was unwilling to discuss matters that he had already shared with investigators. But he was not unwilling to offer indirect confirmation of information that Woodward and Bernstein managed to obtain on their own. When Bernstein wrote a story suggesting that CRP officials had made an organized effort to cover up involvement with the Watergate burglary and detailing reports he had obtained on destruction of records at committee headquarters, for example, Sloan confirmed their account.[10]

Sloan provided other information, too. A short while later, he confirmed the reporter's information indicating that Mitchell had authorized the expenditure of campaign funds for illegal activities while serving as the nation's chief law officer. He also provided tacit confirmation to the pair's growing suspicion that the White House chief of staff H. R. Haldeman was the man with ultimate control over such funds. His confirmation confronted the *Post* with a problem. Should it go with a story that carried the growing Watergate mess into the White House? Or should it hold back and stop short of saying that the men around the President and, by implication at least, perhaps even the President himself, were involved in illegal activities?

Caution would have been understandable. Nor would anyone have faulted the *Post* for waiting. But the paper, feeling that it had to press ahead on the story, decided to go with what it had.

So did other news outlets. On October 5, the *Los Angeles Times* carried an interview with Alfred C. Baldwin, whom it identified as CRP's security consultant. Baldwin told a tale of telephone taps, and of Howard Hunt watching in panic from the Howard Johnson's across the street from the Watergate as the five burglars were led away by the police, who had intercepted and arrested them the night of the break-in.[11]

The *Los Angeles Times* story spurred the *Post* team to renewed efforts. The following day, Woodward and Bernstein ran a story naming CRP aides Robert Odle, Jeb Stuart Magruder, and J. Glenn Sedam as recipients of tape logs from illegal wiretaps. The story produced a denial from CRP, and for once CRP was correct: Woodward and Bernstein had gone beyond the facts and were wrong.

But Deep Throat soon set them straight again. A short time later, he offered Woodward the key to the Watergate knot by telling him of CRP's interest in what it called "offensive security," a term that described what others would call simple "dirty tricks." The President, the men around him, and those running CRP, Woodward's source explained, felt that it was not enough to run an efficient campaign themselves. They felt that they had to throw a more-than-symbolic monkey wrench into the Democrats' campaign machinery.

And, it quickly became clear, they did. Deep Throat told Woodward that the notorious "Canuck letter," a forgery in which Democratic presidential candidate Edmund Muskie supposedly spoke disparagingly of French-Canadians was "a White House operation." It was, he said, produced inside the gates surrounding the White House.[12]

So, it turned out, were other "dirty tricks." A September 28 tip from a Tennessee Democrat alerted Woodward and Bernstein to the existence of a Californian named Donald Segretti who, they were told, had tried to recruit some army buddies to help him to play what seemed rather childish pranks on the Democrats. According to what the two reporters were able to learn, Segretti wanted his friends to infiltrate and spy on Nixon's Democratic opponents, and to disrupt their campaigns by doing such things as calling up the owners of halls and rescheduling rallies or by sending out provocative letters over Democratic signatures. Flying out to the Coast to confront Segretti, the reporters learned that his operations were well financed. Checking what they had managed to learn with sources at the Justice Department, they uncovered information suggesting that the scandal over Segretti's pranks reached all the way into the White House and may have involved not only such top presidential aides as Ehrlichman and Haldeman, but the President himself.[13]

The pair was preparing to put what they had learned into print a short time later; they and their editors were, in fact, planning a three-part package consisting of a Woodward and Bernstein piece on "offensive security," a Bernstein story on Segretti, and a Woodward article on White House involvement in the Canuck letter. But while they were working, a new element was injected into the affair. *Post* reporter Marilyn Berger mentioned that White House aide Clawson told her that he was the author of the infamous Canuck letter.

Confronted with this claim, Clawson tried a variety of tactics. He denied that he had ever met with Berger, denied that he had had drinks with her at her apartment, denied, though not convincingly, that he had actually written the letter. The *Post* team could never determine whether Clawson was boasting when he made his original claim, or trying to cover his tracks later. But they did not need to. They had enough information to tie the letter to the White House, and they went with it. "FBI Finds Nixon Aides Sabotaged Democrats" read the four-column headline of the story that ran on page one of the October 9 issue of the *Post*.[14] The story itself detailed some of Segretti's activities, as well as the Clawson claim.

Other stories went even further. A few days later, the *Post* carried a story tying key Nixon aide Dwight Chapin directly to Segretti's dirty tricks. That same weekend, *Time* published a story that went into even more detail. *Time* said that Chapin, once described only as Segretti's contact, had actually hired the political prankster. It further asserted that Gordon Strachan, an aide to Haldeman, was involved, and reported that Segretti had been paid $35,000 for his services by none other than Herbert W. Kalmbach, the President's lawyer.[15]

The *Post*'s stories attracted any number of readers in Washington and outside. But they infuriated the White House, which singled the paper out for its most scathing attacks. White House spokesmen issued statements blaming the *Post*'s stories on Senator George McGovern who, they said, was engaging in the "politics of desperation" as he saw an election defeat facing him. They also accused the *Post* of hypocrisy, noting that it had failed to investigate the GOP's claims that it, too, had been the target of various dirty tricks. The *Post,* to its credit, refused to be intimidated; even White House spokesman Clark McGregor issued a scathing attack on it. Instead, Bradlee responded with a statement that said: "Time will judge between Clark McGregor's press release and *The Washington Post*'s reporting of the various activities of the Committee for the Re-election of the President." The statement noted that "not a single fact contained in the investigative reporting by his newspaper has been successfully challenged."[16]

The White House persisted in its denials. But those newspapers and magazines that stuck with the story continued to undermine its position. On October 18, *The New York Times* ran a story based on telephone records that showed that Segretti's credit card and telephone had both been used for calls to the White House and to the Chapin home in Bethseda, Maryland. The records cited by the *Times* also showed that Segretti's credit card and telephone had been used for at least twenty-one calls to Howard Hunt. The White House did not like the story, but it was unable to offer a convincing denial.[17]

To Woodward, Bernstein, and their editors at *The Washington Post,* it was beginning to look as if all roads led to White House Chief of Staff Haldeman. The information the reporters had obtained from Deep Throat, from Hugh Sloan, from an FBI agent involved with the case, all suggested that Haldeman was the man behind the scheming that went on between the White House and CRP. So it was with a sense of certainty that Woodward and Bernstein went into print on October 24 with a story saying that the fifth person in control of campaign funds for political espionage was none other than Haldeman.

This story, however, was quickly shot down. The White House fired the first salvo at its credibility by issuing a statement saying that the references to Haldeman were untrue. Hugh Sloan fired the second salvo with a public statement in which he denied that he had ever named Haldeman in his answers to investigators.[18]

The two reporters were stunned. Both believed that they had been told that Haldeman was involved. Both believed that Sloan, among others, had given them this information. Where, they asked themselves, had they gone wrong? What had they failed to understand?

Plenty, as it turned out. When they talked to Sloan, they learned that he had not misled them; they had misled themselves. Sloan had told them that he believed Haldeman was involved. He had, he explained, never told this to officials investigating the case, however, and for a good reason: he was never asked.

The mistake, which the *Post* was forced to acknowledge, was serious. Deep Throat implied that Woodward and his partner had blown their chance to nail the White House Chief of Staff, warning them that they had to have the goods on someone so highly placed before they could name him in print.

Their despair, however, quickly turned to elation when McGregor went on television and admitted the existence of the fund for political espionage. McGregor flatly denied that Haldeman was one of the five who authorized or received payments from the secret fund; he said that the five were Mitchell, Stans, Magruder, Porter, and Liddy. But by acknowledging the fund's existence, he confirmed one of the charges that the *Post* had been making from the beginning: that the roots of Watergate reached into the highest levels of government.

Chastened by the fact that the story that elicited this admission had been wrong, the *Post* ran its piece on McGregor's statement on page two. *The New York Times,* though, had no such reservations. It ran the story on page one and included in it its own information that disbursements from the fund totalled $900,000.[19]

That same day, *Time* magazine went even further. It issued a release on a story it was running. The release was sure to attract attention, for the story it described cited FBI files and said that Chapin had admitted hiring Segretti, whose payment was set by Kalmbach. It went on to say, however, that there was no evidence for the *Post*'s charges against Haldeman.

Woodward and Bernstein were thus forced to correct themselves, admitting that the *Post* was incorrect in identifying Sloan's grand jury testimony as the source of information on Haldeman's link to the fund.[20]

The *Post* did not let its error dampen its enthusiasm for the story. Early in November, the paper sent Bernstein out to California to see Segretti. The baby-faced Segretti proved cooperative—at least up to a point. Speaking off the record, he admitted that he was hired by Chapin and gave Bernstein to understand that, as far as he knew, Chapin took his orders from Haldeman. That, however, was as far as he would go. For the record, he would say nothing, leaving a frustrated Bernstein to return to Washington with little he could use in print.[21]

Following Nixon's landslide election, the Watergate story seemed to quiet down. The *Post* team was unable to come up with anything new. Nor, apparently, were *The New York Times*, the *Los Angeles Times*, or *Time*, the three other publications that had been pursuing the story the hardest. Woodward and Bernstein wondered whether the story was over and felt that it was only a matter of time before they were sent back to what they had been doing before the burglary. Others expressed similar concerns.

Their fears, as it turned out, were ill-founded. The original Watergate burglars were about to go on trial before U.S. District Court Judge John J. Sirica, a no-nonsense jurist known, from his habit of handing out stiff sentences to those convicted in his court, as "Maximum John." Woodward and Bernstein expected that they would be assigned to cover the trial. But they were disappointed. In order to make sure that its coverage was both unbiased and perceived to be unbiased, the *Post* decided that a third reporter would be assigned to cover the court proceedings; Woodward and Bernstein would attend on alternate days and look for leads that would help them cover the unsolved aspects of the case.

Separating the trial from other aspects of the story, however, proved easier to plan than to do. *New York Times* reporter Seymour Hersh saw to that when he reported that the four Miami men arrested during the burglary had been promised payments of up to $1,000 a month for such time as they spent in jail. The payments, similar to those made to mafiosi, suggested that someone—someone with money—wanted the men to take their punishment and keep their silence. The suggestion picked up some support as the trial got under way for, it quickly became clear to all concerned, the defendants were not interested in explaining their actions; they were only interested in getting the trial over with quickly so that the light of public and press scrutiny might be focused elsewhere.

The trial of the Watergate burglars got underway on January 10, 1973. And, it quickly became evident, it was no ordinary criminal trial. For, as first the prosecutor and then the defense attorneys offered their opening statements, it was evident that no one had—or wanted to—look too deeply into what had happened at the Watergate and why. The first to offer such evidence was prosecutor Earl Silbert, who outlined a case that seemed, at least to Judge Sirica, to be severely—and dangerously—limited. "Silbert

made it clear, as everyone had already read in the newspapers," wrote
Sirica in his book on the case, "that the defendants had been paid by the
President's campaign committee. Porter, Magruder and Hugh Sloan, the
Deputy at the finance committee, had all known about Liddy's assignment
to gather intelligence. But Silbert said not a word about whether or not
they had known in advance about the break-in and bugging. And the fact
that only a small fraction of the money Liddy had been given had been
traced signaled to me that Earl Silbert and the prosecutors hadn't yet
found out the full story of the Watergate affair."[22]

Nor were the defense attorneys any more helpful when it came to getting
at the truth. They said that their clients had been misled and believed that
they were acting to safeguard American security. But, they indicated,
they were not prepared to name those who may have misled them. And,
it quickly became clear, at least one of the defendants was willing to go
to jail rather than risk being questioned in court. For before the trial had
actually gotten under way, Howard Hunt's attorney announced that Hunt
wished to plead guilty to three of the six counts against him.

Sirica refused to rise to Hunt's bait. "If Hunt simply pleaded guilty,
took his medicine and went to jail, the chance that we would ever find
out what was going on in the case would be reduced," Sirica wrote.[23]
Insisting that no one had coerced him into making his plea and maintaining
that no higher-ups were involved in the affair, Hunt pleaded guilty to all
six charges. His action caused an apparent change of heart on the part
of the four Miami men arrested with him: they insisted that their lawyer
assist them in pleading guilty, and when he refused, they replaced him.

The major publications covering the case—*Time, The New York Times,*
and *The Washington Post*—responded to this development with stories
saying that the defendants had been paid to keep quiet. Sirica, though he
could not say so, apparently agreed. Albeit reluctantly, he accepted the
guilty pleas, then rejected arguments from the two remaining defendants
that a mistrial be declared. Instead, he played an active role in the trial
of Liddy and McCord, exercising his right to question uncooperative
witnesses from the bench.

The trial did not take long. At 4:30 on the afternoon of January 30,
the jury retired to consider its verdict. At 6:10, it returned and announced
that it had found McCord and Liddy guilty on all the counts against them.
Its finding gave Sirica the opportunity he wanted. Foregoing his right to
sentence the defendants immediately, the judge decided to delay sent-
encing and announced that he would make his final sentences conditional
upon cooperation. Meanwhile, the defendants could consider themselves
sentenced to the maximum allowed for each offense.

His action proved effective. A short time later, John McCord appeared alone and unannounced and tried to hand Sirica an envelope. Cautious lest it contain money, Sirica refused to accept it; he told McCord to deliver it through his lawyer or probation officer. The envelope contained a letter in which McCord admitted that he was caught between the rock of an impending invitation to testify before a Senate committee investigating Watergate and the hard place of the long prison sentence that Sirica had promised him. Thus caught, McCord said, he wanted to talk. In sentences that came as no surprise to Sirica, he said that political pressure had been applied to the defendants to make them plead guilty and remain silent, that perjury had occurred in the trial, that others involved in Watergate had not been identified and that, whatever the four Miami men may have been led to believe, the burglary was not a CIA operation. McCord, it was clear, was ready to expose the cover-up, a cover-up so extensive that he did not trust either the FBI or the Justice Department to uncover it.[24]

That a cover-up was under way was by now painfully evident. L. Patrick Gray, undergoing staff questioning at Senate hearings on the confirmation of his appointment as Director of the FBI, had vindicated the beleaguered *Washington Post* by turning over to the Senate documents establishing the link between Segretti, Chapin, and Kalmbach. The White House, in a desperate effort to control the damage to itself and the presidency, had instructed its staffers to defy Senate subpoenas. CRP's subpoenas of *Post* staffers had been thrown out of court.[25]

But no one expected the bomb that Sirica dropped when he walked into court on March 23 to pronounce sentence on the Watergate defendants. Sirica's reading of the letter shook the White House and spurred Silbert into reconvening a grand jury to take testimony from McCord, Liddy, and Hunt about who had authorized the break-in. It produced a defensive letter from Attorney General Richard Kleindeinst. It also led to a spate of stories in the newspapers, including one in the *Los Angeles Times,* reporting that Magruder and White House aide Dean had both had advance knowledge of the Watergate break-in and bugging.[26] By March 28, McCord was testifying before the grand jury, telling what he knew. Within a few days, too, the conspirators in the Watergate cover-up had begun seeking legal counsel; Magruder and Dean were just as soon meeting with prosecutors, bartering their testimony for favorable treatment. The Watergate case and the cover-up were unraveling.

And once it did, it came apart quickly, for most of those involved sought only to save themselves, and some spoke freely, especially to the press. On April 19, the *Post* reported that Mitchell and Dean had approved and helped plan the Watergate bugging. The story cited Magruder as the source of this information.[27] *The New York Times*, meanwhile, gave first-page play to a story relating how Kleindeinst was disqualifying himself from the case and describing Dean's readiness to implicate others should he himself be indicted.[28]

The following months brought other startling revelations. There was, for example, the disclosure that there was a mysterious eighteen-and-a-half-minute gap in a taped record of conversations within the Oval Office, and the discovery that other records had been destroyed. In February 1974, there were guilty pleas to perjury charges from Magruder, Porter, Segretti, Kalmbach, Egil Krogh, and Dean, plus Chapin's indictment for perjury. Mitchell and Stans, meanwhile, found themselves on trial for obstruction of justice. On March 1, a Washington grand jury indicted Haldeman, Ehrlichman, Colson, Mitchell, Strachan, Mardian, and lawyer Kenneth Parkinson for obstruction of justice.

But the biggest breaks in the case were yet to come. The first came when a reluctant Nixon, still insisting that they would exonerate him, turned over to the House Judiciary Committee tape recordings that proved that he and his aides had discussed ways of stifling the Watergate investigation. The tapes constituted the "smoking gun" that Nixon's foes needed in order to impeach him; they constituted proof to Nixon's friends that the President's position was indefensible. The second break came when the House Judiciary Committee voted to impeach the President of the United States for his role in the affair and when even Republican senators, before whom the impeachment case would be heard, told the President that they could no longer support him. After that, all was anticlimax, as a tearful but unrepentant Richard Nixon accepted the inevitable and became the first American president to resign his office in disgrace.

Did the press bring Nixon down? Popular mythology holds that it did and credits a skeptical, diligent press with seeing through the lies and evasions to dig out the truth behind Watergate and the people involved. But the myth is misleading; the American press as a group slept through Watergate. Most papers, in fact, barely covered it. Press historian Ben Bagdikian calculated that of the 433 Washington reporters available for assignment during the Watergate years, only 15 were actually assigned to stay with the story. He also found that of some 500 political columns written between June and November 1972, only 24 dealt in any way with Watergate.[29]

His finding reflects little credit upon the print press, which could easily have done more with Watergate. But at least they show that some newspapers and magazines paid attention to Watergate. A look at television programs broadcast during the period is more discouraging. It reveals that television gave little time to telling the Watergate story and shows that television commentators virtually ignored it.

But those who did cover Watergate did it well. *Time* did more than a dozen cover stories on the case and kept its reporters constantly digging for new information; the magazine also broke its own tradition by running an editorial urging the President to resign. *The New York Times*, the *Los Angeles Times*, and *Newsday* turned the resources of their Washington bureaus, as well as other investigative reporters on their staffs, to the task of ferreting out information and finding out what happened.

No paper, however, did more than *The Washington Post*, which devoted more of its manpower, resources, and space to the story than any other American newspaper, and which managed, even when things were slow, to keep the story alive. The *Post*'s publisher, Katherine Graham, its editor, Ben Bradlee, and the two reporters who spent most of their waking hours with the story, Woodward and Bernstein, knew that they were facing a formidable foe as they pursued the story. They knew that the President and his people could damage the paper economically, as indeed they tried to do by persuading some advertisers to withdraw their business and by threatening not to renew the license of the paper's television station. But they persisted. Congress, the reformed Justice Department, and the American people may all claim part of the credit for tracing a third-rate burglary to the very desk of the President of the United States and for deposing a chief executive who had betrayed the public's trust. Most of the credit, though, belongs to the *Post*.

## Chapter Six

# Winners and Sinners

We've had our good days and our bad days. We remember the good days with feelings of pride. We'd just as soon forget the bad ones.

THOMAS WINSHIP, Editor Emeritus
*The Boston Globe,* 1985

Winship's words are understandable, and not merely by journalists. Everyone prefers to dwell on his triumphs, forget his failures. The press can hardly be faulted for sharing this desire, especially in the light of its recent history. For, as a glance at this record reveals, the press has had some very good days during the last decade or so. It has had days when everything seemed to be going its way, when information essential to good stories, information essential to its performance of its self-imposed duties seemed to be, if not readily available, then certainly obtainable, with no more than a modicum of effort.

But the press has had its bad days, too. It has had days when little seemed to go right, when information was unobtainable, when the public's view of it and its members was far from favorable and when, to make matters even worse, some of its own members did just the kinds of unforgivable things that the public has so long suspected journalists of doing, giving comfort to its critics and causing fear and trembling among its own members.

The good days for the U.S. press came in the wake of the Vietnam War. The press had succeeded in bringing home to American viewers and readers the realities of the war. They had shown the public how the war was being fought and at what price. They had exposed the differences between official statements and the facts, revealed how the government had engaged in a systematic campaign of distortions, half-truths, and outright lies. The press did not turn the American public against the war. But it certainly provided the information that helped, or in some cases, forced the public to alter its views about the war and the U.S. role in it.

The American news media thus entered the decade of the seventies riding a wave of public confidence. Americans, it seemed, liked the press, admired journalists, and felt that both had and would continue to bring them important information about the actions of their public officials and corporate leaders that these people would never provide on their own.

Americans had good reason for this belief. The press had learned and informed them, for instance, that two of President Nixon's nominees for seats on the U.S. Supreme Court were unqualified for the positions to which the President wished to appoint them. Charles Haynsworth was so lacking in distinction as a jurist that only one loyal Republican was able to think of a reason why he should sit on the country's top judicial bench. Nebraska's senator, Roman Hruska, conceded that Haynsworth's record as a judge was mediocre but argued that the United States was full of mediocre people who should be represented in government. Richard Carswell turned out not only to be a member of a club that systematically excluded blacks, but a man with a long record that suggested racial prejudice. Clearly, neither man was fit to sit on the same bench that had once accommodated jurists like Felix Frankfurter, Louis Brandeis, and Earl Warren. And, thanks to the work of the press in exposing their almost complete lack of qualifications, neither man did. Faced with the opposition that newspaper and television reports generated to their appointments, both men withdrew from consideration before their nominations could be voted on in the Senate.

The press did not, however, concentrate its fire solely on Republican appointees. When Richard Nixon's tearful resignation catapulted House Minority Leader Gerald Ford, an undistinguished congressman who had risen through the seniority system into the White House, the news media responded to the new chief executive's affability with a show of tolerance of their own. The media treated the new President well, at least until he issued his blanket pardon, absolving Nixon of all crimes he may have committed while serving as President. The pardon triggered a search by the press for evidence that some kind of deal had been struck, that the promise of a pardon had been Nixon's price for stepping down and letting Ford occupy the Oval Office. The search, however, proved fruitless. The pardon may have seemed hasty. It may have been ill-advised. But the press found no evidence that it was Ford's *quid* for a Nixon *quo*.

For the most part, the press treated Ford as a genial bumbler, making much of his proclivity for stumbling or banging his head as he entered or left presidential planes and helicopters and taking ill-disguised glee from an incident in which the golfing President sliced a drive that beaned another golfer. But the news media never really went after Ford, in part because they regarded him as a caretaker President, one who was merely keeping the presidential chair warm until such time as he could either win election on his own or step down to make way for a rightfully elected successor.

The media did not, though, hesitate when it came to Ford's successor. Early in his campaign for the presidency, the press checked out Jimmy Carter's credentials and reported that the Georgian, or at least someone on his staff had . . . well, overstated one of his purported qualifications. Some Carter campaign literature listed the one-time Governor of Georgia as a nuclear physicist; other material described him as a nuclear engineer. Of the two, the latter was certainly the more accurate description. For, as the media established, while Carter's experience in Admiral Hyman Rickover's nuclear navy unquestionably gave him a background to under-stand the principles of nuclear power and the mechanics of nuclear reac-tors, it hardly qualified him to call himself a nuclear physicist.

Nor was this the only instance in which the press looked critically at candidate Carter. The media looked closely at the Carter family and its business dealings, and raised questions that made at least a few Americans wonder whether the Carters of Georgia might not be just a little too much like the Snopes family of William Faulkner's fictional Yoknapatawpha County to occupy the White House.

But the press took its most probing look at Carter after he was elected. The occasion for the examination was Carter's appointment of one of his friends, fellow Georgian, campaign coordinator, and adviser Bert Lance to the post of head of the powerful Office of Management and the Budget. For some time, the press had been hearing stories about the strange deal-ings in which Lance had engaged while president of an Atlanta bank. Once Lance was nominated for a federal post, the reporters began to check out these stories more carefully.

What they found made for interesting reading. Lance, it seemed, had used his position as president of the bank to make unsecured loans to his friends, including the President's bumptious brother Billy and the Carter peanut warehouse. Lance had borrowed from the bank himself, too. No one suggested that Lance had done anything criminal; in fact, investi-gations revealed that his way of doing business was not uncommon in Georgia, where bankers and their clients tended to know each other. But a large segment of the media found his actions as bank president "irreg-ular" and wondered, in print and on the air, about the wisdom of naming a man who followed such apparently informal banking practices to a post in which he would be responsible for managing large amounts of the public's money.

Annoyed and upset by the implications of the news stories, Carter responded by defending his friend and questioning the motives of those responsible for the revelations. Angry, he charged the media with destroying a man, impugning his character and blackening his name for no reason except to show their power. Carter's defense of his friend did not, however, deter reporters from pursuing the story. Finally, even the combative Carter had to surrender to the media's *force majeure* and agree to an investigation of his friend and his financial dealings. Bert Lance's name was withdrawn from consideration; someone else got the job.

The press pressured Carter in other ways too. The media had a field day with brother Billy, a good ol' boy who liked his beer but who had never lived up to the family's expectations when it came to business. The press learned that Billy had finally found himself a way to make money. In a move that may not actually have been illegal but that certainly betrayed a consummate lack of sensitivity, Billy had hired himself out to the Libyan government as a lobbyist and "consultant." The Libyans' intentions in hiring Billy, who was clearly not qualified to consult on much more than fishing, softball, or the relative merits of different brands of beer, were evident. In the Middle East, a President's brother could be expected to have the ear of, and at least some influence with, the President. The Libyans obviously assumed that the same was true of Billy.

Billy's Libyan connection proved yet another embarrassment for a President who often acted as if he wished his brother would simply go away. When asked about Billy's courtship of the Libyans and theirs of him, a testy Carter replied in almost biblical terms, suggesting that he was neither legally responsible for nor, as it happened, really capable of controlling his brother. He had, he said, expressed his disapproval of Billy's actions. But he had not been able to persuade him to do otherwise.

Carter may have hoped that his statement would put a period to the tawdry affair. But unfortunately for him, it did not. Reporters reminded him that agents of foreign governments were required to register and declare their incomes and sought to know if Billy was complying with this rule. An embarrassed Carter had to admit that he was not, and to concede, as well, that Billy's advice was neither solicited nor heeded in the councils of his administration. His statement proved annoying to Billy, who registered as the agent of a foreign government and ultimately paid back a large "loan" the Libyans had made him. It embarrassed Carter and made him even more leery of the press than he had previously been.

Through the early seventies, the press basked in its reputation as a watchdog and enjoyed the public's approbation of its performance. But by the mid-seventies, that reputation had been eroded enormously. One thing that helped cause this erosion was what the press itself erroneously described as the "Iran Hostage Crisis," a 444-day-long siege that saw a government-led Teheran mob storm the U.S. embassy, capture some fifty Americans, and hold them prisoner while the U.S. government tried ineffectually to obtain their release.

The event in Iran, from the rioting that challenged the rule of the Shah to his eventual abdication and the assumption of power in the country by the fanatic Ayatollah Ruhollah Khomeini, caught the U.S. press unaware and made at least some newsmen realize ruefully how little attention they had paid this important country and how badly they had informed both themselves and their public about it. For the American press, at least, was clearly caught completely by surprise by what happened there. The press had, in a word, been suckered.

During the late sixties and early seventies, the press, or at least that portion of it that paid any attention at all to Iran, had been taken in by what must be seen in retrospect as an intensive public relations campaign. To anyone who would listen, the Shah of Iran had talked of his "white revolution," of his royally imposed efforts to yank Iran into the twentieth century. There was even some truth behind all the talk. The Shah, whose oil-rich country was nothing if not wealthy, had taken steps to modernize its armed forces, purchasing a great deal of expensive American weapons and portraying himself successfully as the U.S. ally in the campaign to contain Communist expansion in the Middle East. The Shah, who invited hundreds of American bigwigs, including more than a few newspaper and magazine editors, to see him crowned in an elaborate ceremony at Persepolis, was regularly depicted as a hero, a man who was trying to help his benighted people by building schools and hospitals, by creating a new medical school at the University of Teheran, by building roads and sewers, by making his country a model of progress in the area.

These depictions were not entirely inaccurate. The Shah did, in fact, build the roads, hospitals, and schools he claimed to be creating. But his "white revolution" was not all it was touted as being. For despite the Shah's modernism in some areas, he was completely traditional in others. He was, as it turned out, an insecure man whose response to dissent was to turn SAVAK, the Iranian intelligence service, loose to imprison and torture those who spoke out against his reign. He was also unable to realize that if he was ever truly to modernize his country, he must control the members of his family, who managed to get a finger or more into just about every Iranian pie, who were corruptly lining their pockets and increasing their own already enormous holdings, and who were, as it turned out, even more assiduous than he in tracking down and stamping out dissent.

Iran, as it happened, was seething with unrest. But the press, to the extent it covered the country at all, gave the impression that all was calm. In fact, writes media critic Anthony Smith, "the press failed almost totally to understand the internal politics of Iran."[1] Instead, Smith notes, it relied on official handouts and pursued stories only within the limits of official policy.

This lack of initiative on the part of the press proved perilous, for as the revolution that was to depose the Shah began to gather steam, the news media failed completely to understand the extent to which the exiled Ayatollah Khomeini and his tenets of Islamic fundamentalism had captured the Iranian imagination.

The media's ignorance was to prove to be anything but blissful, for the Ayatollah was a man with no love at all for things Western and, at the same time, a man who felt ordained by God to return Iran to a more traditional way of life. In ignoring the Ayatollah, in failing to help him spread his message, the press did more than make itself unpopular with the man who would succeed the Shah; it made itself the Ayatollah's opponent.

Like the U.S. government, the press stayed with the Shah almost to the end. As the Iranian revolution gathered strength, as the anti-Pahlevi mobs rioted in the streets of Teheran, the American media continued to assume that the Shah would somehow manage to weather the storm that was raging against him. It was only toward the very end that the media, realizing that the Shah was doomed, began to turn against him and speculate openly on how much longer he could hold on to his throne.

The Shah's departure from Iran was greeted as a hopeful development by most of the media; few newspapers or television news broadcasters believed that he was merely leaving the country until things settled down. But the conduct of the government that replaced the monarch puzzled the media, for few reporters, including some with no lack of familiarity with the Middle East, could fathom the passions that drove the Iranian people into the arms of the Ayatollah or understand their desire to forsake the progress they had made toward westernization and return to a social system most Americans believed to have died out at the conclusion of the Crusades.

This does not mean that the media failed to cover the fall of the Shah or its aftermath. In the days following the Shah's departure, nightly news broadcasts were filled with film footage showing throngs of Iranians kneeling in worship, flagellating themselves with whips, and beating their breasts in religious fervor. They showed the increasingly familiar face of the Ayatollah as he appeared to his followers and as he denounced the United States as "the great Satan" and enemy of all that was holy. They showed pictures of women who had once dreamed of owning the latest in Paris-inspired dresses abandoning western fashions for the severe discipline of the *chador,* a plain black garment that so covered them from head to foot that only their eyes were exposed.

But few newsmen seemed to understand what they were reporting and, along with the U.S. government, few took seriously the warning that Iran's new rulers would consider it a hostile act for the United States to admit the Shah, who was by then seeking medical treatment for the cancer that would eventually kill him. The U.S. government, acting out of what it described as humanitarian motives and unwilling not only to abandon but to be seen as abandoning an old ally, allowed the erstwhile ruler of Iran to enter the country in order to seek medical treatment at New York Hospital–Cornell Medical Center. A few days later, the mob that had made itself a regular feature of life in Teheran by gathering outside the U.S. embassy to chant anti-American slogans, stormed into the compound and seized those who remained within its walls, threatening to execute them unless the United States turned over to them the person of the Shah.

Once opened, the hostage drama continued for more than a year. (It was not a "crisis," which the dictionary defines as a single point at which action must be taken.) Once begun, too, the hostage drama dominated American news coverage. The media assumed at first that the situation would be solved swiftly, that the government would either disavow the actions of the mob and obtain the freedom of the Americans on its own, or that U.S. pressure would secure the release of the captive Americans. The media's assumption, like that of the U.S. government itself, proved erroneous. The government of Iran quickly allied itself with the rioters and approved their actions; eventually it took control of the hostages itself and reiterated their demands—the hostages for the Shah.

The media covered the story copiously. The television networks hastened to produce and air special reports that stressed the theme that America was being held hostage. ABC News began ending its broadcasts by having its anchormen sign off with the information that they were saying good night on the fifth, six, or four hundredth day that Americans were being held in captivity. They presented the usual interviews with Middle Eastern scholars who tried, not always successfully, to explain the phenomenon of Islamic fundamentalism; international affairs experts like former Secretary of State Henry Kissinger, who explained what they would do if they were advising the President; and members of the hostages' families, who pleaded with the President and his people to free the captive Americans.

The press coverage of the hostage drama increased the pressure on the President both to act and to be seen to be acting. Few days went by in which Americans were not reminded that some fifty-odd of their fellow citizens were being held, probably mistreated, certainly threatened, while the most powerful nation on earth seemed helpless to force their captors to free them. The coverage also forced the President and his people to do much of their negotiating in public, and to telegraph their negotiating positions via the electronic or printed press. Pressure from the press, in fact, may finally have forced the President to authorize a daring commando raid into Iran to free them. This stress pushed a normally cautious President into heeding the advice of those military officials who felt that such a rescue mission was possible and ignoring the counsel of those who felt that such an operation, while fine in theory, would probably become a cropper in practice.[2]

That the rescue attempt was a disaster is well known. Unrealistic planning, weather conditions that should have been, but were not, foreseen, and problems to which even the best conceived of such operations are heir combined to create a fiasco. Had it succeeded it would have been the kind of military triumph that would have made Carter a hero and might have kept him in office. Instead, the United States was put in the position of having to ask Iran to return the bodies of those servicemen killed in the attempt. The military shambles and the press's attempts to find out what happened and why put the President, whose unfortunate habit of acknowledging the limits of power had already cost him support from a public that liked to believe that American power was limitless, solidly behind the political eight ball. As the Iran hostage drama dragged on, Jimmy Carter was increasingly perceived as a loser, as a man incapable of protecting the country's citizens or its interests.

As the weeks and months went by, Americans also began to change their perceptions of the press. Once they had applauded the press for its coverage of the situation, believing that media attention assured that the hostages would not be forgotten. But after a while, they began to wonder, along with some officials, if the press wasn't paying the situation too much attention. Was the press allowing the hostage drama to edge more important stories off news broadcasts or newspaper pages, forcing the Administration to ignore other problems in order to concentrate an undue amount of its efforts toward obtaining the release of the captive Americans?[2] They also wondered whether the media attention was not playing right into the hands of the Iranians, to whom the situation was providing direct access to U.S. newspapers and television and an unprecedented opportunity to influence American public opinion. "America is not being held hostage," *The New York Times*'s Tom Wicker reminded his readers. "Americans are."[3]

Throughout the 1980 presidential campaign, the hostage situation haunted Carter, who was running, and according to all the polls, running badly for reelection. It also played right into the hands of his opponent, former California Governor Ronald Reagan. Reagan, whose personal conduct during the campaign (though not always that of his supporters) always followed the high road, never criticized Carter for his handling of the hostage crisis; all he said was that if he were President, he would see to it that no one dared to commit such an outrage against the United States or its citizens. Nor, when asked directly to outline what he would do in such a situation, would Reagan allow himself to be drawn into the debate. "We have only one President at a time," he said repeatedly, "and I support him."

That, as it turned out, was all he needed to say. Reagan exuded an air of quiet strength and decisiveness not unlike that of the cowboy heroes he had so often played in a host of "B" movies. Carter, the Iran situation hanging around his neck like the Ancient Mariner's albatross, exuded an air of uncertainty and self-doubt. The American news media may have thought Reagan an intellectual lightweight. But they—not to mention the American people—clearly preferred someone who made them feel good about America and themselves to someone who made them wonder about their country's worth. The press, as its coverage made clear, may have been appalled, amused, or just intrigued at the idea of an actor in the Oval Office. But it was obviously unhappy with the man who occupied the White House, and while many newspapers endorsed Carter for reelection, few did so enthusiastically.

Nor did the public feel as enthusiastic about the press as it once did. Candidate Reagan and his fellow conservatives raised questions about the press during the campaign, suggesting that the U.S. news media were seriously out of touch with the feelings, the hopes, the desires of the majority of Americans and implying that reporters and editors were part of a self-appointed liberal elite that was considerably farther to the left than the great bulk of the public they claimed to serve.

Reagan and his people had even more reason to dislike the press once they were in office. For it was media exposure, more than anything else, that forced the President to pay attention to an agency he would, from his actions, seemed to have preferred to ignore. It forced him to conduct the first shake-up in a part of the government that he, at least, was convinced was running smoothly.

The problem began late in 1981. The agency in which it occurred was the Environmental Protection Agency, charged with enforcing rules on various types of pollution.

The matter concerned EPA's failure to enforce its own rules. The failure came as no surprise. As a candidate, Reagan had frequently complained about the plethora of rules under which U.S. companies were forced to operate and had promised to simplify things and enable business to move more freely by reducing or eliminating what he considered unreasonable or unnecessary regulations.

Reagan's promise, however, proved easier to make than to keep. Congress was not ready to oblige him by rewriting the rules covering air and water pollution or the disposal of toxic wastes. So Reagan opted for a policy of selective nonenforcement. He made it clear that certain rules would not be enforced. And, to make sure that they were not, he, or more specifically his financial advisers, cut back the staffing at selected enforcement agencies, including the EPA.

This was fine as far as EPA administrator Ann Gorsuch was concerned. She cooperated happily in the dismantling of her department, and helped to demoralize an agency that had long been troubled by seeing to it that those who disagreed with the Administration's policies were transferred. This was fine, too, with Rita Lavelle, the head of the section charged with overseeing the laws and regulations concerning waste disposal. She met with California businessmen and assured them that they need not worry about what they were doing; the rules that might affect them would not be enforced.

Their actions, or rather the lack thereof, did not go unnoticed, at least by the press, which had spent a good part of the election year of 1980 writing or broadcasting stories about toxic wastes and the threats they posed to the environment. *The Washington Post, The New York Times,* and the *Los Angeles Times* ran stories on meetings between Lavelle and those she was supposedly regulating. There were stories of favoritism shown to companies owned by campaign contributors.

Finally, there was a congressional inquiry, at which Lavelle first refused to discuss what she had done, then told tales that turned out to be somewhat less than true. Forced out of her job by an administration eager to avoid embarrassment, she was indicted for perjury and ultimately convicted and sent to jail. Gorsuch, Washington's fabled "ice queen," who boasted

frequently about how she was undoing environmental protection legislation that had taken previous administrations years to pass, was suddenly
perceived as an embarrassment by the Reaganauts and "allowed" to resign.
Both Gorsuch, who had since married and become Ann Gorsuch Burford,
and Lavelle, put much of the blame for their plight on the press. Reagan
and the men around him, who had never had much love for the media,
felt the same way.

Other politicians went considerably further than Reagan. Some more
ideological conservatives felt that the media had an obligation not only
to report on and reflect public opinion, but to mirror it. They noted that
the press, or at least the most visible members thereof, seemed to be
considerably far to the left of a public they insisted was moving toward
the right. Their strong suggestion was that the press had better become
more conservative if it wanted, as it claimed, to speak for America.

Still others had more specific complaints about the press. They charged
that the news media were simply inaccurate, accusing them of paying
scant attention to those facts that were ascertainable and of inventing facts
when the latter were not. Their accusation was not unusual; people have
long accused journalists of distortion, exaggeration, or simple invention,
particularly when they do not happen to like the information they present.
Many an official, embarrassed by the repercussions of remarks made to
reporters, has turned around and denied uttering words attributed to him,
denying things that both he and the reporter involved know to be true.
People, particularly those in public life, often make it clear to reporters,
even as they are passing them information, that they will deny everything
if the information in question is attributed to them. Many people, too,
feel that any story must be wrong if it fails to reflect their views of events
or, worse, if it reflects contradictory views.

Some of these accusations are based on simple misunderstanding. People
assume that their recollections of events are accurate and assume, further,
that recollections that differ from theirs must be incorrect. But some of
these accusations are based on fact. For there have been occasions on
which newsmen, or their editors, or their publishers, acting on a whole
congeries of motives, have ignored facts, distorted them, and in some
cases, simply invented them for the sake of making a political point,
selling newspapers, attracting listeners or viewers, or advancing their own
careers.

The "yellow press" of the late nineteenth and early twentieth centuries
was famous for playing fast and loose with the facts. When a reporter,
sent to Cuba by William Randolph Hearst to cover the war between Spain

and the United States, told Hearst that there was as yet no war, he was told not to worry. "I'll provide the war," Hearst told his reporter. "You provide the reporting."

The practice of manufacturing stories fortunately fell into disuse as the American press grew. The sheer size and scope of the press and the tendency of each newspaper or television outlet to keep tabs on what its competition was up to made it difficult for anyone tempted to fake the news to do so; the chances of being caught were too great, as was the embarrassment of being exposed.

But this does not mean that some newsmen, whether through ambition, laziness, or other motives, did not occasionally engage in the practice. Some were practitioners of the so-called "new journalism," which had a brief vogue in the late sixties and early seventies, and which saw reporters, mainly those working for magazines like *New York, Ramparts,* and *Mother Jones,* as well as for such establishment publications as *Harper's* and *The New Yorker,* compressing time, combining quotes, and taking other liberties with the facts in order to convey a "higher truth" about the subject under discussion.

Most of these distortions were of less than startling significance. Jim Bishop revealed that his "day in the life of the President" was not, in fact, a factual report of a single day spent with President Lyndon Johnson. The President, it turned out, really had very little to do the day Bishop visited. Indeed, as former presidential press secretary George Reedy conceded in his book, *The Myth of the Presidency,* many of the Chief Executive's days were filled with inactivity. But, Reedy reported, a myth has grown up around the presidency, and one of its credos is that the President, as leader of the free world, is busy twenty-four hours a day. To foster this myth, and to oblige a writer and satisfy his readers, the activities, the meetings and appointments covering several days were described as if they took place in a single day.

As sins go, this was hardly a mortal one. Newspapers and television stations have done essentially the same thing on a local level, sending a reporter out to spend a night on patrol with the police, then finding out that the night they selected turned out to be the quietest anyone can recall occurring in a decade.

But as sins go, it is still a bad one, for it results in reporting that, despite its good intentions, misleads and fosters myths that happen to be untrue. It also undermines the credibility of reporters in general. The reputations of all who claim to deal in facts took a bit of a beating, for example, when a writer for *The New Yorker* told journalism students that the quotes contained in an article he had written on Spain had been largely invented, and that events described in the article as having taken place on the same day had actually occurred several days, or in one case, several weeks apart. The writer defended his action, claiming that the invented quotations merely conveyed the sense of what was being said in more colorful, more dramatic language. Using the "higher truth" defense, he insisted that despite the freedom he had taken with specific facts, the overall impressions conveyed by his article were accurate.

The writer's admission proved embarrassing to *The New Yorker,* which takes great pride in the abilities of its research staff and which insists that its articles are reviewed carefully to insure their accuracy. It proved equally embarrassing to the writer, who found his credibility called into question, and who finally admitted that the practice was less than professional.

But *The New Yorker* was not the only magazine at which faces were red in recent years. In 1981, newspaper readers in Washington and elsewhere were stunned when reporter Janet Cooke wrote and *The Washington Post* ran a story titled "Jimmy's World." Their shock was understandable; the story described the life of an eight-year-old heroin addict who had been introduced to the drug and taught how to inject himself with it by his stepfather, himself a junkie.

Well written, the story was nothing if not dramatic. Within days of its publication, it was being quoted throughout the news industry. It was also being envied by newsmen who wished that they could find themselves pint-sized addicts about whom they could write.

One of the most spectacular stories of the year, "Jimmy's World" won the *Post* and Cooke journalism's most coveted award, the Pulitzer Prize. The *Post* patted its own back in a full-page ad in various trade publications. But, as it turned out, it congratulated itself too soon. The story was a phony.

The first inkling that all was not as it should be came when papers reporting on the Pulitzer ran a short bit of biography on Ms. Cooke, reporting, because they had no reason to question the material they had been given, that she was a graduate of Sarah Lawrence College. College officials, anxious to show their students that one of their graduates had done rather well for herself, checked their records before making any claims and found out that Ms. Cooke had attended the school for a year, but had transferred to another school to complete her college work.

Their discovery led to other questions, a few of which had been asked around the *Post* newsroom ever since the story first appeared. The questions—and the absence of answers—prompted the *Post*'s editors to ask. They demanded that Ms. Cooke give them Jimmy's real name and address. Confronted, she reacted with confusion. At first, she said that she would try to produce the youngster; finally, as the pressure mounted on her to do so, she broke down and admitted that the story was false. There was no such youngster, she confessed. Having heard that there were juvenile junkies and having staked her reputation on her ability to find one, she said, she had looked in vain and then, desperate to produce a story, had yielded to temptation and invented one. "The child never existed," she admitted. But then, neither did the confident young lady who had managed to parlay her good looks and the facts that she was both a woman and black into a job with the *Post*. Cooke, it turned out, had not gone to the prestigious Eastern schools she listed on her résumé; she had merely claimed to have done so in order to impress the *Post*'s editors who, as it turned out, set great store by such things. Nor could she do some of the other things she claimed to be able to do, including speak fluent French, a claim that could have been checked out quickly by any French-speaking person on the staff.

Embarrassed, the *Post* made no attempt to excuse its error. The paper returned the Pulitzer Prize, printed a front page story admitting that the story was false, and allowed Cooke to resign. It also launched a painful investigation to find out how such a thing could happen while its editor, Ben Bradlee, admitted that he put too much value in some applicants' apparent qualifications and not enough in records of proven performance.

*L'affaire* Cooke rocked the news business and made most newspapers and television news operations look harder at their own standards. The media had barely started this "agonizing reappraisal," though, before they were rocked by a second scandal. For several weeks, editors at the New York *Daily News* had been looking into rumors that columnist Michael Daly may have been stretching the truth when he wrote his dramatic stories about the tension in Northern Ireland. Only a month after the Cooke affair broke, they learned that at least some of the rumors were true. Daly admitted that he had made up the name of a British soldier who, he had reported, had shot a youngster while he was on patrol in Belfast. At the same time, editors found that the story contained other errors of fact as well.

Daly conceded that he had changed details in several of his stories from Northern Ireland, but maintained, in classic "new journalism" fashion, that altering the facts had not, in any significant way, lessened the truth of the stories he was telling.

Wondering, perhaps, if they might be the next to be found guilty of telling their readers something less than the truth, newspapers were slow to point the finger of guilt at either the *Post* or the *News*. Their caution proved commendable; seven months later, the rash of fraud spread to *The New York Times*. It erupted after the *Times*'s Sunday magazine published a piece by freelancer Christopher Jones that purported to be an on-the-scene report from Cambodia. It was, as it turned out, considerably less. After readers wrote to note errors, incongruities, and anachronisms in the story, the *Times* conducted an in-house investigation and learned that Jones had not traveled to Cambodia to report the story; he had written it from his home in Spain. He had also plagiarized part of it from André Malraux's 1930 novel, *La Voie Royale,* or *The Royal Road*.[4]

These scandals could not have pleased media critics more, for they seemed to support exactly what they had been saying all along. They had been claiming that the major media twisted, slanted, or invented "facts." Now, they could cite examples of three major publications at which this was done and suggest, since it was done at three of the country's most prestigious papers, was it not likely to be done at smaller, less respected publications as well?

Journalists, put on the defensive, pointed out correctly that deceptions like those practiced by Cooke, Daly, and Jones were anomalies, oddities rather than regular occurrences. They also noted, aptly, that the deceptions involved unusual stories, not major news stories, which are covered by so many news organizations, both print and electronic, that deception is all but impossible. They noted that the presence of a small army of reporters, from the major newspapers, network television, and the wire services, makes it virtually impossible to fake a story from the White House, or from anywhere else on Capitol Hill, for that matter. They also noted that the fabrications in question were quickly exposed, in large part because of questions from rival or complementary news organizations. They noted, too, that action was taken quickly in all three instances. Cooke and Daly speedily found themselves dropped from their papers; Jones's name was struck from the *Times*'s roster of freelancers. No one, either in print or in broadcasting, approved of the fakeries; most news organizations lost no time reviewing their procedures to make sure that their staffs understood that fraud would not be tolerated. Some news organizations imposed stringent rules on themselves, such as outlawing the use of unattributed quotes, or making it clear that any reporter who insisted on using a quote without identifying its source could be asked by his editor to identify the source.

The spate of trickery did not seriously undermine the credibility of the papers at which the frauds occurred, let alone that of the media in general. But it did point up a problem that has long plagued the media—and long will—and that is that throughout, editors rely almost entirely on the honesty of their reporters. Dealing with reams of copy every day and working under the pressure of weekly, daily, or in the case of the wire services, hourly deadlines, editors have little choice but to assume that the material being handed them by their reporters is honest and, to the extent that this is humanly possibly, accurate. "I can't go questioning every correspondent about every story he files," *Time*'s Ray Cave once replied to a critic who asked why the magazine had not questioned a report that later became the basis of a drawn-out libel suit (see Chapter 9). "I've got to assume that the stories they file are accurate."

His attitude is understandable. No editor has the time to quiz his reporters about each of their stories; the only times most editors are likely to call in a reporter and make him prove that the story he has just presented is accurate is when the piece in question differs dramatically from what other newspapers, magazines, or broadcasters are reporting or when the story is riddled with internal inconsistencies.

Few reporters willfully invent facts or resort to deliberate distortions, and for reasons that should be obvious. One of these is that most reporters respect facts and pride themselves on their ability to ferret them out and to present them coherently. Most, in fact, go out of their way to double-check their facts and their interpretation of them before they write or hand in their stories. The other reason is that distortions are quickly discovered. Newspapers and radio and television news operations pay careful attention to what their competition is carrying and move quickly to follow up on any good stories, particularly those that seem too good to be true. Any reporter who resorts to inventing his facts is likely to be exposed before he gets a chance to do it again.

But this does not mean that the press does not make mistakes. Human beings constantly make mistakes, and those in the press are no exception to this rule. Most of these mistakes, though, are accidental. Rather than the result of deliberate distortion, they are more likely to be the product of a combination of overaggressive reporting and inadequate checking.

Whatever their cause, people notice them. Notes Robert MacNeil of public television's "MacNeil-Lehrer News Hour": "More and more people have had the experience of being interviewed or being at an event that has been covered and they know that what they see on the screen is not the way it was."[5]

Examples abound. *The Kansas City Times* charged in a series of stories on athletic recruitment practices that the mother of a youth recruited to play basketball at Wichita State University had received a new automobile and a house as a payoff for her son's success with the team. *The Wichita Eagle-Beacon* looked into the story and corrected the record. It found that the money for both purchases came from the settlement of a medical malpractice suit.

The *Atlanta Journal & Constitution* ran a series of page-one articles in 1982 alleging that people who worked at or lived near a plutonium plant in Aiken, South Carolina, were suffering disproportionately from a rare blood disease. After reviewing its stories, the paper published a page-one retraction of the claim. Wrote editor Jim Minter: ". . . our reporters had obviously confused statistics and scientific data. We did not ask enough questions as the series was being prepared."[6]

Journalists have approached other stories uncritically, too. Responding to alarms from Washington, a large segment of the press has reported that illegal immigrants are streaming over the border from Mexico into the United States in such numbers that the ethnic and economic stability of the country are both threatened. Many continued to do such stories, even after the National Academy of Sciences released a research paper declaring that "There is no empirical basis for the widespread belief that the illegal alien population has increased sharply . . . entry attempts may have increased, possibly for no other reason than that the efficiency of the Border Patrol has increased, causing more entries to fail early and thus be repeated."[7]

The continuing stories on the increase in illegal immigration are the result of much of the media's refusal to look beyond the hysterical, head-line-grabbing allegations of a handful of politicians more interested in exposure than accuracy. The same is true of stories on the "epidemic" of teenage suicides. Triggered, at least in part, by the well-publicized suicides of several youngsters from the same suburban community near New York, the stories suggested that American youngsters, particularly the affluent and overindulged, were dying at an alarming rate, either by their own hands or as a result of an increase in accidents and drug use. The stories are misleading. The rate of deaths from accidents among Americans in the fifteen- to twenty-four-year-old group has declined steadily since 1979, and in 1985, dropped below its 1960 rate. Newspaper and television stories to the contrary notwithstanding, the adolescent suicide rate has remained constant over the years.

Nor, as it turns out, are children disappearing at anywhere near the rate news stories would have the public believe. Stirred by the fact that an undetermined number of American children are kidnapped (some by their own parents) or run away each year, some newspapers and broadcasters have reported, without question, the claim put forward by the National Center for Missing and Exploited Children, and told their readers that 1.5 million youngsters vanish each year.

But the claim, as columnist and occasional press critic Nicholas von Hoffman wrote in *The New Republic,* simply does not stand up to scrutiny. He pointed out that there were some 30 million children aged five to thirteen in the United States and noted that if the Center's claim were correct, it would mean that 5 percent of them, or one out of every twenty, was disappearing every year. Said he: ". . . if one child in twenty was disappearing every year, every church group, every PTA, every orga- nization remotely connected with kids and families would be in the streets demonstrating." Von Hoffman also noted that in 1984, California logged no more than 800 people of all ages as missing, meaning that they were gone more than 30 hours. Since California comprises 10 percent of the total U.S. population, and since children might account for as much as 75 percent of the missing, he figured, it should be possible to assume that nationally about ten times that number, or somewhere around 7,000 children, are missing for more than thirty days. If the 1.5 million figure for missing children were correct, von Hoffman noted, there would have to be 150,000 children, 250 times the reported total, missing from Cali- fornia alone.[8]

Errors like these have several causes. One is a tendency, especially among young reporters, to believe the worst in every situation and to see a potential scandal and, hence, fame and fortune for exposing it, in every story. "Every kid I get out of journalism school wants to have some major exposé under his byline," says Rosann Doran, editor of Colorado's Broomfield *Enterprise.* "Sometimes they cannot accept the fact that something is not crooked."[9]

But sometimes erroneous information gets into print and goes out over the airwaves because journalists, whether reporters or editors, simply do not stop to examine the premises of a story or to question the claims of "experts," who are often grinding a variety of philosophical or political axes. ". . . when the topic is drugs or sexual molestation of children or functional illiteracy or homosexuality or you name it," writes von Hoff- man, "then the ten percent law is invoked. According to this law, what- ever it is, ten percent of the population do it or have it done to them or suffer from it."

The abuse of this law is widespread, von Hoffman says. "When most journalistic disasters are detected," he writes, "the 'responsible' press gets exculpated, but on these imaginary stories, there's no difference between *The Wall Street Journal* and *The National Enquirer.* Either one will print any kind of cretinous nonsense if it be uttered by a *soi-disant* expert . . . In Newsland there are only two unknowns: the cure for cancer and the common cold.''[10]

Despite his hyperbole, von Hoffman is on the mark. The press has made mistakes. But most of its mistakes have been inadvertent, the kinds of errors that human beings make in a variety of areas, from adding up columns of figures incorrectly to installing electrical appliances improperly. The fact that a small number of people in the press have been caught cheating does not prove for an instant that, as some claim, "everybody does it." The fact that so few cheats have been exposed proves, instead, that despite some accidental errors, almost no one does.

# Chapter Seven
# The Media Held Hostage

> For the price of a 25-cent newspaper or a 19-inch
> television, a group of hijackers who only represent the
> back pew of some mosque have a very elaborate intel-
> ligence network.
>
> > Defense Department spokesman
> > MICHAEL BURCH, June 1985

The Pentagon's pique was understandable. It was bad enough that a group representing one of the most radical elements of Islamic funda- mentalism had hijacked a Trans World Airlines jet and was holding some three dozen Americans hostage. It was bad enough that the hijackers were demanding that the United States, which claimed that it lacked the power to do so, force Israel to free some seven hundred Lebanese Shiites it had rounded up and interned in order to facilitate the withdrawal of its troops from Lebanon. But it was, from the Pentagon's perspective, even worse that the hijacking was receiving so much attention from the American news media in general and from television in particular. For, argued a good many government and military spokesmen, media coverage of the 1985 Lebanese hijacking did more than merely give the hijackers the international exposure they wanted to advance their ideas. It hampered U.S. efforts to free the hostages by putting unnecessary pressure on the President and by giving the hijackers important information about Amer- ican intentions or the troop movements involved in acting on them. "The media," said one State Department official, "took control of events away from the government and placed it completely in the hands of those who were holding Americans hostage."[1]

Ever since Americans were held hostage for 444 days in Iran back in 1979 and 1980, government—as well as the media's own internal and external critics—have wondered what newspapers and magazines, radio and television should do when confronted with a similar situation. Should the press—both print and electronic—play into the hands of hijackers, kidnappers, and assorted other terrorists by providing them with complete coverage of their complaints and demands? Should the press ignore the incident, cutting terrorists or simply crazies off from the coverage they so desperately covet and allowing government, military, and police officials to operate unsupervised? Or should they follow some middle course, submitting to what amounts to official censorship or exercising some form of self-control that may amount to the same thing?

Americans and the American media had let these questions languish in the years since Iran had released those it was holding and allowed them to return home. So neither the government nor the media were prepared when, with a sense of déjà vu, it seemed, the whole thing happened again.

It happened on June 13, and it happened quickly. TWA's Flight 847, en route from the Middle East to New York, had barely left Athens after a scheduled stop when three men, all Arabs, rose from their seats, produced weapons, and took over the aircraft. For the next twenty-four hours, they forced pilot, crew, and passengers to participate in a hegira, directing the plane to fly to Algeria, where government officials refused to play a role in their ad-lib drama, then eventually back to Beirut, where the plane's pilot ignored the objections of ground controllers and set the plane down. In the process, the hijackers, joined by others, beat and robbed many passengers and murdered Robert Stethem, a U.S. Navy frogman who had the misfortune of choosing that flight for what was to have been a trip home. Then, settled on the airfield at Beirut, they let the remainder of their non-American hostages go and presented their demands. The Americans, they said, could go free when Israel freed the seven hundred Shiite militiamen it was holding. The United States, they insisted, must make Israel do their bidding.

The U.S. government's response was predictable. It announced that it would not negotiate with terrorists while they were holding U.S. citizens hostage. Release the Americans, said the U.S. government, and it would be willing to talk.

The U.S. news media's response was equally predictable. To them, the hijacking of a plane and the taking of American hostages was a story. Within hours, U.S. newspapers, magazines, and particularly television news operations, most of whom had all but abandoned Beirut and pulled their people out of the city because life there was too dangerous, were dispatching reporters, photographers, cameramen, to Lebanon. What had started as an international incident was about to become, willy-nilly, a media event.

It never reached the proportions of the Iranian captivity, which the news media, apparently unaware of the meaning of the word, persisted in calling a "crisis." It was over in a mere seventeen days, which suggests, if nothing else, that Ronald Reagan is inherently luckier than his hapless predecessor, Jimmy Carter. But it lasted long enough. For a fortnight, it dominated the front pages of American newspapers, commanded the covers of the country's weekly news magazines. For a fortnight, it forced almost every other story off the network news broadcasts, and dominated the television-formed American consciousness completely. For as long as it lasted, it *was* the news. The networks interrupted their regular programming to provide up-to-the-minute reports on developments that turned out, more often than not, to be nondevelopments. They broadcast a seemingly endless series of interviews with those who had been released as well as with the friends and families of those who were still being held. They carried live coverage of news conferences at which the hostages appeared with their captors, even showing one at which the competing journalists became so unruly that the terrorists took over to restore order. And in the end, the media, or at least most of them, refused to look at themselves and their performances critically, concluding, after only the most shallow of self-examinations, that they had done a good job and that anyone who criticized them for their obvious excesses was advocating censorship. The media, critics concur, did not cover themselves with glory when it came to covering the TWA takeover.

Are the critics correct? Did the news media mishandle the story and if so, how? What should it have done to cover the story?

The questions are easy to answer in the abstract. But they become more difficult when they center on specifics.

From the start, television dominated the story. The networks interrupted their coverage to report the initial hijacking of TWA Flight 847, breaking into regular programming to announce that the plane had been taken over. It continued to do so as the plane shuttled from airport to airport in the littoral, looking for a place to land. It managed to cover its final landing at Beirut live, airing not only the words of the ground controller who insisted that the airport was closed but the tense voice of pilot John Testrake as he answered the tower, explaining that he was not about to argue with people who were threatening to kill his passengers.

From then on, the television networks stayed with the story. Television executives, realizing that a hostage drama made good television (hostage dramas work on "Kojak" or "Hill Street Blues," don't they?), set aside large blocks of time to cover it, forcing their news operations to find ways of filling that time. The news organizations rose to the challenge. Sparing no expense, they tracked down the relatives and friends of those being held and asked them not only some rather inane questions, like how it felt to know that a husband, brother, sister, was being held by gunmen (or "armed gunmen," as one television reporter insisted on calling them, apparently unaware that a gunman cannot very well be unarmed) but less inane questions like what they thought should be done to free their loved ones. They sought out experts on Islam, terrorism, and international tensions and interviewed them, sometimes in an effort to learn who the hijackers were and what they wanted, sometimes merely to fill up airtime.

The television networks, along with newspapers and magazines, also sought out government officials in an effort to find out what they were doing to free the hostages. Both the print and the electronic media, in short, did whatever they could to cover the story.

But, as it worked out, television could—and did—do more. It did because of its very nature. Newspapers and magazines must be written, edited, and printed before they can be read. They cannot present events as they are happening, offering them undigested or unedited. They must select, from the plethora of facts available to them, those that are relevant and significant, then present them in a context that makes them understandable. Television can air information immediately. The cameras can show events as they are happening, the television reporter on the scene can—and frequently must—describe what he sees before he is fully aware of what he is seeing. He can—and often must—report facts before he understands their meaning or significance. The writers and editors who assemble something like the "NBC Nightly News," can look through a day's worth of film and select that footage that seems to explain the story best, write copy that gives meaning to the pictures. The reporter wielding a live microphone and backed up by a live camera cannot.

The hijackers realized the difference only too well, and used television masterfully to make their cases. Television, for better or worse, helped them.

It helped them, in part, by giving little thought to what it or its people were doing, at least as they did it. It helped them, in some cases, by putting competitiveness before common sense. Television competition is always brutal. In a situation involving American hostages, it became even more so, partly because the public is more attentive during such a situation, partly because media stardom is at stake, as it turned out to be for ABC's Ted Koppel during the Iranian hostage drama. He, after all, managed to parlay his appearances on a nightly program titled "America Held Hostage" into a post as moderator of ABC's justly respected "Nightline."

Given such attitudes, TV could have been expected to pass up no opportunity to get the hostages, their captors, or others involved with the story on film. Given such attitudes, the television networks lived up to expectations. Any qualms that their coverage might play into the hands of the hijackers or run counter to U.S. national interests were quickly forgotten, or at least placed at the backs of executives' minds. What occupied the front spot was the story itself.

For a day after their arrival in Beirut, television crews had to content themselves with long-range shots of the hijacked jet and pictures of the hijackers waving from an open door or cockpit window, or interviews with Nabih Berri, the Lebanese leader who leaped into the situation and, for reasons having more to do with internal Lebanese politics than anything else, attempted to act as broker between Shiite militiamen and those seeking the release of the hostages.

Then ABC got a break. Correspondent Charles Glass, whose writing in the British magazine, *The Spectator,* suggests that he is sympathetic to the Arab position where Middle Eastern affairs are concerned, managed, reportedly through Berri, to interview the pilot and copilot of the plane. As one of the hijackers held a pistol to the interviewees' heads, the interview was considerably less than penetrating. Glass reported that Testrake was smiling. He asked how the crew was being treated and was told that it was being treated fine. He asked about the food and was told that it was wonderful. He asked if the pilot thought the United States should mount a military rescue mission and was told no. "I think we would all be dead men if they did because we're continually surrounded by so many guards," replied Testrake, clearly voicing the views of his captors.[2]

Some segments of the press thought ABC guilty of scoring a cheap shot for getting—and airing—its brief interview with four people under intense pressure. But not ABC's competitors. Both CBS and NBC left no doubt that they envied ABC and made this clear by denying the network quick satellite transmission of its tape unless they, too, were permitted to use it. ABC refused; it knew that in the competitive climate of television, it would get nothing but kudos for its coup. In fact, it did the day after its broadcast when *Washington Post* television critic Tom Shales wrote: "ABC news scored the most sensational journalistic coup of the six-day hostage crisis: exclusive videotaped interviews with the pilot and two of his crew aboard hijacked flight 847 as it sat on the Beirut airport runway."[3]

The following day's coverage proved even more interesting. On June 20—Day 7 in televisionese—the well-armed Shiite militiamen holding the hostages paraded five of them before reporters and cameramen at an impromptu news conference that quickly turned into a free-for-all. Jostling for position, television and print reporters alike began shoving and trying to get closer to the hostages, creating a scene so disorderly that even the hijackers were appalled and threatened to call off the entire exercise. Indeed, it was not until the hijackers began brandishing their weapons that reporters calmed down and settled into something approaching decorum. Led by Allyn Conwell, a handsome petroleum engineer whom they had chosen to act as their spokesman, the hostages told reporters that they were fine and, through Conwell, repeated Testrake's caution against a rescue attempt. But they also aired a good part of their captors' case, making the argument that the 766 Lebanese, most of them Shiites, being held in Israel were hostages in the same way that they themselves were, forgetting, apparently, that the Shiites were soldiers, while they were tourists.

The news conference raised more questions about television's role in the situation. Most agreed that the hostages, their lives at stake, had little choice but to buy their captors' arguments and find a phony moral equivalent between their situation and that of the Lebanese held, but slated for release, by Israel. But many wondered if the networks, which ran the news conference unedited, helped the United States in its efforts to secure the hostages' release. Some felt that television's tendency to personalize the story forced the government to take the position that the hostages' safety would be its prime consideration, effectively preventing it from considering military options even if it had wanted to. Nor were all of television's critics impressed when the networks reported, early in the drama, that the U.S. government had ordered the army's elite Delta Force, the special forces unit that attempted unsuccessfully to rescue the Americans held in Iran, to the Middle East. It made little difference that the reports remained unconfirmed and that the government never said where Delta Force actually was. Merely mentioning it, they felt, conveyed information to the terrorists that they might not have been able to get elsewhere.

Such criticism, though, left the networks unfazed. They continued to broadcast interviews with worried relatives, most of whom pleaded with the President to pressure Israel to release the Shiite prisoners it was holding. They also aired interviews with so-called "average Americans" that helped increase the pressure on the President by featuring people who insisted that Israel must bear much of the blame for the situation.

Indeed, it was not until June 24, the eleventh day of the drama, that the networks showed anything even approaching sensitivity to the strain the hostages were under. The networks' recognition followed shortly after they had aired the views of former Secretary of State Henry Kissinger.

Kissinger was livid at the idea of a hostage press conference, which he described as "a humiliation for the U.S." And, he was equally upset at the coverage the conference had received. Decrying the "huge media coverage these dog and pony shows receive," Kissinger advocated that the media not cover such staged performances, thus robbing the terrorists of the publicity they desired.

"The U.S.," Kissinger said, "cannot afford to give in to the terrorists' demands," and he advocated a hard-line stance against such outrages. What he did not reveal, however, was what he would do if he were in charge of winning the release of the hostages. Nor, to the extent they tried, were TV newsmen able to get him to be specific. Kissinger, as always, told newsmen only what he wanted to tell them. And newsmen, both print and electronic, did what they had always done with Kissinger. They published his remarks as he uttered them.[4]

So, having been successfully manipulated once again by Kissinger, newsmen were understandably a little more perceptive when, on June 24, the Shiite hijackers released films they had made five days earlier of a dozen hostages who insisted that they were being treated just fine. It was obvious, even to the least perceptive journalist covering the story, that any film showing a hostage saying anything other than that which his captors wished him to say would not have been released. So CBS, at least, accompanied the film with a few lines questioning the candor of the hostages' remarks and noting that "What you heard was what their captors wanted you to hear."[5]

The networks may have been obliged to air every foot of film they managed to get of the hostages; the hostages were, after all, celebrities, and Americans, as everyone knows, take celebrities and their activities seriously. But were the networks equally obliged to air every foot of film they were able to obtain on the victims' families? Probably not. But they did so anyway, filling morning and evening news programs with an apparently endless flow of footage of brothers, sisters, wives, husbands of hostages, most of whom did little more than express their understandable anxiety for their safety and urge the President and his policy advisers to follow a course designed to assure their safe return.

Some television executives insisted that neither they nor their reporters had gone looking for hostage families, maintaining that many had come to them seeking exposure. NBC Vice President Tim Russert told Fred Barnes of *The New Republic* that "every network received calls from families who wanted to be on. Psychiatrists say that for many of them it's cathartic."[6]

The exposure may indeed have been cathartic for those who could do nothing but hope and wait as government negotiators tried to free their families. But the exposure added little in the way of meaningful information. CBS's decision to set up a round-robin of interviews at hostages' homes as relatives watched the staged interviews, allowed viewers around the United States to share the anguish those people felt. But the comments that this son or brother "looked well" or "seemed to be holding up," merely showed television's lack of judgment; the hostages' families clearly had no way of knowing how anyone was doing.

The effect of this attention was obvious; it personalized the hostages and their families and turned them from mere names to people with real families who were suffering real emotional crises. But the attention may not have helped the Administration in its efforts to attain their freedom, for the coverage tended to make the hostages' safety the major, if not the only consideration, and effectively forced the Administration, to the extent that it had ever thought seriously of doing so, to drop any idea of using force to free the captive Americans.

This was not the only effect of the coverage, which saw reporters asking both the President and former Secretary of State Alexander Haig whether they might not be conciliatory if members of their own families were held hostages. The coverage, with its emphasis on obtaining the release of the captives at any cost, also forced the Administration to treat Berri, whom the press quickly classified as a "moderate," with more deference than it may have wished. In print, reporters like *The New York Times*'s Anthony Lewis urged the Administration to accede to Berri, pointing out that Berri had jumped into the affair in an attempt to demonstrate that he was a leader. He noted that "the risk for any such figure is, unless he gets results quickly, the radicals will take over for him—and escalate demands."[7] Television reporters were similarly sympathetic. NBC's Bonnie Anderson called his position precarious and observed, with something short of profundity, that "his support among the extremist elements is very tenuous." Worse, other television reporters bought without question the hijackers' idea that their action was somehow similar to that of Israel. On June 21, Day 8 of the drama, ABC's Don Kladstrup interviewed a Lebanese man whose two sons were in Israeli prisons and quoted him as saying: "My sons are hostages, too." His report contained no mention of the fact that Israel had announced its plan for releasing the Shiite prisoners it held well before the hijacking took place.

Television's trespasses did not, however, end when the hostages were released. The circus continued as the freed Americans were feted at a farewell dinner that turned out, at least for television's purpose, to be a love feast between them and their captors. It continued, too, as the former hostages were flown to a U.S. military hospital in West Germany. Each of the television networks had assured itself access to at least one hostage and his family by flying relatives first to New York for interviews, then on to Europe for the forthcoming reunion. This meant that hostages' relatives who arrived in Wiesbaden before the hostages themselves reached Germany were unavailable to any reporters but those who had sponsored them. It also meant that, by the time the hostages themselves arrived, reporters were frustrated and angry and eager to take their anger out on anyone who might be available.

Predictably, then, the homecoming turned into a media circus. The Reagan Administration, ever aware of the impact of the visual over the written, took a part in stage managing the actual arrival. When the plane carrying the former hostages touched down at dawn, a press pool was allowed out onto the runway with Vice President George Bush and a group of dignitaries. The pool did not include any print journalists; the only ones allowed to witness the landing were television cameramen and photographers.

From there, things continued to deteriorate. The former captives were whisked into buses and taken twenty-five miles to the hospital. The Iranian situation featured a mass press conference in which most of the released hostages participated. But no such session was scheduled for the Beirut 39. Instead, officials decided, reporters who wanted to speak to individual ex-hostages could submit written requests for interviews. Those who wished to respond could send messages out to the reporters to whom they wished to speak.

Few chose to speak to anyone. By 10:00 on the morning of July 1, the hospital's press office had received hundreds of requests for interviews, and reporters were lined up outside the facility waiting for answers. They were slow in coming. At noon, hospital commander Colonel Charles K. Maffet met with reporters to report that the ex-hostages were in good health, had firm handshakes, and did not seem to be suffering from any psychological problems. At 1:00 P.M., the hospital gates opened and reporters surged forward, only to be stopped by Air Force guards who said that only the networks, requested by the hostage families they had sponsored, were to be allowed entry.

But even the networks' apparent triumph was short-lived. Inside the gate, the networks set up their equipment on the lawn, waiting to go on the air live with interviews with the former hostages. The waiting went on, as technical problems caused first short delays, then longer ones.

Without the live connection, the newsmen seemed less interested in the one-time hostages, more interested in protecting themselves from the rains that were threatening to turn the whole scene into a sodden mass.

At three o'clock, a military spokesman walked to the gate and told a wet and angry press corps that something had gone wrong. The networks, which had made arrangements with some hostage families, had managed to see some former hostages and get the story, but no one else was even getting close to it.

The networks did little with their advantage. Most broadcast reporters confined their questioning to the obvious, asking the newly released hostages how it had felt to be held prisoner and questioning them as to whether they were glad to be free. Not surprisingly, all said they were.

In the end, in fact, it was the hostages who saved the press. For by day's end, most seemed to have grown tired of their privileged position. A few wandered down to the fence to talk with those still interested in hearing their stories. Others headed to nearby Frankfurt to find themselves a good restaurant.[8]

Hostages and hostage family interviews continued, of course, but with hostages no longer being held, reporters quickly turned to trivialities. On NBC's popular "Today" show, Jane Pauley suggested to the photogenic Conwell that he was a hero. Conwell responded by making his strongest statement to date about the killing of fellow-hostage Stethem. "We didn't find the murder pleasant," he said. Pauley did not, apparently, have the wit to ask him if they had expected to.

Meanwhile, Phyllis George suggested on the "CBS Morning News" that Conwell use his newfound celebrity to run for political office, apparently convinced, possibly on the basis of her own experience, that celebrity alone is a qualification for a life in the public eye. She did not, fortunately, suggest where Conwell might go to seek political office, leaving that open to the viewer's imagination.

The drama over, the postmortems began, as the press and its critics both began to wonder, usually aloud, whether they had helped or hurt the situation, whether they had been used by the terrorists, and whether they should have done things differently. Perhaps predictably, most media spokesmen found little to fault in television's performance. David Hartman, host of ABC's "Good Morning America," expressed the view that "the media did quite well." He took some satisfaction from the fact that television was able to show "that those hijacked—with the obvious exception of Robert Stethem, who was brutally murdered—were at least alive and functioning, although they had guns pointed at their heads."[9] ABC's Sander Vanocur took a similar view of television's performance, noting with pride that the medium "now has the capacity to be almost everywhere at once." Vanocur also took issue with those who charged that television had been used. "I think that what we did was not only very helpful to the families of hostages," he said, "but also helpful in breaking through a great many of the difficulties that governments sometimes have in communicating with each other."[10] CBS correspondent Lesley Stahl took a similar tack. Rather than the instruments of the hijackers and the terrorists, she said, television was much more "the spokesman for those otherwise not having a voice, the hostages and their families, and in a way we contributed to their power."

Stahl admitted, though, that television was used. "We were used by just about everybody, by the White House, by the hijackers, by Nabih Berri and his group, and by the hostage families," said she. NBC's Chris Wallace admitted as much, too. "Of course we were used," said Wallace. "One of the things that terrorists wanted was to get their message out, to express their grievances." But, Wallace insisted, being used is simply a fact of life for those in television. "On a more benign level," he said, "we are used by public officials, as well as those who want to sell their books or movies. The reporter has to decide whether the story is good, informative, and true, and the fact that you are serving someone else's purpose must come second."[11]

ABC's Sam Donaldson defended television as a negotiating tool, but admitted that "we overdid it a bit." Still, he felt that on balance television had performed well, even when it came to airing the hijackers' well-staged news conferences. "TV has no choice," said Donaldson. "If you are in the news business, you can't say you will not show hostages or interview hostages because it might intrude. You have to do it."[12]

Is Donaldson correct? Does television really have no choice? Some of his colleagues think that it has. NBC's senior commentator John Chancellor admitted that he was worried lest the Beirut hostage story become institutionalized. "By institutionalized," he said, "I mean that the media could well have covered it the way they did the Iran hostage crisis: Ending a story telling the audience good night on whatever evening of the hostage story they were reporting on or putting on special programs relating to the crisis or turning over entire pages in the newspapers to the crisis . . . One trap that is relatively easy to fall into is that the press can get so deeply involved covering an issue—especially such an important issue as the Beirut hostage crisis—that it is hard to stop reporting on it, even when there is nothing new to report."[13]

Chancellor's colleague, Bernard Shaw, the Cable News Network's Washington anchorman, agreed. "We have to do the most serious postmortem ever," said he. "Clearly we were a factor in the motivation of the terrorists, whether journalists want to admit it or not. The U.S. government is mounting [a] worldwide campaign against terrorism. We should look closely at whether what we do complements or detracts from this policy.

"We were used," said Shaw. "Absolutely. They wanted a worldwide platform and they got an international stage."[14]

Other media critics concurred. *The Washington Post*'s Tom Shales charged television with trivializing the hostage drama. "Even when the crisis was in full swing," he wrote, "the hostage-taking didn't seem to inflame the American public, in part because we could see the hostages and their captors all but nuzzling on the air as the crisis grew old, in part perhaps because persistent exposure to televised calamities has given us all asbestos sensibilities."[15]

"Television," said Shales perceptively, "turns everything into television; it denatures events, even tragedies. It tidies up calamity and cools it out. One week a jokey, campy massacre on 'Dynasty,' a few weeks later news film of a real massacre on a network newscast. It's hard to keep one's bearings in videoland."[16]

Indeed, Shales concluded, "other than the genuine bravery shown by some of the reporters and technical crews on the scene in Beirut, none of the networks has a great deal to be proud of as this dismaying story is wrapped up and put away."

Shales was not the only media critic to take television to task for its coverage of the Beirut outrage. Syndicated columnist Mary McGrory wrote an evaluation of television's performance that scored the medium for its shallowness and its interviews for their apparent unwillingness to ask difficult questions. What upset her, she admitted, was not so much the fact that pilot John Testrake and Jeffrey Ingalls, a close friend of the slain Stethem, described their kidnapping as a "learning experience," but the fact that television commentators failed to question their description of their ordeal. "Once the initial horror of Stethem's murder had passed," McGrory wrote, "the whole episode took on the surreal coloration of some kind of exchange program, a seminar in the U.S.-Mideast relations conducted under the gun. Apparently, after long bull sessions on religion and politics, both sides came away with a new appreciation of the other fellow's point of view."[17]

McGrory, however, was serious in her assessment of television's impact on the evolution of the Beirut hostage drama. As far as she was concerned, the Shiite militiamen who took the Beirut 39 hostage understood only too well that television could be manipulated to serve their ends. And, she says, they manipulated the medium with skill. "The Amal Shiites," she wrote, "had figured out that TV sanctifies people for Americans. By showing them on the home screen, over lunch at a seaside restaurant in Beirut, attending a last supper with their guards and kissing their captors goodbye, the terrorists personalized the players and restricted Reagan's options. The Amal Shiites craftily made the hostages into members of the national family."[18]

McGrory's point is well made. At the beginning of the Beirut captivity, Reagan was being urged to take the hard line by such experts as Kissinger and conservative columnist George Will, both of whom urged him to put the "national interest" before the mere saving of lives. But their advice soon became politically fatal to follow. "The battle," noted McGrory, "if there ever was one, was finished once the first mad news conference flashed on the box. The Amal Shiites had turned the hostages into television celebrities, and Americans take their television celebrities seriously. No harm must come to them, no matter what abstract principle of foreign policy may be at stake."[19]

Television came in for criticism from other sources as well. Stephen Klaidman, a research fellow at Georgetown University's Kennedy Institute of Ethics, took to the op-ed page of *The New York Times* to accuse television of helping the hijackers. "The hostages 'press' conference staged in Beirut is a perfect example of how terrorists manipulate the media," he wrote. "Because television must find ways to make the drama of the hostage situation explicit, it is easy for gangsters like the hijackers to exploit the hostages, play on the sentiments of the American public— especially the families of the hostages—and thereby undermine Washington's efforts to cope with the crisis."[20]

Suggesting that commercial reasons—"coverage is driven by ratings not news judgment"—dedicated the networks' decisions to devote so much time to covering the hijackers, Klaidman charged that television coverage, by its very nature, "tends to exaggerate the importance of a particular event in comparison with everything else going on in the world at that time." In addition, he said, television used analogies that, while partly relevant, may be mainly false, such as comparing the Beirut drama with the much longer Iran hostage ordeal. But television's worst offense, said Klaidman, is to interfere in government and political processes. "Finally, and most important," said he, "excessive and distorted television coverage can frustrate American policymakers and limit their options . . . Journalists know that terrorists seek as much publicity as possible. Yet by pumping up the story daily, journalists insure that it dominates the news, playing right into the terrorists' hands."[21]

Government officials expressed similar sentiments. Some suggested that the press exercise self-control, meaning self-censorship, and impose a virtual news blackout on stories about hijackings and hostage takings. Attorney General Edwin Meese III told the American Bar Association that news organizations could adopt a voluntary code of restraint in reporting terrorist incidents. The attorney general also approved subpoenas against the national news networks asking for *all* the film footage they shot during the seventeen-day standoff, including their "outtakes," or material not aired for the public.

Meese won a certain amount of applause for his action, especially from conservative groups, which have traditionally favored fetters on the freedom of the press. But he won no praise from civil libertarians, who noted that the government did not cite any specific investigative or prosecutorial need when it asked the networks for their material, and that it did not limit its demand to specific materials or state the purpose of its subpoenas. The purpose of the subpoenas, in fact, was plain: the idea behind them was to intimidate.

Recognizing this, and assuming that the government was conducting a fishing expedition designed to make them appear as the Amal's accomplices in the hostage affair, the networks negotiated a narrow response to the subpoenas. They agreed to turn over any material that could help identify or prosecute those responsible for the hijacking. But even that agreement seemed unnecessary. The Administration had been insisting, almost from the onset of the affair, that it knew the identities of the original hijackers and had eyewitnesses to their crimes.

Meese's attitude is not unexpected. Recent U.S. governments, from that of John Kennedy through that of Jimmy Carter, have increasingly held the press responsible for the problems it publicizes. The Reagan Administration has intensified this tendency, and has sought on several occasions to limit Americans' access to information and to control the way in which the news is gathered and disseminated.

But Meese's attitude is unfortunate, for it attempts to solve a problem by attacking one of its potential solutions. And it ignores an important fact of American life, which is, quite simply, that the news media, and television in particular, exist. Television, in fact, has become a condition of being, a means by which, in our modern, technological society, information is exchanged and people in the global village get to know one another.

Television can, on occasion, be intrusive. It can be inconvenient. It can be harmful. It can be inane. It was all of those things during the Beirut hostage drama. It broadcast too much and said too little. It occasionally blurred the line between electronic theater and news. It diverted the attention of many Americans from the fact that other things were also happening in the world, like the murders of several Americans in El Salvador or the death by starvation of hundreds of people in famine-torn Ethiopia. But it also showed more than just a semblance of responsibility. Those who were so quick to criticize television coverage of the hostage situation never mentioned that the press knew but did not reveal that one hostage was a member of the National Security Agency, an action that probably provided him with at least some measure of protection. Nor did the media reveal, despite the fact that some reporters were privately told, that the Reagan Administration did not, its statement to the contrary notwithstanding, expect to succeed in its demands that seven other Americans held hostage since before the taking of Flight 847 be released along with those kidnapped from the plane.

The media will not help themselves by refusing to reassess their performance during the Beirut hostage situation, or by assuming that anyone who suggests that they do so is seeking to censor them. Dan Rather could be understood for defending television from its critics when he said, "Journalism isn't a precise science. This is a crude art, even on its best days. With it all, I'll take the free press to the controlled media, which some self-serving political types in this country seem to really prefer."[22] But Rather's remarks go a bit too far if they prevent either him or anyone else in television from taking a good hard look at their coverage of the hostage story or from asking themselves the question: If, or more likely when, this kind of story breaks again, would we do it differently?

The question is one that needs to be answered, and not merely by those in the news business. Politicians need to take a good hard look at the hostage drama and realize that America was never held hostage; Americans were. Nor need American interests ever be held hostage merely because Americans are. The nation is only as powerless in a hostage situation as it perceives itself to be. And this perception of powerlessness will be unaffected by whatever the media report. Terrorists, to be sure, seek publicity. Those who set off bombs in crowded marketplaces or machine-gun school buses are not interested in either quiet diplomacy or private protest. But ignoring these outrages does not make them go away any more than ignoring the fact that thirty-nine Americans were held hostage would necessarily have made the hijackers release them.

But focusing the often pitiless eye of the television camera on terrorism can help protect terrorism's victims. Most experts agree that, having produced hostages who assured television viewers that they were being treated well, the hijackers who held the Beirut 39 became considerably less likely to harm them. And most agree, too, that terrorism produces little or no long-term sympathy for those who perpetrate it. The American hostages may have spouted their captors' party line while they were being held against their wills, but most had not been home for too long before they disavowed those statements uttered under duress and called for action to apprehend and punish those responsible for their ordeal.

Looking back, it is obvious that the U.S. news media in general, and the television networks in particular, overcovered the ordeal of those aboard TWA Flight 847. Television devoted an inordinate and inappropriate amount of its time to the story, continuing to report on it even when nothing was happening and, in the process, giving the events it described far more importance than they deserved. Television should learn from its mistakes and alter its approach accordingly.

Which does not mean that it should ignore or downplay the story the next time—and there will be not only a next time but a time after that— Middle East terrorists decide to take hostages in an attempt to prove— or win—a point. Television should report what has happened. It should report what is happening. It should report what may or will happen to the extent that its information is accurate and its doing so will not obviously undermine U.S. efforts to secure its citizens' freedom. For, as Morton Dean, a former CBS correspondent who now serves as New York anchor for the Independent News Network, has observed, "Nothing is gained in a free society from hiding ugly truths. The U.S. has been at its best when it has confronted the stains of injustice: More light means less darkness."[23]

But it should also keep its reporting in perspective. Endless live footage of a plane parked on a runway does nothing to increase a viewer's understanding of what is happening; it merely demonstrates that the station or network he happens to be watching has managed to get a camera and crew to the scene. Endless interviews with hostage relatives, most of whom have less accurate and up-to-date information than those interviewing them, demonstrate little more than the fact that television, as everyone already knows, is ubiquitous. Endless apologies, coupled with the insistence that the media can do no wrong, show simply that television has not learned anything from its experiences.

Television—and the rest of the media—should resist efforts, especially on the part of government, to determine what they can print, broadcast, or show. The government, as it has only too amply demonstrated, does not always know best. But the media should exercise more control over their own actions. For, as their conduct during the 1985 Beirut hostage situation showed, any organization willing to spend enough money can get the story. But just getting the story is not enough. It is getting it right and getting it in perspective that count.

## Chapter Eight
# A Tilt Toward the Left or a Pull Toward the Right?

I charge that the major media in the United States are a bunch of slanted liberals who have systematically, over a long period of time delivered the liberal line.

> WILLIAM RUSHER, publisher,
> *The National Review,* on
> ABC-TV's "Viewpoint,"
> April 17, 1985

This is the most nonsensical thing I've ever heard in my life. The idea that the press of this country, whether at the national or at the state or at the local level, is dominated by liberals is, by any liberal standard, an absurdity.

> HODDING CARTER III,
> TV commentator and columnist,
> responding to Rusher on
> the same program

Okay, so who's right? Are the major American news media dominated, as Rusher charges, by a pack of liberal publishers, editors, writers, and broadcasters, all trying, not without success, to force a liberal point of view on their readers, listeners, and viewers? Or is Rusher's charge ridiculous, as Carter, whom Rusher would undoubtedly label a liberal, says it is?

The questions are not easily answered. American conservatives, who are unquestionably growing in numbers and becoming more influential in American life, but who are nowhere near the majority they would like to be, have long suspected that the American news media have been more partial to people like the late Adlai Stevenson, Senator William Fulbright and Arthur Schlesinger, Jr., than they were or are to people like the late Senator Joseph McCarthy, Senator Barry Goldwater, or Ronald Reagan. Their suspicions have long been, if not secret, then certainly soft-pedaled. Conservatives, after all, have not wanted to sound paranoid.

But in recent years, the conservative claims that the media are biased against them have become louder and more public. They became particularly so, in fact, about midway through 1985 when Rusher and conservative activist Phyllis Schlafly appeared together on ABC-TV's "Viewpoint" and used their appearance to limn what they perceived as the evils of the liberal press. Schlafly put the ball in play by asking whether the media, by hanging the sobriquet "Star Wars" on President Reagan's Strategic Defense Initiative, were not trying to discredit the program. Rusher returned her serve neatly by saying that this was what the liberal media were indeed attempting to do. Their use of this "deceptive" term was, he said, an attempt to "smear" S.D.I. and was ". . . another example of the classic liberal bias of the principal Washington media."

The Rusher-Schlafly exchange might have been dismissed as so much silliness, an intellectual effort on the same level as numerology, if it were the only such accusation. But Rusher and Schlafly are not alone in their belief that the American news media are dominated by liberals. In the course of their quixotic attempt to take over CBS, Senator Jesse Helms and his Fairness in Media organization charged that the nation's best-watched network was a veritable fount of left-wing propaganda. President Reagan's science adviser, George Keyworth, meanwhile, declared publicly that the national press was drawn largely from a narrow fringe element on the far left and, worse, that it was "intent on trying to tear down America."[1] Others, both in government and outside, have also insisted that political coverage by America's major media is slanted against conservatives and for liberals. Nationally syndicated columnist Robert Novak said that he could not help noticing "the intensity of feelings for Walter Mondale among my colleagues in the media" during the 1984 presidential campaign.[2]

Is there any basis to these charges, or are they merely the complaints of people whose ideas have never won the approval they believe they deserve? There is. The charges flow out of two studies. One of these studies was a survey conducted by Stanley Rothman, a professor of government at Smith College, S. Robert Lichter, an assistant professor of political science at George Washington University, and Linda Lichter, a sociologist at the same school. This trio interviewed 240 journalists and news executives at the three major television networks and the Public Broadcasting Service, the three national news magazines and *The New York Times, The Washington Post* and *The Wall Street Journal.* They found—and reported—that between 1964 and 1976 those interviewed had voted for Democrats for President by a margin of more than five to one. They also reported that large majorities of those interviewed favored such "socialistic" ideas as redistribution of income, and described themselves as liberals rather than as conservatives. When it came to social issues, 90 percent endorsed women's right to choose to have an abortion while 97 percent believed that the government should not attempt to regulate sex. When it came to foreign policy, 56 percent believed that the United States exploits the Third World and helps cause poverty.[3]

The other study, which political scientist Michael Robinson reported in the *Washington Journalism Review,* found that the three television networks gave decidedly more negative coverage to Ronald Reagan and George Bush during the presidential campaign than they did to Walter Mondale and Geraldine Ferraro.

Tending, as they do, to support some long-held but heretofore unprovable belief, the two studies, especially the Rothman-Lichter report, were quoted widely, both by conservative spokesmen and corporate officials. Herbert Schmertz, vice president of public affairs for Mobil Oil, expressed the view that the studies show that "the views of America's leading journalists are frequently in direct opposition to prevailing American values." In one of his Mobil "public service" ads, titled "The Myth of the Crusading Reporter," Schmertz cites a Rothman-Lichter study finding that 40 percent of the students at Columbia University's Graduate School of Journalism favored public ownership of corporations. And, he warned, "if [journalists] use the press to crusade on behalf of such beliefs, they do the public a great disservice."[4]

Mobil was not the only corporation to cite the findings of the Rothman-Lichter study. United Technologies ran an ad titled "Where the Media Stand." The ad, which ran in several publications, warned that journalists were "out of step with the public."[5]

Others also found the Rothman-Lichter study good grist for their political mills. Terry Dolan, head of the National Conservative Foundation (formerly the head of the National Conservative Political Action Committee) used the Rothman-Lichter study to justify a well-financed campaign aimed at alerting the public to the media's bias. Michael McDonald of the American Legal Foundation has employed the research to help in court cases and complaints to the Federal Communications Commission about what he described as the media's "liberal outlook."[6]

Nor have journalists themselves been above citing the results of the study. *New York Times* television critic John Corry, *Time* associate editor William Henry III, who was then writing the magazine's "Press" section, and Dan Seligman, associate editor of *Fortune,* among others, all mentioned the study in articles, giving almost official credence to the survey's conclusions that journalists are members of a liberal elite.

Citing from the study would be an understandable action on the part of everyone, from corporate executives to journalists, if the study said what everyone thinks it does. But unfortunately for those who would regard it as gospel, the Rothman-Lichter study is, from a scientific point of view, flawed. The methods employed by the three researchers were less than sound or impartial; the conclusions they reached from their data are not, in all cases, supported by the data themselves. The researchers carefully selected from the data that which would support the thesis they seemed intent upon proving and ignored that which did not. Examining the study and its assumptions in a long article in the *Columbia Journalism Review,* Herbert Gans, a professor of sociology at Columbia and a senior fellow at the Gannett Center for Media Studies, found that Rothman and the Lichters "hide a political argument behind a seemingly objective study, highlighting the data which support that argument."[7]

"The argument," Gans goes on, "is conservative-populist: to show that journalists come from prestigious backgrounds and, holding very liberal views, are therefore out of step with the rest of America. They are described as irreligious, hostile to business and supportive of homosexuality and adultery, as well as of affirmative action."[8] Moreover, Gans notes, the attitudes expressed by the journalists interviewed are compared to the conservative views of a sample of corporate managers who were also studied, as well as those of Middle Americans who are presumed to be even more conservative, though this is difficult to determine because Rothman and the Lichters neither identify this group nor supply research about its beliefs. Still, after testing journalists by the criteria of corporate managers and conservative Middle Americans, the researchers conclude that the journalists are "cosmopolitan outsiders" and find that they possess an "anti-bourgeois social perspective." The researchers do not explain why journalists should be compared with corporate managers rather than other professionals. Nor do they explain why journalists should be expected to share the attitudes of one particular segment of the American population.

These, though, are not Gans's only problems with the Rothman-Lichter study. What bothers him even more is the fact that the researchers report findings that do not accurately reflect the answers to the questions they asked. Rothman and the Lichters did not ask the journalists polled for their opinions; they asked them whether they agreed or disagreed with certain statements. They asked their subjects, for example, whether they agreed or disagreed with a statement that said: ''The government should work to substantially reduce the income gap between the rich and the poor.'' They concluded from their answers that a majority of journalists favored the idea of income redistribution.

But the greatest flaw in the Rothman-Lichter study is that it fails to show that journalists' liberal ideas, if these are indeed the ideas they hold, affect their work. They fail, in short, to answer the question raised by Stephen Hess of the noted Brookings Institute, an occasional adviser to Republican politicians and someone who has written frequently about the Washington media. Hess believes that Washington-based reporters are generally more liberal than the rest of the American public. But having made that statement, he asks the question: ''So what?'' Newsmen's personal beliefs are important, Hess feels, only if they affect their news coverage.

The second study contrasts sharply with the Rothman-Lichter work. Robinson's study is a content analysis of the coverage the three major television networks gave the 1984 presidential campaign, with particular attention to the ways in which the networks played or handled certain stories. Robinson and his coworkers found that the Republican presidential ticket had received twelve times as much ''bad'' press as it did ''good'' coverage, while the Democratic ticket got slightly more good press than it did bad.

On its face, the Robinson study could be taken to suggest that the press treated Mondale and Ferraro better than it did Reagan and Bush. But that, in fact, is not what the study says at all. Looking closely, Robinson found that fully three-quarters of the news reports studied were either neutral or could not be considered favorable to either ticket. Analyzing more than 800 stories, he found that fewer than 3 percent, or only 24, contained any identifiable bias at all, and that those that were biased were almost evenly divided between favoring the Republicans and the Democrats. Where issues were concerned, Robinson reported, the networks demonstrated ''near total objectivity.''[9]

Furthermore, Robinson believes, the fact that Reagan and Bush received slightly more negative coverage than Mondale and Ferraro was due largely to nonideological factors. He expresses the view that the negative treatment Reagan received during the 1984 campaign was due largely to what he called the "four I's": incumbency and journalists' tendency to warn their readers against its political advantages; impishness, or journalists' desire to turn the campaign into a contest; irritation at the President's ability to manipulate the media; and finally, irrevocability, or journalists' reaction to the realization that 1984 was their last chance to cover a Reagan campaign.

Robinson's latest survey ties in well with one done a year earlier to refute Helms's allegations of a liberal slant at CBS. After completing a content analysis of CBS News reports, Robinson concluded that fully two-thirds of the network's stories were not slanted toward either side. Of the remaining third, he found, 16 percent were slanted in favor of the liberal side while 17 percent favored the conservatives.[10]

Robinson's research might not satisfy some conservatives, a few of whom insist on calling CBS the Communist Broadcasting System. But it should convince most open-minded people that, whatever Helms himself thinks, CBS is hardly a vehicle for left-wing propaganda.

A detailed examination of various studies, though, is hardly the only way to refute the charge that the media are dominated by liberal ideologues. All that is really necessary is a dollop of plain, garden-variety common sense. All one really has to do to realize the inanity of Rusher's charge is think back no further than the 1980 campaign. Were the media really kinder to Jimmy Carter than they were to Ronald Reagan? Neither Carter nor his supporters would say so. They felt that the press, constantly reminding the public that Americans were still being held in Iran and constantly calling attention to Carter's inadequacies, never gave their man a chance. To be sure, Reagan aide Pat Buchanan got a going-over from the media, but his treatment at the hands of the press was nothing compared to that accorded Carter's chief of staff, Hamilton Jordan, who was variously reported to have spat a mouthful of liquor at a woman he had tried unsuccessfully to pick up in a bar and to have insulted the wife of the Egyptian ambassador. Both stories, based on information from unidentified sources, were widely circulated. Neither story stood the test of careful checking.[11]

The coverage accorded both Jordan and Buchanan frequently verged on the irresponsible. But anyone who studies it carefully with as much objectivity as he would hope to see on the part of the press, will see that the coverage reflected few ideological biases. It reflected, rather, the fact that both Jordan and Buchanan viewed the press as parasites and expressed their views frequently. The press, it is clear, reciprocated their feelings.

Obviously, being contemptuous of the press has its perils; the press has the power to repay this contempt in kind. But just as clearly, cultivating the press has its rewards. Former Secretary of State Henry Kissinger, one-time Democratic National Chairman Robert Strauss, and Treasury Secretary and Reagan adviser James Baker have all enjoyed excellent coverage in the media, and for reasons that need little explanation. All have courted the media with the passion (and occasionally the grace or lack thereof) of an octogenarian pursuing a chorus girl. All three have made themselves available to reporters, sometimes on the record, sometimes off. All have given at least lip service to the idea that the media are important. All have shown respect for editors and reporters. And all have been accorded respect in return. Even reporters who personally consider Kissinger a Machiavellian manipulator or a Metternich manqué treat him courteously and do nothing that might compromise their access to this important and generally informative individual.

Which calls attention to a situation with which no responsible reporter working in Washington is comfortable. Reporters in general are suckers when it comes to access to powerful officials. And reporters in Washington in particular are, to a greater extent than many are willing to admit, captives of their sources. For reporters in the nation's capital need access in order to work, and few are willing to risk that access by publishing stories that will anger or upset those upon whom they rely for their information. Indeed, an examination of the stories published by at least some leading Washington reporters suggests that they are more interested in assuring access or obtaining invitations to White House functions than they are in informing their readers and viewers. And a further examination shows that conservatives are just as likely to do such stories as liberals.

But anyone who knows anything about the news business will find the Rusher-Schlafly charges ridiculous for still another reason, and that is the nature of the news business itself. For in newspapers and magazines, on radio and television, the news is shaped by forces that have little to do with ideology. Reporters may be liberal, conservative, or something in between where their personal politics are concerned. But where the news is concerned, most of them are newsmen and newswomen and most are far more concerned with getting stories, getting them accurately, and getting them into print or onto the air—preferably before their competitors do. As Gans found when doing the research for his 1979 book *Deciding What's News* and as others who have studied and spoken with journalists at work have also discovered, journalists' personal beliefs have little or no influence on the way they report the news.

Which is understandable. News coverage, except at clearly identified journals of opinion like the avowedly conservative *National Review* or the just-as-avowedly liberal *Nation,* is shaped less by ideology than by other factors, such as the size of the news hole, the news budget under which a publication or broadcaster happens to be operating, the information available, and by considerations unique to each medium, such as television's need for stories that can be told visually. When anyone's personal beliefs are expressed in news stories, they are rarely those of newsmen or editors involved. Instead, they are likely to be those of the President or of the other high-ranking federal, state, and local officials whose statements and actions make the news.

What gets printed or aired is also determined, in good part, by the audience. News readers and viewers do not want or need to hear such good news as the fact that the nation managed to get through a whole day without some threat to its security, or a murder, or a natural disaster like a flood, or a manmade one like a plane crash. Such "good news" is really no news. It is bad news that makes news. People pick up their newspapers or switch on their television sets to hear the details of a terrorist outrage, or to learn that an auto company is closing and laying off workers, or to find out that the national deficit is rising and threatening to beggar those whose taxes finance the Social Security system. Politicians have always been unhappy about bad news, whether they happen to be liberals or conservatives or something in between. Lyndon Johnson once called upon the Washington press corps to try, in their stories, to emphasize the good aspects of an occurrence over the bad. To oblige him, one newsman came up with a news lead that said: "Yesterday, 499 students at Central High School went about their studies quietly and diligently. Meanwhile, another student shot the principal . . ."

Presidents like John F. Kennedy, Johnson, and Carter were unhappy about what seemed to them a plethora of bad news while they were in office and, presumably, responsible for or at least responsible for doing something about much of it. That conservatives are the ones who are today unhappy about bad news does not mean that there is more bad news than ever. It means merely that the conservatives are the ones in office and thus presumably responsible for or at least responsible for doing something about it.

This does not mean for a moment that at least some journalists do not have strongly held political beliefs, or that many, perhaps even a majority, of those working as journalists in the United States today hold beliefs that must, by all standards, be considered liberal. After all, as one old wire service editor once said, "You start out working in this business at $100 a week if you're lucky, and it's hard to be a conservative when almost everyone you know is making more money than you are."

But few newsmen get to express their opinions in news columns. Some may get to do so in syndicated or featured columns, to be sure. But the opinions that are most often expressed in newspapers and on television programs are likely to be those of editors, publishers, and news executives, most of whom tend to be considerably more conservative than the members of their staffs. And strong opinions, either liberal or conservative, are most likely to be expressed in local newspapers or on local radio or television stations, which have monopolies in their markets and which can get away with being strongly opinionated, or which can cater to particular local audiences. They are not often expressed in mass-circulation newspapers or magazines or on television stations that reach large catholic audiences.

Still, many of the opinions expressed seem more likely to displease conservatives than they do liberals because journalists are by nature reformists and are likely to respond to unfairness by calling for changes. They are likely to react to the fact that people are homeless or hungry or unemployed by calling upon someone in a position to take action to do something about it. They are likely to see something basically inequitable in the fact that some Americans face nothing but the despair of dead-end lives while, say, oil companies, are reporting record profits.

And journalists are not, Rothman and the Lichters notwithstanding, the only ones who feel this way. While many Americans subscribe to such conservative credos as the need to take a strong stand against communism or the notion that government should interfere as little as possible in the lives of individuals, many of these same people also feel that the government should do more to create jobs or provide food or clothing for the needy or assure equality of opportunity.

Which means, *pace* Rusher, that while the American public may—and does—feel that the press has its flaws, it does not necessarily believe that the media are prejudiced against conservatives. An April 1984 Roper Poll asked a sample of some two thousand people for their responses to questions about groups that the press is ''out to get.'' Only 12 percent agreed that the press was out to get conservatives. Interestingly, the exact same percentage agreed that the media was out to get liberals. The public, in short, may not like the press and may indeed feel that many of its members fail to share the values of the American community at large. But few feel that the press is biased against one side of the political spectrum or the other.

Facts like these will not prevent some conservatives from seeing the press as their particular adversary, or from agreeing with former Interior

Secretary James Watt, who stated on ABC's "Viewpoint" that the press's mandate was to pursue the truth, asking if the press was doing a good enough job and answering with a resounding no. Watt felt that the press held "partisan, biased points of view."[12]

But ABC's Sam Donaldson, who has annoyed many conservatives by his aggressive behavior and probing questions at presidential news conferences, put things in perspective when he responded to Watt. He said that he had no problem with Watt's description of the media's mandate to pursue the truth "as long as truth does not represent one political point of view, one ideology, one administration." Said Donaldson: "People who are conservative believe their message isn't getting across at this time. Twenty years ago, it might have been on the other foot. But truth is truth, and it's not something that can be measured in an ideological framework."[13]

Donaldson's point is well made. Many members of the media think of themselves as liberal and hold ideas that would certainly be so labeled by those who think of themselves as conservatives. But this does not mean for a minute that news coverage, whether in print or on the air, is biased against conservatives. In fact, a careful study of what gets printed or broadcast will show that newsmen generally have only one identifiable bias, and that, even critics of the media will agree, is a healthy one. It is a bias in favor of the truth.

There are, though, those who would like to impose a bias of another sort on the news media. They include the current occupant of the White House, who has called persistent reporters "s.o.b.'s."[14] They include right-wing politicians and the religious right, who have tried to convince both Americans in general and the press in particular that they speak for the majority of the U.S. population. They include big business, which has used some not-so-subtle persuasion, including threats of lawsuits and economic pressures, to try to convince news organizations to see things their way.

Some of the activities in which these antimedia forces have engaged occasionally border on the childish. The White House Correspondents' Association has discerned a pattern of harassment by the Reagan Administration, in which members of the news media are kept at bay in the name of protecting the President. Basing their accusation on a three-month survey of veteran White House reporters, the members of the organization complained of a "growing degradation of civility" among the Secret Service agents protecting the President. Longtime White House journalists complained of having their equipment repeatedly searched; a few reporters claimed that they missed events because they were subjected to second or third searches in the course of the same trip. "When they stop you and know full well who you are, you have to conclude that they want to show who's in charge," said United Press International's Ira Allen.[15]

In addition, reporters complain, they are generally kept far away from the President, to the point that they are unable to hear what he is saying or tell what he is doing. Nor do those reporters in the "pool," the small group allowed to accompany the President when a larger group would be unwieldy, find themselves getting any access. "In previous administrations, the White House press pool was permitted to follow the president at a reasonably close distance in all public places," the survey said. "Under Reagan, however, pool access to the president has eroded to such an extent that many reporters fear that the pool system is on the verge of extinction."[16]

Other forms of harassment have also been noted. Reporters claim that the White House press office often assembles them for announcements, then keeps them waiting until their deadlines are close in order to prevent them from asking too many questions. Some complain of being physically harassed, of being pushed and shoved, by White House aides and Secret Service personnel.

At the same time, White House reporters note, those journalists who represent papers or news outlets with a more conservative view, or those who hold such views themselves, do get at least some access to either the President or his chief aides. The message to them is clear: See things the White House way or you might not get to see them at all.

Some of the other attempts to pull the press toward the right have been a bit more serious. North Carolina's Senator Jesse Helms and Accuracy in Media won more than just a little public support for their efforts to buy a controlling share of CBS. Their idea, which included encouraging like-minded conservatives to buy shares of CBS stock, then turn them over either to AIM or to vote them the way Helms and AIM suggested, seemed, at least at the outset, like a serious threat against the network. Helms boasted of what he would do if he were Dan Rather's boss and made it clear that he would see to it that there were some changes made in the way CBS, which he perceived as a hotbed of liberalism, reported the news.

The Helms effort failed however, and for a couple of rather simple reasons that demonstrate both his and AIM's occasional inability to deal with reality. One was that many conservatives, including some who cheered loudest when Helms announced his plan, were unwilling to put their money where their mouths were. Another was that much of CBS's stock is held in large blocks; anyone who sought to take over the network would

clearly have to offer stockholders more than the current market value for
their shares, something that Helms's followers were either unwilling or
unable to do.

A far more serious effort to take over CBS was made by Ted Turner,
the freewheeling Atlanta millionaire whose Cable News Network has risen
from an idea to a major journalistic force in only a few years. Turner,
like Helms, proposed to make some changes at CBS. He would make its
approach to the news more "pro-American," he told all who would listen.

Turner, who knew his way around the world of finance far better than
Mr. Helms, went about his campaign to acquire CBS with more care.
With the help of E. F. Hutton & Co., he proposed a novel, no-cash,
leveraged buyout that would have been worth some $5 billion. He proposed
paying $175 a share for CBS stock, something on the order of 60 percent
more than the price of the stock just prior to his offer. But there was less
to his offer than met the eye. In a normal leveraged buyout, the would-
be acquirer raises money by borrowing against either the assets or the
cash flow of the target company. Normally, he gets his money by selling
high-yielding debentures, or "junk bonds," to private investors, then
buys the target company's shares for cash. Turner, however, offered no
cash. Instead, he asked CBS shareholders to participate in the buyout by
trading their stock for a package of securities that would include the junk
bonds as well as some equity in the new company.[17]

Turner's offer clearly had some appeal to at least some CBS shareholders, who saw the value of their holdings beginning to increase. But
it upset CBS, which mobilized its not inconsiderable resources and talents
to fight it. The network battled Turner financially. It also battled him in
the courts and before the Federal Communications Commission. Labeling
Turner's hostile bid "wholly unrealistic," CBS petitioned the FCC to
block it, claiming that a combination of CBS and Turner Broadcasting
System Inc., would reduce the diversity of television news and lessen
competition for advertising dollars. CBS charged that Turner, whose TBS
Superstation is primarily an outlet for old movies, lacked the skill to run
a major news network, and CBS won support from some two dozen civil
rights, religious, labor, and public-interest groups.[18]

Turner countered by urging the FCC to approve his bid promptly. But
in the end, his offer went unaccepted, and not because a timid, indecisive
FCC blocked it. In the end, it was the marketplace that ended Turner's
attempt to buy CBS and make it into a network that would reflect his
essentially laissez-faire views. The longer they had to study his offer, the
less interested shareholders seemed in exchanging their stock for a mess
of bonds that might, on balance, prove to be worthless.

The Helms and Turner efforts may have failed. But they could not help but frighten reporters and editors, who needed little imagination to figure out what would happen if CBS, or any other news organization for that matter, were to be taken over by people who believed that journalism should serve a particular point of view. And it made at least some news executives wonder if perhaps they shouldn't be at least a little nicer to the right wing, out of both a desire to keep its friendship and to prevent it from considering a takeover that might just succeed. "I won't deny that the attempts to take over CBS have made us more careful about what we do," admitted a news executive who was too embarrassed by his disclosure to go on the record. "We've tried to at least achieve a sort of balance in what we print. My publisher spends a good deal of time seeing that all points of view are equally represented in our paper. I know it's not good journalism. But it is safe journalism."[19] It may also be irresponsible journalism. Merely representing all points of view equally ignores the fact that some are better grounded than others.

Business has also increased the pressure on the press. Mobil, angry at news stories about the company, cut off all corporate contact with *The Wall Street Journal* and withdrew all its advertising from that publication. The Bechtel Group pressured ABC to run a report challenging the allegations in a segment on the company on the network's popular "20/20" program. Kaiser Aluminum & Chemical, angered by another "20/20" broadcast, filed a slander suit against ABC in the California courts. Eventually, ABC gave it unedited airtime to broadcast a rebuttal to charges about the danger of aluminum home wiring.[20]

The President, the political and religious right, and big business are all trying their hardest to turn the American news media from skeptics to cheerleaders. What would happen if they succeeded?

Americans got an answer to this question in mid-1985 when the Public Broadcasting System ran an hour-long rebuttal to its Emmy Award-winning thirteen-part series titled "Vietnam: A Television History." A scrupulously researched effort, the $5.6 million PBS project was first aired in 1983. Shocking, at times painful to watch, it approached its subject with few identifiable biases and seemed, to most of those who watched it, to be as dispassionate as a program on such a subject could possibly be.[21]

But AIM, among others, objected to the program, and, feeling pressured by the fact that much of its money comes from the public, PBS agreed to allow it to present a rebuttal. The result was a two-hour program called "Inside Story" that included, in addition to the AIM rebuttal, a brief history of the PBS series, an examination of AIM's major charges, and a twenty-two-minute panel discussion of the issue.

The program produced by AIM was nothing if not unpolished. Slickly narrated by actor Charlton Heston, the program was nonetheless dry. It also spent far less time pointing out errors in the PBS program than it did impugning the motives of those who made it. One of those quoted in the program, Douglas Pike of the Institute of East Asian Studies at Berkeley, stirred up shades of Spiro Agnew and his demand that newspapers print good news by charging that the original program did not "produce anything on the screen that an American could be proud of." Heston blamed the press for the U.S. military defeat in Vietnam. "In the end," he said, "words—disinformation, deception—were the deciding factors in the Vietnam War."[22]

Reed Irvine, chairman of AIM, hailed the program as a precedent-setter. "It marks the first time that a network will air a criticism of its own program," he said. "Besides doing a good deal to set the historical record straight, it will set a precedent for airing professionally produced critiques of TV shows on the same system that aired the original program."[23]

It is just this precedent that many news executives find disturbing. Broadcasters, acting under the FCC's "Fairness Doctrine," have long allowed editorial replies to their broadcasts, just as newspapers have frequently allowed guest editorials to appear in their op-ed pages. But allowing those who differ with a program airtime to question the patriotism of those who produced it is a different matter. Broadcasters regularly exercise some judgment as to who they will allow on their airwaves to respond to their broadcasts. Broadcasters regularly deny airtime to those who approach an issue from a purely ideological viewpoint, and most say they would have no hesitation turning down a request by, say, a Communist group that wished to critique a program on capitalism, or an Islamic fundamentalist group that sought airtime to defend its terrorist attacks on non-Moslems.

But PBS clearly felt that it could not avoid airing the program, not without offending the conservative zealots who currently control the Corporation for Public Broadcasting. Its attitude is understandable, and leaves little doubt that left-wing bias is not the major problem plaguing the American news media, which are considerably less biased in their coverage than their critics claim. The problem is not at all that the American news media lean to the left. The problem is that they are being pulled from the right.

# Chapter Nine

# A Case of Libel

"Here's this morning's New York Sewer!" cried one. "Here's this morning's New York Stabber! Here's the New York Family Spy! Here's the New York Private Listener! Here's the New York Plunderer! Here's the New York Keyhole Reporter! Here's the New York Rowdy Journal! Here's all the New York papers! Here's full particulars of the patriotic locofoco movement yesterday, in which the Whigs was so chawed up; and the last Arkansas gouging case; and the interesting Alabama dooel with Bowie knives; and all the Political, Commercial and Fashionable news. Here they are! Here's the papers, here's the papers!"

CHARLES DICKENS,
*Martin Chuzzlewit*

The press may be sovereign, able to print—or broadcast—whatever it wishes. But it is not, no matter what its critics say, answerable to no one. Even the most independent of newspapers, magazines, or broadcasters can be held accountable for what they publish or air. Even the most outspoken media outlet can be called to account under the laws governing libel, sued, and, if found guilty, forced to pay damages to those whom they have libeled.

Webster defines libel as "a written or oral defamatory statement or representation that conveys an unjustly unfavorable impression," or as "a statement or representation published without just cause and tending to expose another to public contempt." American courts have long followed a similar definition. One could print derogatory statements about individuals or institutions whenever one wished. But one could also be held legally liable for the damages these statements might cause. A newspaper that called a banker a crook, a minister a wenching libertine, or a scout-master a child-molesting syphilitic could be hauled into court and, if the jury agreed that damage had been done, forced to pay compensation for the harm it had caused to an individual or his reputation.

Unless, of course, the publication could show that the statement in question happened to be true. For truth has long been and remains an absolute—in fact, the only absolute—defense against a charge of libel. A newspaper that calls a minister a degenerate may damage his reputation irreparably and assure that he will never again hold a pulpit. But it cannot be successfully prosecuted for libel if it can show that the clergyman in question has regularly been intimately involved with the boy sopranos in his church choir. A paper that destroys a politician's career by calling him an ex-convict cannot be successfully sued if it can show that the man had indeed served a jail sentence.

Most responsible publications had few problems with laws that required them to prove the truth of what they were printing. But they did have one major problem. What would happen, they wondered, if they made an honest mistake? What would happen if they published something that they believed at the time to be true, only to learn later that it was not?

And in addition, what would happen when a paper attempted to exercise one of its primary functions and criticize a public official for his perform-ance in office? Could a politician take umbrage at being called an incom-petent and challenge the paper to prove that he was not doing a good job? Could the threat of a libel suit be used to muzzle the press, to keep it from performing its critical role?

The U.S. Supreme Court agreed that it could. And, in the 1964 case of *New York Times* v. *Sullivan,* it took action to rectify the situation. Until then, libel laws varied somewhat from state to state. But basically, all provided the same protection. They required the plaintiff to show that the press had published a statement that damaged his reputation. They then required the defendant to prove that the statement was true.[1]

In *Sullivan,* the Court let these basic rules stand in most instances. But it decided that a different set of rules should apply in the case of public officials (and, it subsequently decided, public figures, too). They could not collect for libel, said the Court in a unanimous opinion, unless they could meet two criteria: they must prove not only that the story or state-ments at issue were false and defamatory; they must prove that they were published with "actual malice." Plaintiffs, in short, would have to prove that those involved in the publication of a defamatory statement knew that it was false or that they went ahead and published it with "reckless disregard of the truth'' or without making any serious effort to determine whether it was true or not.

A bold and unprecedented step for the Court, the *Sullivan* decision was described by lawyer/legal philosopher Alexander Meiklejohn as cause for "dancing in the streets."[2] It was described by others in similar terms; most saw it as an affirmation of the right, indeed the responsibility of the press to critique the performances of those holding public office.

But the *Sullivan* decision also raised some questions in the minds of the public, the most important of which were these: Why should the press have such latitude when it came to dealing with public officials? And why should officials who feel themselves wronged not have the same rights to seek redress as other citizens?

Justice William Brennan, who wrote the Court's opinion, supplied the answer. The United States, he wrote, had made a "profound national commitment to the principle that debate on public issues should be uninhibited, robust and wide open.'' If journalists had to fear libel suits from officials over statements printed or broadcast in good faith, both reporting and public debate would be seriously hampered. Therefore, said Brennan, journalists should not be punished for error or carelessness as long as they were convinced that what they were reporting *was* true. The public, Brennan continued, had an overriding interest in being informed as to how public officials are carrying out their duties. Such officials, he said, accept their offices voluntarily, knowing their burdens and risks. They have vast powers to command press coverage, to defend themselves, to talk back. They can say virtually anything in the course of performing *their* jobs without the risk of being sued.[3]

For several years after the *Sullivan* decision, the freedom of the press was virtually untrammeled. Judges almost routinely dismissed libel suits brought by public officials, holding that it was all but impossible for them to prove actual malice.

Their attitude, however, eventually changed. In 1979, Chief Justice Warren Burger expressed the view that too many libel suits were being dismissed, and judges, responding to his urging, began to interpret *Sullivan* less liberally. Later that year, in the case of *Herbert* v. *Lando,* the Supreme Court held that a former military commander who alleged that statements in a CBS documentary about him were the result of actual malice was entitled to examine reporters' notes and view unused film footage to find evidence of their intentions.[4]

The impact of this decision was enormous. Newsroom files had always, at least in theory, been subject to search and seizure in court cases. Now, under the Court's newest ruling, the newsman's mind was subject to the same scrutiny. The ruling meant that what journalists did not report could become as important in a court case as what they did. It meant, ironically, that cautious, conscientious reporters could be more vulnerable than their less professional colleagues, because their questioning of sources could be interpreted as evidence not that they were careful, but that they had doubts as to the accuracy of their stories.

Burger's suggestion, and the response of state and federal judges, coupled with an emerging desire on the part of many Americans to punish a press they felt had become too arrogant and powerful, led to an increase in both the number and size of libel suits. Suddenly, it seemed, more and more people were taking newspapers, magazines, and broadcasters to court and demanding and getting large libel awards.

Some of these suits were well justified. People in and out of Hollywood applauded when comedienne/actress Carol Burnett successfully sued the *National Enquirer* for a story reporting that she had been drunk and disorderly in public.

But a great many of the suits were aimed less at obtaining redress for actual damages than they were at intimidating the press. In mid-1979, for example, *The Tampa Tribune,* a generally well-regarded Florida daily with a circulation of 225,000, carried an article that described serious management problems at a local solar energy company. Claiming that he had been defamed, the owner of the company sued the paper. The case went to trial in 1981, ran for ten days, and resulted in a judgment ordering the paper to pay $380,000. When the *Tribune* ran daily stories about the trial, the plaintiff sued over those, too, claiming, among other things, that the paper had erroneously called his company bankrupt when it should have said instead that it had entered Chapter 11 proceedings. The paper was prepared to go to trial again when the reporter who had covered the case became ill and his doctors told the court that he should not be compelled to testify. The paper settled out of court.[5]

A similar case occurred in El Paso, Texas. This case developed when, at the end of a well-publicized 1978 drug conspiracy trial, reporter Ron Dusek wrote a column in *The El Paso Times* questioning the fairness of the federal justice system in the community. The column was particularly critical of U.S. Attorney Jim Kerr, asserting, among other things, that he had lied in his closing arguments. Kerr responded to the allegation by slapping the paper with a $40 million libel suit.

The case took nearly six years to come to trial. But once it did, it went quickly. Kerr made an emotional appeal to the jury to cleanse his name. The paper's case suffered when it came out that Dusek's column had been written quickly and published without editorial review. The jury responded by handing Kerr one of the biggest awards ever made in a Texas libel case. It gave him $3.5 million, $3 million of it in punitive damages.

Kerr's award was reduced on appeal to $600,000. But the impact of the case remained powerful. For as David Crowder, a reporter for the paper, granted, "The verdict had a very great effect. It scared the hell out of the publisher and editor. That definitely trickled down to us—to the point of near hysteria."[6] Crowder felt that the Kerr case and the threat of other lawsuits affected the kinds of stories *The El Paso Times* was willing to do, that it had an impact on the paper's willingness to take risks. A *Times* political writer took issue with his evaluation, but most of the papers staffers did not, and reporter Molly Fennell, who was called off a story on a contempt case after she had ferreted out all the facts, said simply, "We're less aggressive now."

Paul Hogan, managing editor of *The Tampa Tribune*, said that the suit his paper lost affected its temerity. "You can never prove that a story didn't get into a paper," he told a writer for the *Columbia Journalism Review*, "but I'm going to say that there are things that should have gotten into our paper that haven't." Since the court case, he admitted, "We've been a little less aggressive. There are situations we haven't covered that we otherwise might have."[7]

Libel suits such as these get little more than local attention, except from students of the media. But in 1984 and 1985, a quartet of cases claimed national attention. One was a suit brought against *The Washington Post* by William Tavoulareas, then president of the Mobil Corporation. One was a suit against CBS by retired General William Westmoreland. One was a suit against *Time* magazine by Israel's General Ariel Sharon. And one was a suit against *The Boston Globe* by unsuccessful gubernatorial candidate John Lakian.

In some ways, the cases were similar. All four plaintiffs charged the newspapers, magazine, and television network with carrying stories that were not only untrue but that damaged their reputations. All four sought large awards. Westmoreland asked for $120 million. Sharon, Lakian, and Tavoulareas all sought $50 million.

There, however, the similarities ended. For the cases and their outcomes were quite different.

Of the four, the case of *Tavoulareas* versus *Washington Post* was the most straightforward. In 1979, the *Post* carried a story by reporter Patrick Tyler stating that Tavoulareas had used Mobil's resources to help set his son Peter up in business in a London shipping management firm. The story also asserted that Representative John Dingell's House Energy and

Commerce Committee was conducting an investigation into Tavoulareas's action.

Tavoulareas did not act in haste. He asked the *Post* to retract its story. The *Post* stuck by it. Tavoulareas asked again; he asked several times, in fact. But each time, the *Post* stood by its story and refused to print a retraction. Finally, nearly a full year after the story first appeared, Tavoulareas and his son, contending that the story had defamed them, held them up to ridicule, and embarrassed them, sued the newspaper.

The Tavoulareas' suit, like so many cases, took a while to come to trial. Once it did, though, it went their way. On July 30, 1982, the U.S. District Court jury in Washington ruled that the newspaper had libeled the elder Tavoulareas, though not his son. And it awarded the Mobil executive $2,050,000 in damages.

Tavoulareas was pleased with his victory, which he called a vindication. The *Post,* clearly, was not. It appealed the ruling and on May 2, 1983, scored a temporary victory when Judge Oliver Gasch threw out the 1982 jury award.

Gasch said that the article fell "far short of being a model of fair, unbiased investigative journalism." But he also said that he saw "no evidence in the record . . . to show that it contained knowing lies or statements made in reckless disregard of the truth."[8]

The *Post* was naturally cheered by Judge Gasch's ruling. But it was less than pleased when, nearly two years later, the U.S. Circuit Court of Appeals, in a 2–1 decision, overturned Gasch's decision and reinstated both the jury's verdict and the damages against the newspaper. The Appeals Court's majority opinion said that Tavoulareas had demonstrated "clearly and convincingly that the falsehoods contained in the article were published not merely through negligence or inadvertence, but with reckless disregard of whether they were false or not."

Which does not mean that the case is over. The *Post* has appealed the case to the appelate court's full bench and is awaiting a further ruling.

The case of *Lakian* v. *Boston Globe* was a bit more complex. The *Globe* has long been a thorn in the sides of local politicians, many of whom have found themselves embarrassed by the paper's hard-hitting investigative reports. The paper became a thorn in Lakian's side during Massachusetts's 1982 gubernatorial primary when it carried an article by reporter Walter Robinson noting that there appeared to be "a pattern of discrepancies between what [Republican gubernatorial hopeful John Lakian] says and what the records show about his upbringing, schooling, military service and business career."[9]

The article noted, among other things, that while Lakian claimed to have been a Republican since 1970, voting records in the six counties where he had lived showed that he first became a member of the GOP in 1980. It reported that while Lakian's campaign material said that he had received a "battlefield promotion" in Vietnam, Lakian himself had acknowledged that the claim was false; it also said that though Lakian said several times that he had taken graduate history courses at Harvard, university records showed that he had never attended the institution. The article noted discrepancies, too, between ascertainable facts and what Lakian claimed about his business career, and noted that the subject of the story had once contended in an interview that embellishing one's record was an acceptable practice in politics and the sales business.

Lakian lost his bid for the Republican gubernatorial nomination, and, holding the *Globe* at least partially responsible, sued, charging that the paper had sabotaged his political career. The case, which came to court early in 1985, gave Lakian and his lawyers a chance to examine the *Globe*'s editorial process and attempt, at least, to determine what was going through the minds of reporter Robinson and his editors as they prepared and published their story. Politicians, including Boston's politically astute mayor, Kevin White, were amazed that Lakian would pursue the case as far as he did; most figured that taking their lumps from the *Globe* was just one of the prices they had to pay for jumping into the deep, often choppy pool of Massachusetts politics. But Lakian persisted, and he claimed at least a moral victory when, in August 1985, the Massachusetts jury handed down its decision. The jury found that although three paragraphs were false, defamatory, and published with "knowing or reckless" disregard, the "gist of the article" was true. Deciding that Lakian had suffered no actual damage as a result of the story, the jury awarded him no damages.[10]

Not unexpectedly, both sides claimed victory. Lakian said that the jury's finding vindicated him, though how he could say such a thing after the jury had ruled that most of the article was accurate seems to say more about him and his character than it does about the newspaper or its article. Francis Fox, the *Globe*'s chief attorney, said that the decision cleared the *Globe*, pointing to the absence of a damage award as evidence that no libel was proved.

Far more complicated than either of these cases were the actions brought against CBS by General William Westmoreland and against *Time* magazine by Israeli Defense Minister Ariel Sharon. Westmoreland's suit was prompted by a program titled "The Uncounted Enemy," a 1982 documentary in which CBS charged, in effect, that the general had cooked the intelligence books in Vietnam and lied to his superiors at the Pentagon, to the President and, by extension, to the American people, about the nature and strength of the enemy the United States and South Vietnam were facing. Sharon's action was in response to an article published in February 1983, in which *Time* reported that he had given at least tacit approval to the 1983 massacre of Palestinian refugees by Lebanese Phalangists.

Both men brought their suits because they felt that their reputations had been damaged. Westmoreland said that he wanted his standing as a professional soldier cleared. Sharon, charging *Time* with perpetrating a "blood libel," claimed that not only he, but the state of Israel and Jews around the world had been slandered.

The trials, which got under way in 1984, "played" in separate courtrooms in the same building, the federal courthouse in lower Manhattan's Foley Square. They played to packed houses, too, as media watchers and courthouse buffs alike vied for seats.

Both trials were emotional affairs. *Westmoreland* v. *CBS* revived the emotions and anguish connected with the Vietnam War. *Sharon* v. *Time* stirred all the embers of the Arab-Israeli conflict, rekindled some of the ashes of the Holocaust, and raised, to the extent that Sharon was allowed to get away with doing so, the whole question of whether *Time* was anti-Semitic.

Both trials, however, were well run. Judge Pierre Leval made it clear to lawyers representing both Westmoreland and CBS that the question of whether the United States should or should not have been in Vietnam was not at issue in the trial over which he was presiding; the case, he declared, concerned the accuracy of the CBS documentary. Judge Abraham Sofaer ran an equally tight ship. The case under question, he said, was whether *Time*'s allegations about Sharon were or were not true; it concerned whether Sharon had been libeled, not whether Jews or the state of Israel had been defamed.

The trials were, in their ways, quite different. The CBS case seemed, at the outset, far shakier than *Time*'s. CBS President Van Gordon Sauter had admitted that "The Uncounted Enemy" had violated some of CBS's own journalistic rules. But, at the time the program was aired, he had rejected Westmoreland's demand for forty-five minutes of rebuttal time. Instead, he had made the aggrieved general a belated offer of fifteen minutes of airtime to refute the allegations contained in the program. The general, knowing that he could not undo in that time any damage the original program had done in an hour, wisely refused the offer.

Even at the time, the CBS program had come under criticism. Many viewers had been upset by newsman Mike Wallace's inquisitorial manner, feeling that he was taking advantage of his ease before the camera to browbeat a man who was clearly unused to this type of questioning. Critics had more concrete complaints. Four months after the program was aired, *TV Guide* branded it a "smear" and accused CBS of distorting facts that might have contradicted the thesis it had set out to prove. Sauter had ordered an in-house probe of the program and later issued a memo conceding that the documentary had violated good reporting practices. But, he insisted, CBS still stood behind it.[11]

The trial, which ran for two months, brought out much about the way in which CBS had gone about preparing the program, and gave substantial support to critics' suggestions that the network, its reporters, and the program's producer, George Crile, had been far more interested in making a point than in learning and presenting the truth. The program, it became clear, had been conceived as an indictment of Westmoreland; any facts that tended to weaken the case against the man who had served as U.S. military commander in Vietnam were played down or ignored. Those who worked on the program were, it seemed, far more interested in making a dramatic impact than they were in trying to determine just who knew what, when.

Nor was this all the trial brought out. The case brought out the enmity that had long existed between the print media and their broadcast brethren. For, it quickly became clear, many print journalists approached the trial with a built-in bias against CBS, a feeling that television, unlike print, was incapable of serious journalism. Some print journalists were obviously jealous of the staggering salaries commanded by some broadcasters. Others said that, as far as they were concerned, "broadcast journalism" was a contradiction in terms. "Television news is not journalism but entertainment," said a newspaper reporter covering the trial. "So-called 'television newsmen' are never sure whether they're after truth or ratings."

But the hostility that print journalists felt toward television was not the only indication of enmity that came out during the trial. Many of those involved in the case left little doubt that they felt that they were involved in a crusade, a campaign aimed at trimming a large, arrogant, dangerously powerful network down to size. Westmoreland's lawyer, Dan Burt, maintained throughout the trial the attitude of a man who saw the news media in general and CBS in particular as a threat that had to be tamed. Though Burt later repudiated the remark, *USA Today* reporter Ben Brown insisted that he had quoted him accurately when he reported him as saying before the trial opened that "We are about to see the dismantling of a major news network."

Many would obviously have been happy if the trial had produced such a result, including several New Right charitable organizations, which helped to defray Westmoreland's large legal expenses. Burt told *The Washington Post* following the conclusion of the trial that Richard Mellon Scaife, publisher of the *Sacramento Union* and the Greensburg (Pennsylvania) *Tribune Review,* an angel of the New Right movement, had contributed more than $2 million of the $3 million it cost to prosecute the case.

Scaife was not Westmoreland's only financial backer. The John M. Olin Foundation gave Burt's Capitol Legal Foundation more than $230,000 between 1982 and 1985, and made no secret of either its support or the reasons for it. Michael Joyce, executive director of the foundation, said in an interview shortly before the case ended that he thought the trial would "air the limits of the media and the role they play."[12] Joyce said he felt that the media had become more powerful in recent years and wondered whether there were sufficient checks on that power.

The Westmoreland case might have shown more about how CBS had prepared "The Uncounted Enemy" and revealed just what footage the program's producers had seen fit to leave on the cutting-room floor. It might have provided an answer or two to Joyce's question as to just what checks and balances exist on the news media in general and CBS in particular. It might, too, have ended in a dramatic defeat for General Westmoreland, whose case, observers agreed, seemed to be going badly.

But it stopped short of doing any of these things. On February 18, after Burt had presented the case for Westmoreland and two days before CBS, which was offering its defense, was due to rest its case, Westmoreland decided to drop his suit.

Why? In a joint statement, both the general and CBS expressed the view that, as a result of the trial, their respective positions had been "effectively placed before the public for its consideration and that continuing the legal process at this stage would serve no further purpose." Both also expressed mutual admiration. CBS said that it "respects General Westmoreland's long and faithful service to his country" and insisted that it had "never intended to assert and does not believe that General Westmoreland was unpatriotic or disloyal in performing his duties as he saw them." The general, for his part, said that he respected "the long and distinguished journalistic tradition of CBS and the rights of journalists to examine the complex issues of Viet Nam and to present perspectives contrary to his own."[13]

Both sides claimed victory. CBS acknowledged that its investigation of the program had revealed "minor procedural violations" of CBS news standards, but insisted that the violations had "in no way compromised the editorial integrity of the broadcast." Said CBS, "Nothing has surfaced in the discovery and trial process now concluded that in any way diminishes our conviction that the broadcast was fair and accurate, and that it was a valuable contribution to the ongoing study of the Vietnam era."[14]

Westmoreland's statement quoted CBS's line from the joint statement and said that had it been made at the time the program had been aired there would have been no problem. Indeed, said Westmoreland, such a statement could have ended the court case at any time.

Others, however, saw things differently. They believed that Westmoreland had grabbed for a face-saving settlement because it was becoming increasingly evident, to his lawyers if not to him, that he could not meet Judge Leval's requirement that he provide "clear and convincing evidence" that the documentary was false. "They turned the cards over one at a time," said Burt after the case was over. "They turned over that one and I said [expletive deleted]. I remember that feeling in the pit of my stomach. I said, 'It's over.' "[15]

Others also saw the decision as a loss for Westmoreland. "General Westmoreland had trouble proving any falsehood," said *The New York Times* in an editorial titled, appropriately, "A General Surrenders." Continued the *Times*: "At the end he stood in imminent danger of having a jury confirm the essential truth of the CBS report."

A handsome man, Westmoreland managed to look noble even in defeat. But his ability to walk away from the trial straight-backed did not satisfy some of his backers. Retired General Herbert G. Sparrow, who had helped raise funds for Westmoreland to press his case, said that he was disappointed that the jury had not had a chance to rule. Retired Admiral Thomas Moorer was disappointed in the general, expressing the view that his public image—and perhaps that of the military in general—would have suffered less if he was perceived to have been beaten by the jury rather than capitulating himself. Reed Irvine, of the conservative media watchdog group Accuracy in Media (AIM), was disappointed in everything connected with the case. "It was a very unfortunate move on the part of the general and his counsel to throw in the sponge within sight of the goal line," said Irvine. "The only worse outcome would have been a directed verdict by the judge. I would have told him that this hurts his credibility. If the jury went against him, everyone knows a jury can be fickle."

The case of *Sharon* v. *Time* was a very different matter. From the start, it was clear that there was little or no chance that this case could be settled out of court. What Sharon wanted from *Time* was nothing less than an admission that it had knowingly lied when it said that he had discussed with Lebanon's Gemayel family the need for them to avenge the murder of a family member by Palestinians, and, in the process, placed at least his implicit approval on the El Shatila refugee camp massacre. He needed such an admission, he said, to clear his name. He also needed it, though he did not say this, to keep his foundering political career afloat, for the fact was that many Israelis opposed their country's invasion of Lebanon and held Sharon largely responsible for the international black eye Israel suffered as a result of the massacre.

An admission of error, though, was something that *Time* was not willing to make. The magazine stood firmly by its story and the correspondent upon whose reports it was based. The story, *Time* said, was correct.

From the outset, Sharon fought as much of his battle in the press as he did in the courtroom. In the court, Sharon spent much of his time describing his career and reiterating his regrets that an imperfect world made the skills possessed by him and other professional soldiers necessary. He spoke at length of the horrors of war and of the threats to its survival with which his country had to deal almost daily. He spoke at such length, in fact, that Judge Sofaer, a man more than familiar with Israel and Israeli affairs, had to remind him pointedly to stick to the subject.

Outside the court, Sharon proved equally long-winded. In one interview after another, he insisted bluntly that "*Time* lied," and insisted, too, that the magazine must be punished. *Time*'s article was "written in hatred," he told *The Washington Post,* and it reflected the magazine's antipathy toward Israel. He was pressing his suit, he added, to teach *Time* "a kind of lesson" and to make it "more cautious when it comes to the truth and professional journalism."[16]

*Time* refrained from replying in kind. When questioned by reporters from other publications, the magazine's editors said only that *Time* stood by its story.

The story was a long one. The story, in fact, was an eight-page cover story that dealt with the inquiry by Israel's Kahan Commission into the 1983 massacres at Sabra and El Shatila, where hundreds of civilians were killed by Lebanese Phalangist soldiers. The Kahan Commission had concluded that Sharon, then Israel's defense minister, was "indirectly responsible" for the killings because he had ordered the Phalangists into the camps and should have known what would happen when he did.

Sharon could not question that part of *Time*'s story; the report had been made public. But he did take issue with one paragraph, which said:

> One section of the report, known as Appendix B, was not published at all, mainly for security reasons. The section contains the names of several intelligence agents referred to elsewhere in the report. *Time* has learned that it also contains further details about Sharon's visit to the Gemayel family on the day after Bashir Gemayel's assassination. Sharon reportedly told the Gemayels that the Israeli Army would be moving into West Beirut and that he expected the Christian forces to go into the Palestinian refugee camps. Sharon also reportedly discussed with the Gemayels the need for the Phalangists to take revenge for the assassination of Bashir, but the details of the conversation are not known.[17]

Sharon claimed that the paragraph was false and defamatory. Defamatory it may have been, said *Time,* but it was also true.

How did the disputed paragraph get into the magazine in the first place? The answer to this question, which came out in the course of the trial, upset some people, who had no previous idea how a newsmagazine worked. What is even more interesting is that it shocked some journalists, who should have known.

For, as those who were not already aware learned at the trial, a newsmagazine does not function the same way a newspaper does. Newspapers employ reporters who go out, like the legendary blind men examining the elephant, to "see" that part of the story that may be visible from where they are before deadline time. Newspaper reporters write their stories directly from the field. Sent in to the newspaper, these stories are run pretty much as written, generally with little having been done to check the facts they contain.

Newsmagazines, which are published weekly, also employ reporters. But these reporters or correspondents rarely write directly for publication. Instead, taking advantage of the fact that time is so often on their side, they write more discursive reports, or "files," and send them in to the magazine's main office. There, they are funneled to a single writer, who studies them and then, using them as his research material, assembles them into a comprehensive story. *Time* may use files from a dozen or more correspondents in different parts of the world to assemble a single cover story; *Newsweek,* which was, after all, founded by former *Time* staffers, operates much the same way.

*Time*'s correspondents, however, do more than just file for scheduled stories. Each week, *Time* correspondents in Washington and in the magazine's foreign and domestic bureaus contribute items to a trio of memos, which are circulated internally for the edification and guidance of the magazine's New York–based writers and editors. The disputed paragraph, in fact, first surfaced in *Time*'s "World Memo." It did so when correspondent David Halevy, an Israeli employed in the magazine's Jerusalem Bureau and a man known to have excellent sources in the Israeli government, sent in an item reporting on his conversation with intelligence sources. The item contained a sentence that said, "He [Sharon] also gave them the feeling after the Gemayel's questioning that he understood their need to take revenge for the assassination of Bashir and assured them that the Israeli army would neither hinder them nor try to stop them."

Like all memo items, the Halevy item was not intended for publication. But like many memo items, it aroused the interest of the magazine's editors, who remembered it when, two months later, they were assembling the cover story on the Kahan Commission investigation. The editors went back to Halevy, told him they wanted to use the information, and asked him to go back to his sources and make sure that it was correct. Only after Halevy reported back that he had rechecked his sources and felt secure about the story did the editors of *Time* decide to use it.

During the course of the trial, Sharon and his attorneys tried to make much of the fact that Halevy had once been associated with Israel's Labor Party, which bitterly opposes Sharon. They also brought out the fact that Halevy had been the source of an earlier error that occurred when he reported that then-Israeli Premier Menachem Begin was ill only to have his report refuted by the Israeli government. Sharon and his attorneys also attacked the vaunted *Time* checking system for failing to recheck Halevy's information with his sources. Their attack, however, did more to reveal their lack of understanding of how such a system worked than it did to reveal any failure on *Time*'s part.

Things took a nasty turn when some members of the Sharon legal team, as well as some of the former defense minister's supporters, attempted to show a pattern of anti-Semitism on *Time*'s part. Researchers dug up several unflattering references to Jews in the earliest editions of *Time* and tried, without success, to show that the sentiments that led to their publication still prevailed at the magazine. Sharon supporters also made some unpleasant inquiries, calling several *Time* staffers to inquire about anti-Semitism at the magazine.*

*Time* realized midway through the trial that it had made a mistake. It had said in its story that the information in question came from Appendix

---

*I received one of these calls myself. I was rung up one day by a man who introduced himself as an old friend of my father (who, as it turned out, had never heard of him) and asked, after some beating around the bush, how "good" a Jew I thought *Time* editor-in-chief Henry Grunwald was. When I suggested that he put this question to Grunwald himself, he ended the conversation.

B of the Kahan Commission report. But when, after protracted negotiations with the Israeli government, it managed to get a look at this document, it found that the information was not there. Upon learning this, the magazine printed a correction and an expression of regret. It was not allowed to learn if the information was to be found in any of the report's other appendices.

The admission proved damaging. But it did not prove that *Time* had libeled Sharon.

Nor did the outcome of the trial. Because of the complexity of the case, Judge Sofaer took an unusual step. He instructed the jury to answer three questions separately. The first question was: Were the allegations in the *Time* story false? The second, to be answered only if the jury answered "yes" to the first, was: Were the allegations defamatory?

The third question, to be answered only if the jury answered "yes" to the first two, was the crucial one: Had *Time* acted with actual malice? That is, had it acted in "reckless disregard" of the truth and published a story about which it entertained substantial doubts?

The jury had little trouble answering the first two questions. It came back fairly quickly to report that it found the story false and to chide *Time* for carelessness in allowing it to get into print. It took little more time to decide that the story did defame Sharon.

But the jurors took longer to answer the third question, and when they did, they exonerated *Time* of libel. For the jury found that *Time* had not acted with malice, and with that finding, it brought Sharon's suit to a shuddering stop.

The reaction to the verdict was predictably mixed. Sharon claimed victory, despite the fact that he had spent more than $1 million bringing his suit and had come out of it without a penny in damages. "I came here to prove that *Time* lied," Sharon said. "We were able to prove that *Time* did lie." Sharon's lawyer, Milton S. Gould, also claimed success. "We did not come here for the money," Gould said after the trial. "We got everything we came for."[19]

*Time* also claimed victory. Managing editor Ray Cave and editor-in-chief Grunwald expressed disappointment that the jury had found against the magazine on the questions of whether the story was false and defamatory. But they labeled the final verdict a vindication. They dismissed the mistake in paragraph twenty-two of the story as "a small matter" and repeated their oft-made assertion that the story was "substantially true."*

*\**Time* later settled a suit brought against the magazine by Sharon in Israel. The magazine did so, Grunwald explained, because the Israeli court had declared the New York jury's first two findings

*Time* and its lawyers also rejected the suggestion that the magazine had, in fact, lost the case by being found to have made an error. *Time*'s chief attorney, Thomas D. Barr, whose efforts on behalf of the magazine also cost more than $1 million, indicated, in fact, that he found such suggestions unsophisticated. "A lawsuit is very much like a war," said Barr. "Who wins the battles is not particularly important. Who wins the war is terribly important. The war is over and we won."[20]

*Time* editors insisted, too, that they would have fared better if the trial had been more equitable. Grunwald noted after the trial that *Time* had been denied access to certain documents it considered essential to its defense, and pointed out that Sharon was thus enabled to take at least some refuge in secrecy. It was, he said, "deeply disturbing to see a foreign politician, one who is seeking to promote his political fortunes, come into an American court to sue *Time* for libel while the government of which he is a member controls vital evidence and refuses *Time* full access to it. This could have been an alarming precedent."[21]

But then, so could media interpretations of the trial. For much of the coverage of both the case and the verdict suggested that *Time* had really "lost" the case when the jury answered Judge Sofaer's first two questions, and had only "won" on technical grounds when the jury found an absence of actual malice. Some media critics accused *Time* of "arrogance" for failing to admit its mistake early, thus either preventing a trial or ending it early. "We often make inadvertent mistakes in journalism," wrote Ken Auletta in the New York *Daily News*. "*Time* could have said . . . we openly admit it. Instead of a humility defense, *Time* has hunkered down. It has refused to print a retraction. It has arrogated to itself the task of besmirching Sharon's name . . ."[22]

Many newsmen feel that *Time* should have been more cautious. Some feel that the magazine should not have used the information without physical proof that the incriminating lines were actually in the report, and that the editors should have declined to use the item until they actually had a copy of the document, something they were unlikely to get. Many, too, agreed with Auletta that *Time* should have admitted its mistake earlier.

It would be easier to understand their attitude if it were clear that *Time* *knew* from the start that it had made a mistake. But it is less easy to understand why Auletta et al failed to get their own facts clear in the case. For the facts show that *Time* had little choice as to how it would

---

binding in Israel, but, because of differences between American and Israeli law, not the third. Figuring that the magazine was going into the Jerusalem court with two strikes against it, and convinced that the Israeli government would prove no more cooperative in this suit than it had in the first, the magazine agreed to a settlement.

behave in the case. To begin with, *Time* did not know until well into the case that the information it cited was not, in fact, in Appendix B. The record also shows that *Time* was never asked for a correction or retraction; Sharon initiated his libel suit within days after the story was published. His decision to do so made anything *Time* said or published thereafter automatically part of a legal matter with potential consequences in a large-damage lawsuit. Once Sharon filed suit, in short, he effectively precluded *Time* from publishing a retraction.

Many of *Time*'s readers, however, agreed with Auletta and the magazine's other critics. Of the 316 letters received by the magazine the week following the verdict and *Time*'s own story on the case, 206 condemned *Time*. "Some victory," sneered one reader. "You won the same way many criminals win—on technicalities."

Others concurred. Richard Clurman, former chief of correspondents for the Time-Life News Service, said after the trial that regardless of who had actually triumphed in the courtroom, journalism had lost. "In journalism," Clurman wrote, "there is only one sin worse than being found wrong: an unwillingness to admit it." Sharon may have been defeated in law, Clurman said, "but *Time*—and journalism—suffered a worse defeat by having to invoke the privilege of laws that allow but hardly applaud inaccuracy or unfairness."[23]

But the real fact is that if anyone "won" the Sharon case, it was the public. For in upholding the principle that actual malice is an essential element if a newspaper, magazine, or broadcaster is to be found guilty of libel, the court—and the jury—struck a strong blow for the principle of free debate that is essential to democracy.

"What both Mr. Sharon's supporters and *Time*'s critics fail to acknowledge is the crucial importance of the constitutional rule that knowing falsity must be proved to give freedom of expression the 'breathing space' it needs to survive," wrote Henry R. Kaufman, general counsel of the Libel Defense Resource Center. "This rule," he continued, "is no mere technicality. It recognizes that the press cannot guarantee the truth of every newsworthy statement it publishes. Error is inevitable in free debate. When the issues are war and peace, I would rather have more information, with all its uncertainties, than only the official version of events or those items the press can guarantee to be without error. There is no such guarantee, nor does the First Amendment demand it."[24]

Kaufman's argument is unassailable. But it may not be enough to protect the press—or the public—from the tidal wave of libel suits that has risen in the United States. For the number and size of libel suits *is* rising. Politicians, public figures such as actors and authors, businessmen, and plain "ordinary" citizens, are increasingly hauling newspapers and broad-casters into court. Nevada's Senator Paul Laxalt, a close friend of President Reagan, is suing *The Sacramento Bee* for nearly $2 million over allegations that illegal skimming of profits took place at a gambling casino he controlled. Two justices of the Pennsylvania Supreme Court are suing *The Philadelphia Inquirer* for articles accusing the court of nepotism and conflict of interest. Dozens of other suits are before the courts in almost every state of the union.

The press still wins about half of the libel actions brought against it. But the cost of losing such cases is climbing. A decade ago, the usual award in a libel case was $100,000 or less. Now, the average award runs around $2 million. And some even larger awards are being handed out. When two police inspectors and a former deputy district attorney sued the San Francisco *Examiner* for a report claiming that they had obtained testimony improperly during a murder trial, the jury awarded them $4.56 million.

The effect of the libel boom and skyrocketing libel awards is nothing if not chilling. Major publications and news outlets like *Time* and CBS have the resources to fight libel suits, which not only cost enormous amounts of money in legal fees, but which can tie up large numbers of staffers for long periods of time. But smaller newspapers and local television stations lack the resources to resist lawsuits.

So, understandably, many are protecting themselves by pulling in their horns. They are being more cautious about checking their facts, which is all to the good. But they are also being overcautious and, instead of taking the attitude that they can defend themselves if sued, taking the course of trying to avoid lawsuits altogether. "I have stories now I know are true, but they don't get on TV because I can't cross the threshold," said Richard Belcher, an investigative reporter for Atlanta's WAGA-TV, after the Sharon verdict.[25] Many smaller papers have told their reporters to avoid controversy and have quite deliberately begun to stop doing stories that might stir anyone up to sue. And, even larger publications are wondering if they want to be bothered by lawsuits. Even though *The Washington Post* won the first round in its battle with Tavoulareas, editor Ben Bradlee counseled his staff to caution. "We just don't need that kind of grief," he told them.

His attitude is understandable. Few papers, magazines, or television stations can afford to carry the kind of insurance that would protect them should they lose a libel case. Few news outlets can afford to hire the defense teams necessary to protect them in the event that they are sued. Few, in fact, can afford to settle out of court. *The Wall Street Journal* may have felt that it got itself a bargain when it avoided a suit by paying $800,000 in recompense for a story that charged two former federal prosecutors with improperly trying to persuade a convicted felon to testify against some reputed mobsters. But a payment like that could put some smaller papers right in the hands of bankruptcy receivers.

Is there an answer? Some have suggested, as some Supreme Court justices did at the time of *Sullivan,* that rules be adopted barring public officials from ever suing for libel, a measure that would provide the press with some protection from thin-skinned politicians who cannot stand criticism. But most legal scholars—and a good many news editors, too—feel that such blanket protection is improper. Most find *Sullivan* a good set of guidelines—if judges stick to the original ruling and not try to narrow its definition.

Some suggest that many lawsuits could be avoided if the press were required by law to print corrections when it was proved wrong. But that possibility worries many editors, for, they ask, who will make the determination as to when a newspaper, magazine, or television station is wrong?

But the majority, like *Time*'s Grunwald, realize that there is no easy answer to the problem. Part of the solution must be provided by the media itself, he says. Newspapers, magazines, broadcasters must be even more careful than the majority are now. But, he suggests, they should not be any less aggressive when it comes to pursuing the news and publishing stories that may be controversial or even potentially actionable. "Libel actions," he says, "when we look at them in perspective, are an ornament of civilized society. In most cases, they have replaced a resort to weapons as a means of defending one's reputation."[26]

But part of the solution must come from the American news-consuming public, too. For it is the public, after all, that sits on juries; it is the public that hands out the large awards that can frighten, and in some cases, perhaps, silence, the press. And it is the public that will suffer most if this is allowed to happen.

For the public, despite its misgivings about what it reads or sees, relied and will continue to rely upon the news media for its information. Some segments of the public may like President Reagan's present practice of attempting to bypass the news media and going straight to the nation's television viewers to tell the story as he sees it. Some may applaud when the President does as he did upon his return from his meeting with Soviet Premier Mikhail Gorbachev in Geneva in 1985, addressing a special session of Congress with the express purpose of telling his version of events without having to pass them through the filtration mechanism of a newspaper or a television news program.

But many who claim that they want their news unadulterated by the press may also wonder, at least after a while, if they are getting the whole story or only that part of it that the government or some other institution like business or the medical establishment wants them to know. And when they do, they are likely to decide that the press, despite its failings, is not so bad after all.

It really isn't. The press may make mistakes. It may, on occasion, even be mean-spirited or malicious. It may not always get or give out the whole story. But even on its worst days, it gets and gives out more of the story than either government agencies or vested interests like big business. At least now. The public can allow those who use, as well as those who abuse, the libel laws to intimidate the press. The press will suffer severely if this is allowed to happen. But those who will suffer the most will ultimately be the public.

# Chapter Ten
# The Perils of Polling

I wonder who these people are who prefer Dan Rather to Tom Brokaw, or Camel cigarettes to Marlboros or Ronald Reagan to Jimmy Carter. I hear about polls every time I turn on the tube, but I can't remember anyone ever asking me what I thought.

New York television viewer,
November 1980

The television viewer's bewilderment is understandable. Americans are constantly picking up their newspapers and magazines, switching on their radios and television sets, to be told what they think about politicians and political issues, about restoring prayer to public schools, about the consumer products they prefer. In any given week, American consumers are likely to be confronted by as many as a dozen different surveys. Some, conducted for those interested in selling something, will tell them, usually through the medium of paid advertisements, that two dentists out of every three polled prefer a particular brand of toothpaste or recommend a particular brand of chewing gum to those of their patients who chew gum. Some, conducted by such professional firms as the Gallup Organization, Louis Harris, or Yankelovitch, Skelly and Wright, will tell them that a representative sample of their fellow Americans support, say, the decision of the President of the United States to impose an economic boycott on the Arab state of Libya, believe that children with acquired immune deficiency syndrome (AIDS) should or should not be allowed to attend public schools, or oppose adoption of the Equal Rights Amendment.

And reading these polls, or hearing their results described by radio or television broadcasters, Americans cannot help but wonder how they were conducted. For, despite the plethora of polls being conducted throughout the United States at any given time, the majority of Americans will go through their entire lives without once being contacted by the Gallup,

Harris, or Yankelovitch organizations. Most will never be called in the evening by someone seeking to know which television programs they are watching. Few will be stopped in the supermarket and asked which brand of detergent they prefer. And most will go to the polls on Election Day, pull the curtains of the voting booth behind them, vote, emerge, and go about their business without once being asked to disclose the name of the candidate for whom they cast their ballots.

Small wonder, then, that Americans are somewhat suspicious of polls. Many suspect them because they realize that the numbers of people actually questioned are small. They therefore question just how accurately their views can be said to represent those of the population at large. Many distrust polls because they suspect, not without a touch of paranoia, that their methodologies are flawed. They question whether people answer pollsters' questions honestly, and wonder if questioners are able to distinguish truth from wishful thinking.

And many resent them because they feel, not without reason, that polls influence the decisions of politicians who find it easier to do what they think the public wants than to take a tough stand on a difficult issue. Some resent them even more because they feel that polls exert an undue influence on the public, stampeding people eager to go with the crowd into doing things they might not do otherwise.

Even some veteran journalists have grave reservations about polls. One of them is reporter/author Edwin Newman, who says bluntly that "this country is up to its ears in public opinion polls. Most of the time, they are simply boring. They usually labor the obvious and even when they don't they can safely be ignored. There is not the slightest reason to believe that American life would be poorer if there were no public opinion polling."[1]

Their suspicions are not without foundation. The numbers questioned in any poll are small, at least compared with the population as a whole. A major poll might cover as many as a couple of thousand people, a tiny fraction of an American population of some 250 million. The majority of polls cover something on the order of one thousand subjects; many cover only a few hundred.

This is not surprising; the numbers covered in any poll must be small. Public opinion surveys are not, after all, the same things as elections, in which millions are eligible to cast ballots. They are samplings of what a representative segment of the public thinks on specific issues. And they must often be done quickly, sometimes in a few days, occasionally overnight. Clearly, the number of people covered in them cannot be large.

But Americans' suspicions about pollsters' methodologies are not generally justified. For polling, as the accuracy of polls increasingly demonstrates, has become a science. To begin with, professional pollsters select their samples carefully. They know, more from experience than by any set of scientific laws, how large a sample they need in order for their results to be valid. And they know, too, how to select these samples. Pollsters do not, for example, conduct modern public-opinion surveys by going out into the street and stopping people at random. A major polling organization conducting a survey for, say, a presidential candidate, will try to construct a sample that is representative of the population as a whole. Thus, it will make sure that women are represented in the sample in the same proportion that they are represented in the population. It will make sure that the sample includes members of minority groups, such as blacks and Hispanics, that it spans class and economic lines, that it includes people who identify themselves as Republicans as well as those who call themselves Democrats.

Once it has constructed its sample, a good polling organization will question it carefully. In a presidential election poll, it will ask the members of the sample which candidate they prefer, and this information alone can obviously give an indication of which candidate the public at large will prefer. But the pollsters will also analyze the responses to their questions carefully, to see which candidate does or does not have the support of women, minorities, and voters over or under a certain age. In more complex surveys, such as those that attempt to ascertain attitudes toward religion, morality, sexual conduct, serious pollsters will ask respondents a whole series of questions designed to expose contradictions and determine if those in their sample are answering the questions put to them both openly and honestly.

Having done all this, responsible pollsters will publish more than just the answer to such questions as "Would you rather see Candidate A or Candidate B elected President?" They will disclose the size of their sample and reveal something about how it was selected. They will tell when the poll was taken in order to let those reading the results determine if they might have been influenced by events occurring at the time. Finally, they will explain the poll's margin of error.

The last point is important. A poll that shows one candidate leading another by two percentage points may be meaningless if the poll's margin of error is plus or minus 4 percent, while a poll with a 4 percent margin of error may prove predictive if it shows one candidate ahead by, say, ten percentage points. Obviously, the larger the sample, the smaller the margin of error, which is why a poll based on a sample of one thousand respondents is likely to be more accurate, though not, as it turns out, ten times more accurate than a poll based on a sample of one hundred interviewees.

Polls, at least those done by such established organizations as Harris, Gallup, and Yankelovitch, are, in a word, scientific. They are also accurate. And they are useful, too. They tell manufacturers how consumers feel about their products, let advertisers know how the public is responding to their ad campaigns, inform politicians as to the public's feelings and attitudes on the issues of the day. They are valuable, too, for informing the public, for letting people know that their views are shared by many of their fellow citizens, or conversely, for letting them know that even though they are convinced that their opinion is the only logical one, they are in a minority.

Polls probably do influence public opinion and help to convince at least some people, on the idea that millions of other Americans cannot be wrong, to go along with the majority and support a presidential proposal to commit troops to the Middle East, to cut off aid to a country that is refusing to cooperate with the United States, to vote for one candidate instead of another. They probably help persuade people to buy certain products, too, for much the same reason. But there is no way of knowing just how effectively they do this. Polling organizations have yet to do a poll to determine the persuasive effects of their polls—or at least they have yet to make the results of such a poll public if they have done one.

There is one kind of poll, though, that does seem to influence both people and events, and that is the exit poll, a study conducted sometimes by newspapers and wire services, but more often by television networks, to determine how voters have just voted, and used to make early forecasts of election results. The findings of these polls enable television networks to project, often well before polling places are officially closed, the winners of local, state, and even national political contests. These projections understandably affect the attitudes and actions of those who hear them. After all, a would-be voter might ask himself, upon hearing the Cosmological Broadcasting Network project or "call" the outcome of a presidential election an hour before the polls in his district are scheduled to close, why bother to go down to the school basement and cast my ballot for the Democrat candidate as I had planned to do if the Republican has already won?

The notion of projecting the outcome of political contests is not new. In many ways, it is a logical outgrowth of public-opinion polling. The first of the television networks to use the new polling technology in this way was CBS, which began in the early sixties to use a system it called Vote Profile Analysis.

The idea of the system was simplicity itself. CBS and its pollsters studied election results and demographic data until they could identify certain model precincts, voting districts whose social and ethnic composition and whose voters' performances in past elections made them microcosms of local, state, and national electorates. They then used these precincts as bellwethers, stationing people there so they could get the results of the voting in them as soon as they were available and phoning them in to election headquarters in New York. There, the information was analyzed and, if its meaning seemed clear, used to project the winners of various contests. With Vote Profile Analysis, CBS was able to project, with a high degree of accuracy, that one state or another would end up in the Republican or Democratic column and declare one candidate or the other senator, governor, President, long before the candidate himself felt sufficiently confident in the results to claim victory.*

The other networks quickly realized that they must follow the same road if they were to compete with CBS. So ABC and NBC quickly adopted similar systems. By 1972, the networks were all projecting winners, at least state-by-state, within an hour after the polls closed. By 1976, the polls were able to project that former Georgia Governor Jimmy Carter would defeat Gerald Ford, who was running for a presidential term in his own right. In 1980, the networks projected early in the evening that Carter would be sent into retirement by former California Governor Ronald Reagan.

Carter's defeat came as no surprise. Public opinion polls, both those done by newspapers, magazines, and television networks, and those done by pollsters working for the two candidates, showed well before Election Day that Carter, plagued by the Iran hostage situation, was trailing Reagan badly. Carter's own profiles left him with little doubt, as Election Day dawned, that he was about to go down to a devastating defeat.

---

*Though CBS's Vote Profile Analysis was supposed to be scientific, there were obviously times when science was not enough. In 1964, when I was working for a CBS-owned radio station in Boston, I found myself sharing a desk at election headquarters with David Manning White, the dean of Boston University's School of Public Communication, who was working that night for CBS. Election returns came in slowly that night, and the CBS people in New York kept calling us to ask for some results. When we explained that the returns were coming in late, they responded by telling us that they had called at least one race in every state and needed to call one in Massachusetts. Manning and I consulted for a moment, looked at a list of the races, and decided that Congressman Philip Philbin was as close to a sure thing as one could find in politics that year, then told CBS that he would certainly be reelected. A moment later, we heard the sonorous voice of a CBS announcer reporting that Vote Profile Analysis had just projected a victory for Philbin in his Massachusetts district. Fortunately for us, our prediction proved correct.

But the network projections still influenced the outcome of the election. The networks, using data collected from those polling places that reported quickly once the polls closed, began putting one eastern state after another into the Reagan column, almost, it seemed, as soon as the voting was over. Moving west with the clock, the networks projected a Reagan triumph, saying flatly that Ronald Reagan had been elected President of the United States by 10:00 P.M. Eastern time.

Carter, embarrassed by his dreadful showing and obviously anxious to get the whole ordeal over, bowed to the inevitable. Only minutes after the networks' announcements, he issued a statement conceding the contest and congratulating Reagan on his victory. His action was greeted in some quarters with outrage.

Why? What had Carter done wrong? All he had done, it seems, was face the facts and recognize that his opponent had carried enough states to assure his election. He had made a gracious statement. He had offered Reagan his help. Why should people object to what he had done?

The answer is simple: because his timing was terrible. The polls in California were still open, as were those in other West Coast states, Alaska, and Hawaii. With an hour remaining in which to vote, some voters in those states were just finishing their dinners and getting ready to head for the polling places. Once they heard that Carter had conceded, many, and just how many will never be known, changed their plans and decided to stay home.

Their decision did not hurt Carter that much. Even if he had carried California and a couple of the other states, Carter could not have overcome Reagan's landslide lead. But the decision did hurt some of Carter's fellow Democrats, who had been counting on public interest in the presidential election to bring out the vote and, they hoped, help them, at least, to win election or reelection. For the fact is that those voters who decided that the presidential contest was over never cast their votes for anyone, including some congressional and senatorial candidates who felt that they might have had a chance had Carter not conceded as early as he did.

In the aftermath of the election, everyone involved blamed someone else. Some politicians blamed Carter, who had never had strong connections with or loyalty to the Democratic Party, for not thinking of his fellow Democrats when he decided to concede. Others blamed the networks, insisting that none of this would have happened if they had not been so quick to call the election, and suggesting that, in the future, the networks might have the decency at least to wait until all the polls in the continental United States were closed before they announced who had won the election.

The networks themselves talked about doing this. But their talk was never translated into action, and when 1984 rolled around, the networks' competitive instincts took over. With their polling techniques refined in previous elections, the networks outdid each other—or at least tried to— when it came to calling the results of the political races.

Well before the polls closed in the East, the networks were on the air with their reports. Broadcasters reported whether turnouts in key districts were heavy or light as compared with previous elections. They reported what their exit polls were telling them about who seemed to have captured the imagination, or at least the votes, of those turning out.

By the time the polls closed in the East, the networks were on the air with their full-scale election coverage, flashing results on the screen every few minutes, or cutting to maps that showed first one state, then another, falling into the Republican column. They were, in addition, influencing the vote in those states where the polls were still open, for as American voters watched the making of a second Reagan landslide, some inevitably decided to join in and go with the likely winner, while others, feeling that their votes would make no difference anyway, canceled their plans to go out and vote and instead settled down in front of their television sets with a view toward watching a bit of American history in the making.

There is no way of determining just how and to what extent the vote was influenced by the networks' early—some would say premature— publication of election results or projected results. Democratic presidential candidate Walter Mondale never suggested that the vote would have gone the other way if the networks had been a bit more circumspect and waited until the last of the polls in the continental United States had closed before beginning to project winners on the basis of early results. But he and others wondered if the practice of polling, particularly that of exit polling, had not gone just a bit too far, and if the networks might have influenced American voting patterns more than they should by rushing to project election results before every American had had a chance to cast his vote.

The networks defended their actions, insisting that they had done nothing more than ask people coming out of polling places how they had voted, then used their answers to predict how others would vote. They pointed out that those polled were under no compulsion to answer their questions and expressed the view that not only had most voters made up their minds who they were going to vote for by Election Day, but that few, if any, were persuaded not to vote by reports projecting winners. Politicians, the network line said, were holding the media responsible for their message.

But the network front was far from solid. Television anchormen like

CBS's Dan Rather, ABC's Peter Jennings, and NBC's Tom Brokaw, acknowledged that in a business as competitive as theirs, no broadcaster could decide unilaterally not to broadcast the results of his network's election polls until all polls had closed. To do so would be to concede a competitive edge to the network or networks that did air such reports; the public, for all its supposed resentment of the practice, was innately curious and uniformly eager to know as quickly as possible just who was expected to emerge victorious from each election contest.

Some broadcasters concede that polls can be undesirably persuasive. Edwin Newman believes that ". . . in elections, polls may be dangerous . . . When news organizations conduct them they lead to public impressions about who is ahead, they establish this or that candidate as the 'favorite,' and they risk affecting the outcome of the vote. They also help determine the way in which the outcome will be judged."[2]

Nor does Newman accept the argument that for a broadcaster to abandon election polling would be to concede an advantage to his competition. That idea, he said, is the product of a herd instinct that journalism could do well to abandon. "Everybody does them, so everybody does them," Newman sneers. "But they are a poor substitute for reporting. And they are an interference in the electoral process."[3]

Some television broadcasters and news editors suggested, at least in part in response to a suggestion by some politicians that legislation be enacted preventing the reporting of election results or statistical projections while polls were still open, that they would be willing to hold off on announcing the results of their exit polls if their competitors would follow suit. Their offer of voluntary restraint scored a few points in the acrimonious aftermath of the election. But it was quickly forgotten as the public began turning its attention to other matters.

And, it seems unlikely to be remembered until the next presidential election when television, the candidates, and the public will be faced with the same problem once again. For the problem is not likely to come up, at least not seriously, in the off-year congressional elections of 1988. Though control of the Senate and House of Representatives will be at stake, the elections themselves will be essentially state and local affairs, with states choosing senators and congressional districts choosing representatives. Many of these elections will be decided not on such national issues as the MX missile or the Gramm-Rudman Bill to reduce the national deficit, but rather on such matters as what has good old Senator Jack S. Phogbound done or what does he propose to do about some more local matter, such as the location of a toxic waste dump, or what does his opponent plan to do to prevent a neighborhood factory from closing and leaving several hundred voters—or would-be voters—unemployed.

It is unlikely, then, that senators or congressmen or those who are challenging them for their seats in Congress will seriously claim that their chances of keeping or winning office were seriously affected by a broadcaster's decision to air a report projecting the winner of a congressional race in a neighboring state while the polls in their states remain open. But it is not unlikely that the whole question of when election results or projections should be reported, and how, will come up again before the next presidential election.

And there is every reason why it should. For the time to begin thinking of whether broadcasters should project the winners of each state and, thus, the winner of the presidential election before all the official results are in is not a few days or even a few weeks before Election Day. It is now.

There are a number of questions to consider. One is a question that senators, congressmen, and would-be presidential candidates must ask themselves: Is it proper, right, and constitutional to enact, or even to attempt to enact, legislation limiting what the news media can broadcast in the absence of clear and convincing evidence that such broadcasts will somehow have an adverse effect on the nation's security?

One is a question that the media must ask themselves. Is it really necessary for them to project election winners before the last of the polls has closed so there will be no chance, however small, of influencing the outcome of the contest?

The final question is one that the American news-consuming public must answer. Do the American people want to know the likely outcome of a presidential or other election before all the votes have been cast? The public at large has never been surveyed on the question. But the results of such a survey, should it ever be conducted, could prove revealing.

For, as the election-night habits of most Americans have made clear, U.S. voters and nonvoters alike are addicted to information, follow presidential election coverage closely, and want to know the results of such elections as quickly as possible. This explains why so many Americans switch on their television sets at 7:30 Eastern time on Election Night, at least half an hour before the polls have closed in most eastern states, an hour before they have closed in the Midwest, two hours before they have closed in the mountain states, and a full three hours before they have closed in California and the far west. Americans, it is clear, want to know what is happening as soon as it happens and they want to know what is going to happen as soon as those in a position to say think they know.

A few Americans, learning that one candidate or the other has effectively won an election before they themselves have had a chance to cast their own ballots, may decide not to go out and vote, particularly if the weather happens to be bad.

But an equal number are just as likely to do the opposite. For Americans—better than some of their politicians—know that, good as they are, polls can be wrong, and that a few votes one way or the other *can* make a difference. Some Americans may, to be sure, let a premature projection keep them home on Election Night. An equal number are just as likely to be goaded into action, and hearing that a candidate they do not like is winning or has just carried a crucial state, get out and vote in the hope that they can prove the projections wrong.

Which suggests that many critics are making too much of the issue of exit polling—and that many news organizations are making too much of the fact that they do it. Clearly, outlawing exit polling is unnecessary. All that is necessary is a little common sense. The issue of exit polling is not a major one. It seems likely to disappear entirely if the networks will only exercise a little restraint and refrain from making any projections before the polls have closed in a particular state. If that reform is achieved, neither politicians nor the most easily influenced of voters should be able to complain.

# Chapter Eleven
# Shutting Off the Flow

A sinister wind is blowing through the American Democratic process. We began our society on the principle that government exists legitimately only with the consent of the governed and that consent without significant information is meaningless; the greater the information available to the public, the safer the democracy. But in the last generation, we have reversed that assumption. Thanks to nuclear weapons, the Cold War, and the growing militarization of America, we seem to have accepted the contrary idea that the less the public knows, the greater "the national security."

BEN H. BAGDIKIAN, "The Calculus of Democracy," preface to *Keeping America Uninformed*, New York, 1984

The words sound like those of a hand-wringing Cassandra, seeing doom everywhere. They are not. They are the words of a longtime newsman and student of the American news media, of a professor of journalism at the University of California at Berkeley, of the author of several books on the press. They are the words of a man who thinks before he speaks or writes, who knows only too well the power of words.

The words, unfortunately, are only too true. Press critics like Senator Jesse Helms, the Reverend Jerry Falwell, and Accuracy in Media may be trying to persuade, or in some cases bully, the news media into seeing things their way. But the federal government has increasingly been trying to assure that the news media and, by extension, the public, does not even see some things at all. The government, under the administration of President Ronald Reagan, has conducted a conscious, concentrated campaign aimed at shutting off the flow of information available to the public about what its government agencies, military, and elected officials are doing in its name.

The President, in fact, began to tighten the tap almost as soon as he took office. At his first news conference, held just nine days after his swearing-in, Reagan flashed his 100-watt smile and announced that he would block two rules promulgated by the Carter Administration from taking effect. He would not, he said, implement a rule increasing patient access to nursing home records. Nor, he said, would he require the National Highway Traffic Safety Administration to inform car buyers how their vehicles had performed in crash tests.[1]

The President clarified his attitude toward the media at his third press conference, this one held in July 1981. In that session, the President made a misstatement that aides found necessary to correct later. His error led the wire services, among others, to run stories after every presidential press conference or statement, listing the errors of fact for which the President was responsible.

Angered, Reagan and his aides took out their resentment on the media, blasting reporters for concentrating on the minor errors in the President's statements while ignoring what they considered the import of the President's remarks. ". . . the president's aides argued that it didn't matter whether some of his stories were literally true—his numerous misstatements of fact, his confusion about detail, and his repeated anecdotes about supposed welfare cheats that no one was able to confirm, for example— because they contained a larger truth," wrote Anthony Marro in the *Columbia Journalism Review*.[2]

The larger truth about the Administration's attitude toward the press did not take long to emerge. The President soon made it clear that he felt that too much information was dangerous. On September 30, 1982, he sent a meeting of the Radio-Television News Directors Association in Las Vegas a videotaped message in which he said he was concerned about a lack of balance "between the media's right to know and the government's right to confidentiality in running the affairs of state." Reagan questioned whether intensive coverage had actually increased the public's understanding of the nation's problems and wondered whether in some cases it had not actually "hindered government's functioning and, thus, slowed the solution of our problems."[3]

Shortly afterward, the Administration began to increase the pressure on the news media. Press aide Larry Speakes began calling upon television anchormen to broadcast more positive news. Adviser Edwin Meese accused the news media of "undue scrutiny" of presidential policies. Reagan himself suggested that the press had a duty to be less independent of and more subservient to government. The news media, he suggested, had been responsible for the U.S. loss in Vietnam; now it was interfering with American efforts in the Central American country of El Salvador. The media, Reagan implied, should not play an adversarial role; they should support the government.

Presidents from Jefferson on down have found the press a thorn in their political sides. Lyndon Johnson lamented publicly that the press did not understand or appreciate what he was trying to do, and fairly begged for more favorable, or at least less critical, coverage. Richard Nixon conducted an assault on the press. Under Nixon, newsmen, particularly those whose writings displeased the President and his people, were subject to tax audits, FBI investigations, and, if they happened to be broadcasters, to license challenges. Nixon's campaign was not ineffective; his assault made many newsmen run scared, or at least tiptoe softly. "By orchestrating a barrage of anti-media efforts," wrote Marilyn Lashner in her 1984 study of the Nixon years, *The Chilling Effect,* "the Nixon White House was able to chill dissent in political commentary delivered on network television evening news programs, a feat that it was not able to accomplish in nationally-syndicated columns in newspapers."

Indeed, Lashner continues: "While newspaper columnists—Tom Wicker, Joseph Kraft, James Kilpatrick, Clayton Fritchey, James Reston, Jack Anderson, David Broder and more—were focusing on White House affairs with consistency, a clear and restless eye, and sometimes thunder and fury, the analyses that television commentators reserved for the White House were writ in poetry and balm."[4]

It is not hard to understand why. Nixon's Federal Communications Commission chairman, Dean Burch, the man responsible for the agency that gave television stations their licenses to broadcast, telephoned network heads to request transcripts of commentaries critical of the President. The White House issued several memos to agencies, outlining efforts to curtail media criticism. Nixon's vice president, Spiro Agnew, whipped up anti-media sentiments in his speeches, attacking what he termed "the unelected elite." White House aide John Ehrlichman suggested to CBS that Dan Rather be removed from the White House press corps. The Nixon Administration launched an investigation of CBS newsman Daniel Schorr, whose criticism of its actions was particularly outspoken. The Internal Revenue Service issued a subpoena seeking access to *The Washington Post*'s telephone records.

Still, no President has gone as far as Ronald Reagan to restrict the amount of information the government makes available or to limit press

access to information. Shortly after he took office, Reagan asked cabinet
officials and agency heads to come up with programs aimed at cutting
the flow of information from their departments down to a trickle. His
minions responded with a will, adopting departmental regulations that
discouraged employees, on pain of dismissal, from talking with newsmen,
and otherwise keeping contact with the press to an absolute minimum.
Their purpose and that of the Administration was clear, particularly to
columnist Jack Anderson, who saw the President giving members of his
government what amounted to carte blanche to conceal their errors and
to control what the public would know about what they were doing.
"President Reagan," Anderson wrote, "seems relentlessly determined
to control the flow of information to the American people. He speaks of
security; the correct word is 'censorship' . . . The truth is, of course, that
he hopes to use the security issue to manage the news."[5]

The reason for Reagan's action is equally clear. Neither Reagan nor
the people around him have much tolerance for freewheeling public debate.
They hold a "Father knows best" attitude, believing that the public should
simply put its trust in government and let the White House and the agencies responsible to it handle things. Their attitude may be in sharp contrast
to their philosophical conservatism, which leads them to advocate getting
the government out of people's lives as much as possible. But the incon-
sistency does not seem to bother either the President or his people.

The President, for example, has been critical of the movement opposing
placement of U.S. nuclear missiles in Western Europe and has gone so
far as to call its members "anti-nuclear terrorists." The U.S. Immigration
and Naturalization Service has taken its cue from the President and denied
visas to some noted antinuclear activists.

The Administration has pulled some other stunts, too. In February
1981, it issued a White Paper titled "Communist Interference in El Salvador." Eight pages long, single spaced, the paper provided what the
government described as "definitive evidence of clandestine military
support given by the Soviet Union, Cuba and their Communist allies to
overthrow the established government of El Salvador." The problem with
the paper was that the evidence it contained was anything but definitive.
The press immediately began asking questions about first one claim, then
another, demanding to see proof that the massive Soviet- and Cuban-
directed subversion to which the Administration wanted to respond with
military aid of its own was actually taking place.

The government was unable to provide it. In fact, after six months of
inquiries, the State Department was forced to back down and admit that
it could not vouch for any of the information in the White Paper. The

paper, issued by the Administration in the hope of winning public support for its position, was withdrawn.[6]

The Administration's experience with the White Paper on El Salvador did not, though, prevent it from making other attempts to manage the flow of government information and thus the news. In 1982, the Administration pushed through a piece of legislation called the Identities Intelligence Protection Act. The legislation was simple and straightforward: It made it a crime, punishable by prison, to disclose the names of American intelligence agents or to expose covert agents. The stated purpose of the legislation was to protect agents in the field, something that many thought necessary after a CIA operative in Athens was first identified, then shot and killed. But the effect of the legislation went further, for it allowed the CIA to operate essentially unsupervised.[7]

A year earlier, Reagan had cut off some other information. He imposed a moratorium on the production by government agencies of new audio-visual aids and printed publications, saying that the government was spending too much on public relations. One of the projects killed by this cut was a publication called *The Car Book*. Compiled and published by the National Highway Transportation Safety Administration, *The Car Book* did not make for light reading, for it revealed just how each of the automobiles then available in the United States would stand up in a collision. This information proved valuable to many car owners and buyers, who bought 1.5 million copies of *The Car Book*. It proved upsetting to automobile manufacturers, though, and thus to the White House. Though well on its way to becoming a best seller, *The Car Book* was canned.

Other sources of information were also shut off. In March 1983, the Administration promulgated National Security Directive 84. This required all current and former officials who had or had once had access to classified documents to sign agreements promising that they would not disclose the contents of these documents. The directive covered some 5 million federal civilian and military personnel, plus another 1.5 million federal contractors with access to classified material. It made all of them potential candidates for lie detector tests should the Administration suspect them of leaking information to the press.[8]

This order, combined with an earlier order making it easier to classify material, produced the expected reaction. *The Washington Post* said that the order on classification represented "the flowering of an unwarranted and unbecoming spirit of distrust of the public." Observing that American courts had yet to overrule a government decision on national security grounds, the *Post* speculated that the real reason for the ruling was to make it easier for government agencies to avoid making possibly embarrassing disclosures under the Freedom of Information Act.[9]

Reaction to NSD 84 followed similar lines. *The New York Times* pointed out that leaks are a vital part of government communications. "Leaking," wrote reporter Richard Halloran, "is not solely or even largely the province of the dissident. Rather it is a political instrument wielded almost daily by senior officials within the administration to influence a decision, to promote policy, to persuade Congress and to signal foreign governments."[10]

As Halloran and others pointed out, leaks are a way in which government communicates with itself, enabling members to transmit information unofficially that they may not be able, for a variety of bureaucratic reasons, to transmit through normal channels. Leaks, it was also noted, rarely harm national security. More often they help inform both politicians and voters. They are dangerous largely because they can embarrass the party in power, not because they can provide the "enemy," whomever he may happen to be, with information that he could not obtain otherwise.

Furthermore, leaking is rarely done by the kinds of people the Reagan Administration, or any other administration, is likely to prosecute. For the record shows clearly that the majority of newsworthy leaks do not come from disgruntled civil servants or Republican or Democratic holdovers in a government controlled by the opposite party. They tend to come from high-level officials. Former National Security Adviser and later Secretary of State Henry Kissinger was, whether he was publicly identified or not, a major source of "inside" information during the Nixon years. Several of the major leaks that have occurred during Reagan's tenure have come from White House sources and cabinet officers. Sometimes, these sources are releasing information that they are legally authorized to make public, even though its publication may annoy the President. Sometimes, these sources leak in order to test public reaction to certain proposals. Whatever their reasons, they are not likely to be prosecuted. A low-level civil servant who leaks some information that embarrasses the government may be dismissed or actually prosecuted in order, as Voltaire once put it in a somewhat different context, *"pour encourager les autres" (to encourage the others)*. But the worst thing that is likely to happen to a cabinet officer or White House aide who leaks information that the President would prefer be kept confidential is that he might be asked, or "allowed" to resign.

But even if he does, he may find his freedom to speak or to write restricted. Since the directive requires those who have had access to classified material to clear all future writings or utterances, anyone who has served as a government official could find it impossible afterward to work

as a newspaper columnist or radio or television commentator, or to participate in a political debate or run for office. Indeed, critics of the order
observed, had Reagan's rule been in effect earlier, former officials like
General Alexander Haig or Eugene Rostow would have been unable to
write about their days in government or the Vietnam War. Indeed, in a
supreme irony, a political candidate like Walter Mondale would have had
to have his speeches cleared by the very Administration against which
he was campaigning.

NSD 84 will not, critics contend, do much to curb leaks. But it will
have another effect. It will curb informed debate, which seems, from its
actions, to be exactly what the Reagan Administration wants. For, as *New
York Times* columnist Anthony Lewis wrote at the time: "The promoters
of the secrecy system are fanatics who do not share the traditional American belief that open debate makes this country stronger."[11]

The Reagan Administration has taken several subtle steps to keep the
public uninformed and to shut off debate on important issues. But none
of its actions has been more egregious than its assault on the Freedom
of Information Act.

For those who believe that the public has a right to oversee the actions
of its government, few laws are as important as the Freedom of Information Act. First enacted in 1966, the law provided the first federal
recognition of the public's right to know what the executive branch of
its government is doing. (The act does not cover either Congress or the
judicial branch).

Prior to the passage of FOIA, as the law has come to be known, individuals seeking access to information about government activities had to
demonstrate a "need to know." They had few maps to guide them in
their search; no rules existed under which a seeker of information might
ask a judge to order the release or publication of material that had been
improperly withheld. The decision as to which information could be made
available rested squarely with the government itself; it could decide which
material was secret and which was not.

The idea that government could control what was released about its
activities was not a new one. Presidents Truman and Eisenhower both
held that no act of Congress could require members of the government's
executive branch to release information to either house or to the public.
And they relied for their rationale on a 1789 measure called the Housekeeping Statute, which, enacted at the request of no less a personage than
George Washington, allowed department heads to regulate the storage
and determine the disposition of government records.

The first assault on this law was led by California Congressman John

Moss, chairman of the Subcommittee on Government Information, who began in 1958 to amend the century-and-a-half-old act. Moss declared that not only was Congress being denied information essential to the performance of its role, but that others—journalists, scientists, historians—were having similar trouble getting the information they needed. The Housekeeping Statute should be amended, he said, in order to prevent censorship. It was amended, in one of the least prolix pieces of legislation ever enacted by either house. All the amendment said was this: "This section of [the Housekeeping Statute] does not authorize the withholding of information from the public or limit the availability of records to the public."

Passage of the bill wrought no noticeable changes in the amount of information made available; agencies of the executive branch merely used another law, Section 3 of the 1946 Administrative Procedure Act, to withhold vital information whose release they felt was not in the public interest. Congress and the public had no way of challenging their action; they did not even know what information was being withheld.

So, responding to public pressure, Congress passed the Freedom of Information Act. FOIA gave "any person" the right of access to government records. But not all records. The law exempted classified information about national defense, foreign policy, and trade secrets, as well as personal information. But it did provide an important piece of protection for the public: under the law anyone denied access to government information could request a court to review the denial.

President Lyndon Johnson was not pleased with the measure. But he overcame his displeasure and signed it anyway, saying, in the florid language for which he was well known: "Democracy works best when the people have all the information that the security of the nation permits. No one should be able to pull a curtain of secrecy around decisions which can be revealed without injury to the public interest."

FOIA was a watershed measure. It replaced the criterion of an individual's need to know with that of his right to know. It set up procedures under which an individual could request and inspect government records and provided a legal remedy for those wrongfully denied access to information.

But the law was not without some serious weaknesses, which became obvious as agencies either tried to comply with it, or, more significantly, to avoid compliance by dragging their feet on requests or by charging high fees for copies of documents requested. With critics complaining that the act was ineffective, the House Foreign Operations and Government Information Subcommittee convened in 1972 and held hearings to determine just how well FOIA was functioning. The subcommittee's finding: "Efficient operation of FOIA has been hindered by five years of foot-dragging by the federal bureaucracy."

Following the hearings, the subcommittee began to work on amendments to the act. It had good reason to do so. The Watergate scandal had broken, and the revelations that were making the front pages of the nation's newspapers, coupled with President Nixon's attempts to "stonewall" on any congressional requests for information, spurred the lawmakers to strengthen the law. The committee's members proposed no fewer than seventeen amendments to FOIA. One strengthened the act's section on judicial review by not only allowing judges to review the government's decision to withhold information but to review the basis of the decision. This meant that judges could review withheld information to determine whether it had been properly classified and to order its release if it had not. In 1973, the U.S. Supreme Court had ruled that a federal judge in Alaska lacked the power to review requested documents about underground nuclear tests, saying that there was "no means for Congress to question any Executive decision to stamp a document 'secret,' however cynical, myopic or even corrupt that decision might have been."[12] The Supreme Court's decision had the effect of eliminating from the FOIA umbrella all documents concerning national security. The amendment had the effect of putting at least some of them back.

Other amendments also strengthened FOIA by giving more muscle to those seeking information. They did so by setting out specific procedures that agencies must follow upon receipt of requests for documents. Among other things, they required the government to meet statutory deadlines for responding to requests, forbade it from charging requesters for the cost of excising documents, or blanking out those parts that could be kept secret, required it to surrender investigatory files unless it could show that their release would impair investigations in progress or do other damage, and finally, amended the national security exemption to the law so that the government could not use it merely to withhold information.

The amendments did not permit either Congress or the public to obtain access to any or all of the information either wished. Despite the improvements in the law, certain information remained exempt, including defense and foreign policy material, interagency memoranda circulated as part of a decision-making process, some law-enforcement information, and information whose release would constitute a clear invasion of personal privacy.

The amendments, in short, still allowed the government to keep some secrets. But not enough to please President Nixon or the members of the executive branch, including, predictably, the Central Intelligence Agency and the Justice Department. Nixon might, as he was expected to do, have vetoed the amendments had not Watergate and the threat of impeachment forced him to resign. Nixon's successor, Gerald Ford, did veto them.

But Congress, riding the wave of public outrage over Watergate and suspicion of the government's passion for secrecy, overrode his veto. On November 21, 1974, the House voted 371 to 31 to override the presidential veto. A few days later, the Senate did likewise. Congress also passed the Privacy Act, a measure limiting the kinds of information the government can gather on citizens and restricting the ways in which this information could be used.

The passage of these amendments did not, however, produce a sudden access of compliance. FOIA gave agencies ten days, plus ten more under "unusual circumstances," to reply to an individual's request for information, and required the Justice Department to reply in a similar time frame to an individual's appeal of what he considered a wrongful denial. But in 1976, a newspaper study found that the FBI was taking an average of nine months to comply with requests for information, while the CIA had a backlog of 2,400 cases. The government, meanwhile, faced no fewer than five hundred suits for various failures to comply with the act.[13]

FOIA found a friend in President Jimmy Carter's Department of Justice. In 1977, Attorney General Griffin Bell advised department and agency heads that even though they might find legal grounds for withholding information, they should release it as long as it was clear that the release would not damage the public interest. He also made it clear that his Justice Department would be considerably less than eager to defend any agency that withheld documents for merely technical reasons.

Bell's support helped. But pockets of resistance remained. In 1977, Benjamin Civiletti, who succeeded Bell as attorney general, studied the possibility of introducing a package of amendments that would restrict the range of FOIA by placing a three- to five-year moratorium on the release of criminal files and exempting CIA documents. That same year, the FBI began to shred some of its files, an unauthorized act that would have undermined FOIA to the point of making it moot.

The Reagan Administration did not wait long before launching its own campaign against FOIA. Reagan had not been in office four months before his Attorney General, William French Smith, circulated a memo to all government agencies, informing them that the Justice Department was reversing Bell's policy; it would, he said, defend denials of FOIA requests based on technicalities. In October of that same year, the Administration sent Congress a number of proposals that it said would "fine tune" FOIA, a step Smith said had to be taken because, as he put it, "certain requirements of the act have interfered unduly with proper law enforcement activities and jeopardized national security functions.''

What Smith called fine tuning looked to supporters of the act more like evisceration. The Administration's proposals gave the attorney general vast power to withhold information about terrorism, organized crime, and counterintelligence operations. They gave agencies permission to provide less information than requested about their internal operations. They restricted the right to request information to citizens and resident aliens. They allowed agencies to impose fees for processing and censoring released documents over and above those fees they were allowed to charge for searching and copying. They provided for businesses to be notified about requests for information that concerned them and gave such businesses greater leeway when it came to challenging these requests. Finally, they severely restricted judges' power to review material related to national security.

Several Republican senators, including Utah's Orrin Hatch and New York's Alfonse d'Amato, supported the Administration's proposals and offered proposals of their own to undercut FOIA. They supported CIA Director William Casey, who sought nothing less than a complete exemption from the act for his agency. Casey justified his request on the grounds that foreign intelligence agencies and agents were refusing to cooperate with the CIA for fear that their identities and activities would be revealed through FOIA. Casey, however, proved a poor witness when he appeared before Hatch's Subcommittee on the Constitution. Questioned by Hatch and other senators, Casey was unable to cite even a single concrete example of an agent quitting the CIA because of fear of disclosure. He fell back on the claim that his agency was losing sources of information because of a ''perception'' that their identities could be revealed. But he could not back up this claim either.

FBI Director William Webster made a more convincing case when he gave the subcommittee secret testimony to the effect that his agency had lost informants because they feared disclosure. Webster even cited examples of cases in which organized crime figures had confronted FBI informants with FBI documents obtained through FOIA.

The senators may have found Webster's arguments impressive. But NBC correspondent Carl Stern did not. In a piece published on the op-ed page of *The New York Times,* Stern, who obtained his information through FOIA, showed that the FBI had tried and failed for nineteen months in 1979 and 1980 to collect data to support Webster's claim that the act had turned informants into ''an endangered species.'' There was, it turned out, only one case in which agents agreed that an informant was endangered because of documents obtained under the act.[14]

Despite Stern's study, opponents of the act continued to insist that it hampered law-enforcement activities. Most, interestingly, concentrated their fire on the fear that agents' and informants' names would be revealed, ignoring the fact that this was something that the act did not allow.

Proponents of FOIA argued that the FBI and others were exaggerating the act's impact on their activities. James Wieghart of the American Society of Newspaper Editors noted in his testimony that the majority of improper releases of law enforcement and national security information did not come from FOIA requests; they came instead from high-level officials using the media to leak data. Others admitted that the act could be an annoyance to law-enforcement officials, but noted that judges had not yet ordered the release of any information over their objections.

Hatch expressed concern that groups critical of American foreign and defense policies could obtain information under FOIA. Businessmen said that they were afraid that their competitors could use FOIA to ferret out their trade secrets. Some government officials told Hatch and his committee members that processing FOIA requests simply cost too much. Their argument, however, was quickly put into perspective when friends of FOIA pointed out that the government itself had estimated the cost of complying with FOIA at $50 million a year, or about half the figure it spent on military bands.[15]

Despite objections from civil libertarians and journalists, who, as it turns out, account for only 5 to 10 percent of all FOIA applications (most are from private citizens), the subcommittee reported out the Reagan-Hatch proposals. Fortunately, the bill did not pass but died before the full Senate could vote on it.

But this does not mean that FOIA has thus far survived the Reagan assault unscathed. Provision b(3) of the original law allows agencies to turn down FOIA requests for material that is specifically exempted by laws covering agency programs. Exemptions adopted under this provision need not go through the usual FOIA committee process. Generally, they originate in committees considering authorization bills or other acts dealing with things other than information policy. Thus, b(3) amendments are not examined at public hearings and tend to be passed along with the legislation to which they are attached. Their existence rarely comes to light unless an agency uses one of them as grounds for denying a FOIA request.

Between 1980 and 1984, Congress adopted six b(3) exemptions. One exempted Federal Trade Commission investigations. Another exempted information submitted to the Consumer Product Safety Commission by manufacturers of hazardous products. Still others exempted unclassified information submitted to the Department of Energy about the production and transportation of nuclear materials, the records of the professional review organizations that study the medical practices of institutions that rely upon Medicaid for their funding, and information about nuclear research collected by the Nuclear Regulatory Commission.[16]

Crippling FOIA, however, is not all the Reagan Administration has tried to do—or done—to keep America uninformed. The Administration's penchant for secrecy has permeated government action at every level. The Administration may be able to claim, after all, that it is merely safeguarding national security when it seeks to suppress information about a new weapons system or withhold details of a U.S. negotiating position. But it can hardly use this excuse when it seeks to keep information about environmental hazards or faulty consumer goods from the American public.

Still, this lack of an excuse has not prevented it from damming the stream of information about these and many other things. Never a friend of the environmental movement, the Administration early on adopted a policy of nonenforcement and foot dragging where toxic waste dumpsites were concerned, giving lip service to the idea of cleaning them up while actually doing nothing. By November 1982, twenty-one months after Reagan took office, the Administration could show that only four of the 160 dump sites on the Environmental Protection Agency's priority list had been cleaned up, and that only $74 million of the $265 million Superfund Congress had made available for the purpose had actually been used. Critics accused the Administration of manipulating Superfund for political purposes and hinted at unhealthy relationships between the people heading EPA and the firms the agency was supposed to monitor.

In September of that year, congressional investigators asked EPA officials for information on three sites. But acting on orders from the White House, the EPA refused to turn it over. Noting that the Administration was extending the soiled doctrine of executive privilege beyond the confines of the White House, the House sent EPA chief Anne Gorsuch a subpoena requesting the information. When she followed the White House line and refused to comply with the request, the House acted and cited her for contempt of Congress. When Gorsuch's aide, Rita Lavelle, was found to have shredded documents and was ordered dismissed, the White House's position began to crumble. Gorsuch resigned. Reagan agreed to turn over to Congress those documents he had previously withheld.

Elsewhere in government, the heavy hand of censorship could be felt. It was felt in 1981 when the National Highway Traffic Safety Administration reversed its long-standing policy and decided that it was not necessary to inform the public every time it ordered a recall of defective cars. It was felt in 1982 when the Office of Management and Budget ordered the EPA to stop the distribution of some sixty-odd publications, supposedly on the grounds of economy. Among the publications ordered destroyed because they had already been printed were *What Everyone Should Know about the Quality of Drinking Water* and *The Toxic Substances Dilemma.* It was felt in 1983 when the Department of Energy announced a plan to further restrict information on nuclear power. The Department of Energy plan would allow the department to label certain material ''unclassified controlled nuclear information'' and then ban its release. The material covered in this category would describe such things as accidents at nuclear power plants, health hazards from nuclear radiation, and plans for safeguarding nuclear materials in transit.[17]

The public's access to information was restricted in other ways, too. One of these ways was financial: the government raised the prices of its publications. The price of the *Federal Register,* the official record of federal government activities, climbed from $75 to $300 a year. The *Congressional Record,* which used to be given away to anyone who requested it, had risen to $135 a year by 1983; that year, its price went up to $208.

Meanwhile, people whose ideas proved unpalatable to the Administration were prevented from spreading them by the simple expedient of keeping them out of the country. Not only did the government refuse entry to the United States to Italian playwright Dario Fo, an outspoken critic of the country, but in 1985, it denied entry to Canadian author Farley Mowat, an ardent environmentalist and Canadian nationalist who had objected to the idea of nuclear-armed U.S. planes flying over the Gulf of St. Lawrence island on which he made his home. Mowat fought the exclusion, demanding through FOIA to know why he had been kept out of the United States. He finally received a slim folder containing copies of a few newspaper clips, one of which listed him as a member of the old Fair Play for Cuba committee.

The Administration's most egregious exclusion, though, occurred in October 1983, when it sent U.S. troops to invade the Caribbean island of Grenada. The invasion, like many of the government's actions, was supposed to be conducted in secret. But troop movements can never be kept entirely quiet, so it was not surprising that Washington-based reporters suspected that something was afoot and went to White House spokesman Larry Speakes on October 24 to ask him whether it was true, as rumored, that U.S. troops had landed on the island. Speakes checked with a member of the President's national security staff and got back to the press denying the rumor and insisting that no invasion was planned. The invasion took place the following day.

And it took place without the press. It was, in fact, the first invasion in American history in which the media were not present during the initial fighting.

At the beginning, all information about the invasion came from Washington, which was following the example set by the British government during its campaign in the Falkland Islands and keeping control of the news. Journalists, who had flocked to Barbados, were kept away from Grenada; military spokesmen told them nothing while the commander of the invasion force, Admiral Thomas Metcalf, took ill-concealed delight in telling them that he would tell them nothing. It was not until three days after the invasion, when most of the fighting had ended, that small pools of reporters were allowed to go to Grenada. But even then, they were not allowed to report the story. Loaded onto military aircraft, they were allowed to spend a little time on the island under the strict supervision of military officials, then flown back to Barbados.

Given this tight control, it surprised no one that the story behind the invasion took a while to become public. Washington declined to disclose the number of Americans killed in the invasion. It kept insisting that there was a large Cuban military force present on the island until persistent press questioning forced it to admit otherwise. It failed to report the fact that an island hospital was bombed.

Nor did it always assure that what information it deigned to put out was accurate. Military officials told reporters that they had found large quantities of military hardware on the island. Reporters who finally got a look at the captured arms reported that the weapons were fewer and older than the military had claimed. The government said that it had conducted the invasion to protect the lives of American students attending the island's medical school. The students and other independent sources said that Grenada had promised them safe transport back to the United States.

Predictably, the press was outraged. The press had always been allowed to accompany U.S. troops in the past, respecting the military's need for security by delaying its dispatches until operations had been completed. Editors and television news executives could see no good reason why their reporters could not have followed the same practice in Grenada.

They could, though, see a bad one, and *Time* editor-in-chief Henry Grunwald described it incisively in an essay titled ''Trying to Censor Reality.'' ''Taken together,'' Grunwald wrote, ''the Administration's measures suggest a certain mindset: the notion that events can be shaped by their presentation, that truth should be a controlled substance."[18]

His point is well made and one that should not be lost on those who think that the time has come to trim the wings of the news media. The press may have its flaws; it may tell the public some things it would rather not know. But even at its worst, it provides the public with a lot more information than it will ever get from the government. The government, it increasingly appears, does not want to tell the public anything.

# Chapter Twelve

# As Others See Us

Oh wad some power the giftie gie us
To see oursels as others see us!
It wad frae monie a blunder free us,
    An' foolish notion.

Robert Burns,
*To A Louse,* 1786

The great Scots poet's lines have been quoted—and misquoted—almost from the time he wrote them. But the poet's plea is well offered. Everyone needs, from time to time, at least, to know how he looks to eyes other than his own. And this need is particularly pressing on the part of the news media, which pride themselves on holding a mirror up to the world and letting others, from world leaders and celebrities to the proverbial man on the street, know how they look to newspaper and television reporters and editors.

Some recent surveys have revealed that the nation's news media are not universally loved. Spokesmen for the radical right have tried, and in some cases succeeded, in convincing the press that it is dangerously out of touch with the ideas, beliefs, and values of the great majority of Americans, most of whom perceive it as inaccurate, elitist, and unpatriotic. The leaders of America's powerful electronic churches draw nods of agreement from their audiences when they excoriate the U.S. news media, and, claiming to speak for not only their churches' supporters but for millions of other Americans, warn the media to get back into touch with America, which means, translated, to support conservative aims and causes more.

Influenced by polls and more frightened than most of them will admit by their vociferous right-wing critics, American newspapers have been pulling in their horns in recent years. Few have gone so far as to become cheerleaders for the Administration or for the mythical Moral Majority.

But some, believing or assuming the press's critics to be as powerful as they claim to be, or unwilling, for a whole variety of reasons, to test them and learn just how powerful they really are, have trimmed their sails to what they sense to be a wind blowing from the right.

The attitudes of those who have done so are understandable. No television station or network can survive for very long if it alienates its audience. No newspaper, even in a one-paper town, can thrive if people feel that the opinions it expresses are substantially at variance with those held by the majority in the community.

But the actions of those who have followed this course may be unfortunate. For those who have allowed themselves to be intimidated may be guilty of violating good journalistic practices and acting on insufficient information. For the fact is that, despite a few public opinion polls, despite a few soundings here and there, no one has really taken the time and trouble to conduct an in-depth study and find out just what the American public really thinks of its news media.

At least, no one has done so until recently. For in 1984, the Times Mirror Corporation decided to do exactly that. The corporation had been disturbed by what *Editor and Publisher* had called "puzzling inconsistencies" in current public opinion poll results.[1] And, corporation chairman and chief executive officer Robert T. Erburu noted, the company had been disquieted by the implication of these inconsistencies, for what they suggested was that pollsters had not probed deeply enough to identify the public's true perspectives on the press. "We reckoned that the public might really be telling these pollsters, 'If you're not sure what we really think and feel about the news media, it's because you haven't yet asked us the right questions. Dig deeper,' " wrote Erburu.[2]

To do that, Times Mirror decided to commission an in-depth study of its own. In November 1984, it engaged Professor Michael J. Robinson of George Washington University and the conservative think tank, the American Enterprise Institute, to help form an inquiry. Then, early in 1985, it turned to the Gallup Organization, asking its president, Andrew Kohut, to design and carry out an investigation aimed at uncovering the American public's most basic attitudes toward the news media and to learn, as Erburu put it, "if there were in fact real inconsistencies under the apparent inconsistencies."

Times Mirror had good reason for conducting such a study, ample motivation for finding out how the public really felt about the news media. It is one of America's media giants. Times Mirror publishes eight newspapers: the *Los Angeles Times, Newsday,* the *Dallas Times Herald, The Denver Post, The Hartford Courant,* the (Allentown, Pennsylvania)

*Morning Call,* the (Stamford, Connecticut) *Advocate,* and the (Greenwich, Connecticut) *Time.* It publishes five popular magazines: *Popular Science, Outdoor Life, Golf Magazine, Ski Magazine,* and *The Sporting News.* The corporation owns television stations in Dallas and Austin, Texas, in St. Louis, Missouri, and in Birmingham, Alabama; its fifty cable television systems serve three hundred communities in fifteen northeastern, western, and southwestern states. Times Mirror is also a major book publisher, owning several publishing houses. Matthew Bender & Co., publishes law books; C. V. Mosby publishes medical texts, as does Year Book Medical Publishers. Harry N. Abrams is one of the country's best-known publishers of art books. Mirror Systems publishes computer software; Learning International does training programs. If any corporation had to know what the public thought about the press, it was Times Mirror.

The Times Mirror study, which took a year to conduct, complete, and compile, was nothing if not thorough. All told, the Gallup Organization conducted some four thousand interviews during the summer and autumn of 1985. But more important, it set up its study and its methodology in such a way as to do more than merely note the inconsistencies that seem to arise whenever the public is asked to outline its attitudes toward the press. Among other techniques, it employed one called "double-back interviewing," a method that involved going back to its sources after each wave of research and seeking the answers to questions raised by respondents' replies to the first set of queries. It had to employ such techniques, it explained in its report, for the questions raised by earlier studies suggested that the public's perception of the press was anything but unclouded. Why, it sought to learn, does the public generally express overall favorable opinions about newspeople and news organizations while questioning the fairness of the press in general? Why do both Democrats and Republicans tend to express similar opinions about the news media, even though some critics and a substantial segment of the public accuse the media of a liberal bias? Why is it that although the polls generally indicate that the public approves of the news media, newspeople feel sure that the nation has reached a crisis point as far as antimedia hostility is concerned?[3]

The answers to these questions are reassuring. For the Times Mirror survey's first conclusion was straightforward. "There is no credibility crisis for the nation's news media," it concluded. "If credibility is defined as believability, then credibility is, in fact, one of the media's strongest suits."[4]

The study found out other things, too. It dented the egos of some of the media's stars by revealing that they were less well known than most probably believe themselves to be. It found, for example, that less than half of those polled could identify "CBS Evening News" anchorman Dan Rather from his photograph, despite the fact that his program is watched by more viewers than watch either ABC or NBC. It also found that, despite the fact that he has been identified in *The New York Times* as America's most visible news commentator, fewer than one respondent in eight could recognize conservative columnist George F. Will.

Nor was this all. The report of the survey began by concluding that the press's perception of a crisis may be somewhat exaggerated. ". . . A crisis in confidence, focused toward the media or any other political institution, assumes a lot," said the report. "It assumes that the public thinks about that institution, knows something about its performance and pays attention to the events and issues associated with the growing crisis."[5] But, the survey found, the public does not, in fact, spend a great deal of its time thinking or talking about the press. When the subjects in the study were given a list of nine groups of professionals, including doctors, lawyers, entertainers, and clergymen, and asked to list them in the order in which they discussed them with their friends and acquaintances, they ranked journalists eighth, admitting that the only group they discussed less frequently was scientists.

The public did know several journalists by name; in fact, found the study, fully two-thirds of those polled could name a particular journalist as their favorite. Most, predictably, named television journalists, who are more visible than their print counterparts. But many were unable to identify some of America's most visible journalists. Only ABC's Barbara Walters, as it turned out, was identified by a clear majority of respondents. Others fared less well, despite their high visibility. Fewer than four out of ten respondents could recognize CBS's Mike Wallace, ABC's Ted Koppel, or NBC's Tom Brokaw. More people, in fact, could recognize such "soft" news personalities as Phil Donahue or Ann Landers than could recognize such "hard" news personalities as Peter Jennings or John Chancellor.

The public, according to the survey, proved equally uninformed when it came to major press-related issues. Fully 62 percent told interviewers that they were not concerned about the question of equal time in political advertising. A majority of 51 percent said that they were not concerned with the issue of fairness in the coverage of controversial subjects. Sixty percent knew that General William Westmoreland had sued some news organization for libel. But only 30 percent could identify that news organization as CBS. Thirty percent were at least vaguely aware that a group led by Senator Jesse Helms had tried to buy a controlling interest in a major news organization. But only 20 percent knew that the organization in question was CBS.

The Gallup Organization found that most Americans had some knowledge about the news process. Eighty-five percent, for example, knew that press releases were written statements given to reporters, not pieces written by them. Seventy-nine percent knew that television anchorpeople did not go out and report stories themselves, but read stories that others prepared for them. Three out of four respondents knew that the White House press secretary worked for the President, not the press. A similar number were aware that the national wire services, the Associated Press and United Press International, provided most of the national and international news that went into smaller newspapers.

But, Gallup found, Americans generally knew considerably less about the news business. More than half knew what a newspaper chain was, though nearly half did not. But only 41 percent knew that an editorial represented the official opinion of a newspaper on a given issue. More than half were unaware that radio and television stations were more closely regulated than newspapers and magazines; better than two-thirds did not know that no formal training was required in order to report the news for a newspaper or television station. Most remarkable, the survey found, only 27 percent knew that *Time* and *Newsweek,* which compete fiercely, are owned by different companies. While 60 percent were not sure if the two major national newsmagazines were separately or jointly owned, fully 13 percent believed that they were owned by the same company.[6]

Even more startling, most Americans had little knowledge about what the First Amendment was or said. Journalists may believe that the First Amendment is so well known that it needs no explanation. But only one American in ten knew that the First Amendment was that part of the U.S. Constitution that mentions freedom of the press.

Yet despite these gaps, the study found that most Americans held a generally favorable view of the press, at least as far as its credibility was concerned. "If one defines credibility narrowly, as believability," said the report on the study, "then the public expresses something of a consensus: the public believes the press. In fact, if believability *per se* were the only credibility issue, one could justifiably close the book on the credibility gap."[7]

The Gallup Organization based its conclusion on the answers to more than one question. It asked each respondent whether he or she felt that news organizations got their facts straight or presented stories and reports inaccurately. Fully 55 percent felt that the press was basically accurate. And, just as important, a similar percentage so responded when asked the same question about specific news outlets, such as the major television network news operations, *Time, Newsweek,* and such nationally known newspapers as *The New York Times, The Washington Post,* and the *Los Angeles Times.*

The public also indicated that it felt favorably toward the news media. More than 85 percent of those polled said that their opinions of radio, local and national television news, newsmagazines, and their local daily newspapers were either mostly or very favorable. Their answers suggest that the media may be more popular than many national figures and institutions. The military was regarded mostly or very favorably by 81 percent, Congress by 72 percent. President Reagan, unquestionably one of the most personally popular of any of the people who have occupied the Oval Office in U.S. history, was rated mostly or very favorably by 71 percent, a fact the Gallup Organization found easily understandable. "President Reagan is not in the nonpartisan news business," it noted. "He is in partisan politics." Newspeople, on the other hand, are in "the believability business."[8]

Americans carry their positive feelings about the press into several specific areas. Some 70 percent feel that the press is professional; slightly more feel that news organizations care about their performance and try to do good work. Most reject the notion that the press has treated President Reagan unfairly; in fact, fully 78 percent feel that the press has been fair to the gentleman from California.[9] Just over half, 52 percent to be exact, believe that, the claims of the radical right to the contrary notwithstanding, the press does stand up for America.[10]

But this does not mean that the public perceives the press to be without flaws. For the Times Mirror study found that the public gave the press negative ratings in six areas of performance. According to the study, 45 percent of the public feels that the American news media are politically biased in their reporting, while 53 percent feel that the press tends to favor one side over another in presenting political and social issues. Sixty percent feel that the press pays too much attention to bad news, while fully 73 percent feel that the news media invade people's privacy.

Even more significant to those in the news business, the study found that 53 percent feel that the press is often influenced by the powerful in its presentation of the news, while 55 percent felt that the media tried to cover up their mistakes.[11] Questioned in detail on these views, a significant number of respondents (44 percent) felt that a combination of commercial pressures, including the need for attracting and holding a large audience, and pressures from various special interest groups, kept the press from doing as good a job as it might otherwise do.

The results, in short, were equivocal, as the pollsters had expected them to be. For they showed that while the U.S. news media received high marks for believability, they and their members got low grades for fairness, independence, and even good manners. Why? What explains the public's ambivalence?

By doubling back and asking more questions, the Gallup Organization found an answer to this question. It assumed that Americans might be tolerant about the press's failures if they felt that the press was basically accurate, if they appreciated the press's performance of its watchdog role, if people appreciated the difficulties the press must often overcome to get a story, or if they really liked the news itself. It found that the public's appreciation of the media's watchdog role tended to mute its criticism of the media's failures.

And, it found this attitude reflected in answers to questions about press freedom. For the survey discovered that the value the public placed on press freedom depended quite directly on who was required to pay the cost. On issues pitting the rights of news organizations against those of the government, the public tended to side with the press. But on issues pitting the rights of the press against those of individuals, the public regularly went against the press.

The public, for example, rejected the notion of removing the risk of libel suits from newspapers and television broadcasters; 89 percent felt that the press should face libel suits if the stories it publishes are false. The public also expressed some opinions that should cause the media some concern. Three out of four believed that it should *not* be more difficult for public officials to sue for libel than it is for private citizens, while 67 percent felt that the press should be required to pay damages for libel whenever its stories are false, even if it believed them to be true at the time of publication. The public, in short, regards the libel laws as a reasonable, even desirable, check on the freedom of the press. Nor does the public believe that the news media, specifically television, should have an unfettered right to project election winners before the polls close. Asked whether they felt it more important to report the projected winner of an election or to avoid discouraging people from voting, only 18 percent came down on the side of the media; 72 percent said that it was more important not to discourage people from voting.

The pollsters found the public split on issues involving censorship. Asked how they would rule in a case similar to that involving the Pentagon Papers, those documents on American involvement in Vietnam that *The New York Times* sought to publish and the government sought to suppress, 66 percent said that they would allow publication and let the public know the story. But asked to decide a case similar to the *Progressive* affair, in which a magazine sought to publish material describing how to build an atomic bomb, more than half felt that national security was more important than freedom of the press and opted against publication.

But the Gallup Organization found little ambivalence when it asked the public questions reflecting on the press's role as watchdog over government. Fully 67 percent agreed that press criticism kept government officials from doing things that should not be done, while 54 percent agreed that news organizations and their activities safeguarded, rather than hurt, the democratic process.

This was not all the study discovered, however. Those conducting the research also found vast differences between those who supported the press and those who opposed it, and concluded, disturbingly, that press critics tended to be far better informed about the press and how it worked than those who support the media. Indeed, the study found, Americans could be divided into six distinct groups, or opinion clusters, when their responses to questions about the press were analyzed. Three groups support the press. Three are critical.

The first of these pro-press groups, comprising 21 percent of the study's entire sample, fell into a category the Gallup Organization labeled the "Reflexives." The Reflexives were the least likely to see any problems at all with the press; while all the other groups found at least two things to criticize about press performance, the Reflexives had but one. They found the press too invasive. Otherwise, they saw the press as accurate, fair, independent, professional, interested.

The discovery of this group would seem to be reassuring. But it is not. For the researchers found Reflexive supporters "limited not so much in the degree of their support, but in the quality of that support." Reflexives, they found, were less involved with the news media than any other group. Disproportionately likely to be women, black, and not to have gone much beyond grade school, Reflexives were seen as essentially working- and lower-middle-class New Deal Democrats. They are also the least informed. Though most watch television, few spend much time watching television news; one in four do not read newspapers. Reflexives, it is clear, are uncritical and uninvolved. They are also, the pollsters concluded, unlikely to offer the press much support in time of trouble.

The "Empathetic" supporters, who constitute 26 percent, or just over one-fourth, of the entire population, generally view the press favorably, approve of its practice of criticizing political leaders, and give it high marks for believability. But Empathetics, who tend to be college-educated, liberal women, more than any other group find the press influenceable and believe the media to be less independent than they could or should be.

The group Gallup labels the "Ambivalents" most closely mirrors the view held by the public at large. Comprising 23 percent of the poll sample, the Ambivalents have no problems with either the character or the consequences of the press and its activities. But they have many reservations about press practices, finding the media to be invasive, frequently one-sided in their coverage, often negative in their approach to the news, and easily influenced by various parts of the American power structure from government to big business. Likely to be women, working class, and high-school educated, Ambivalents fall slightly below the national average when it comes to news consumption and understanding of how the press works.[12]

The media's opponents are also divided into three parts. The biggest cluster among those holding basically negative views of the press is that dubbed the "Main Street Critics," which accounts for 15 percent of the population. Main Streeters criticize the press in three of four areas, questioning its independence, its performance, and its consequences. Disproportionately white, Protestant, and likely to live in small-town America, Main Streeters tend to describe themselves as conservative or strongly conservative, to vote Republican, to approve of President Reagan's performance in office. They tend, more than any other group, to see the media as liberal, biased, intrusive, negative, and uncaring. They watch, listen to, and read more news than the majority of Americans and they tend to know more about the press than the members of any of the positive clusters. According to the Gallup Organization, one American in five talks about journalists or the press; among Main Streeters, the ratio is one in three.

Following just behind the Main Streeters in size on the negative side is the cluster composed of what the researchers call the "Embittered Critics"; it is the second largest antimedia cluster and includes 10 percent of the population at large. The Embittered fail the media on every test of performance and are the only Americans who persist in perceiving the press as immoral and unprofessional; 80 percent, in fact, believe that the press harms democracy. But unlike the other negative clusters, the Embittered, who tend to be disproportionately nonwhite, uneducated, and over fifty, tend, too, to be the least involved and least knowledgeable about the press. They are not only alienated from the media, the survey found, but from just about every other institution as well.[13]

Though smallest in size, the cluster called the "Vociferous Critics" seems the most interesting and important group of all. Comprising only

5 percent of the population, the Vociferous share some views with both the Main Streeters and the Embittered Critics. They agree with the former that the press is influenced by special interests; they agree with the latter that the media harm democracy. But the Vociferous hold at least one opinion that is uniquely their own: they believe that the media are independent of the power structure, uninfluenced by the federal government.

What makes their attitude so interesting is the fact that the Vociferous are more involved with the media than any other group. The Vociferous read newsmagazines more than members of any other group, watch more television news, pay more attention to such influential publications as *The New York Times* and *The Wall Street Journal*. They are also more aggressive. Most Americans never get sufficiently exercised by what they see, read, or hear to sit down and write letters to newspapers, magazines, or television stations. Most likely to be professionals, to be educated, and to live in the urbanized East, the Vociferous tend not only to write letters to editors but actually to mail them. They are the ones who are most vocal in their criticism of the press. And because they tend to be informed, articulate, and influential, they are the ones most likely to make their voices heard and their opinions felt. They are, in short, the ones most likely to tell the press that it is out of step and to inform it that it is suffering from a crisis of credibility. And, as the media's own response has shown, they are the ones most likely to make the media believe that what they are telling them is true.[14]

The discovery and identification of the Vociferous Critics helps explain what the pollsters call "the other credibility gap," the belief by the press that the public disapproves of it. Surveys conducted during the past few years have found that as many as six out of every ten reporters consider what they see as the credibility gap as being quite serious. Indeed, despite a number of surveys showing the public to be rather well disposed toward the media, the Gallup Organization reported that it constantly heard newspeople saying that they felt that the public disliked and distrusted them.

This feeling is not beyond explanation. According to the Gallup Organization's research, a few surveys have found declining public confidence in the press. Gallup's own Times Mirror survey, which must, at least until someone polls an even larger sample, stand as the definitive study of the subject, does document some serious public reservations about press performance. Gallup even wonders if newspeople, believing that no one should like the watchdog, might feel better if they sense some public disapproval and enjoy being outsiders.

But, insists the report of the Times Mirror study, "the public does not disapprove. The press is popular with the majority of the American people. The press overstates its image problem."[15]

Why? Possibly because of the criticism of the Vociferous, the report suggests. The Vociferous may comprise only a tiny fraction of the population, but the members of this cluster are generally well positioned, well connected, well informed, and well exercised in their criticism. Because of their positions, they are more than twice as likely as members of other groups to be mentioned in the press. They are thus more likely than members of those groups to be heeded—both by the press and the public—when they voice their criticism of the media. "It isn't the quantitative dimension of opposition so much as the qualitative dimension," says the Gallup Organization in its report for Times Mirror. The press, it says, hears more disapproval than really exists for the simple reason that the opponents are louder than the proponents. Indeed, says the report, it is the loudest opinions, as opposed to public opinion, that have convinced newspeople that there is a crisis. That there is opposition out there in reader-, listener-, and viewer-land is undeniable. It is the extent of the opposition that is being exaggerated. "The opposition," the report concludes, "is still an insurgency, not a rebellion."[16]

This does not mean, though, that it should not be taken seriously. The public may feel favorably toward the press. But this does not mean that Americans may not, on occasion, feel that the media have gone too far or take some delight in seeing the press put in its place. This, according to Jody Powell, who served as President Carter's press secretary, is exactly what happened when President Reagan decided to keep the press away from the U.S. military operation in Grenada. For the public's reaction to the press's exclusion from the action was far more than the usual "shoot the messenger" syndrome. Instead, said Powell, it sprang in part from the ghoulish way the press handled the terrorist bombing of the U.S. Marine barracks in Beirut several months earlier. On that occasion, the media, television in particular, staked out the homes of families awaiting word on whether their husbands, sons, brothers were alive or dead, and, in one exercise in egregious bad taste, actually showed a Marine officer stepping out of a car and ringing a doorbell to bring someone the dreaded news.

Many members of the public complained about such coverage at the time, accusing the press of insensitivity. So many were understandably undisturbed when the media attempting to cover the Grenada invasion found themselves confined to quarters on Barbados. "The press was a clear loser in the fight with the Administration over Grenada," Powell wrote in a book inspired by his experiences in Washington. "It lost in the only court in which such matters will eventually be decided—the court of public opinion. In the immediate aftermath of Grenada, it was sometimes difficult to tell which the American people enjoyed more, seeing the President kick hell out of the Cubans or the press."[17]

But—and this is the message that comes clearly through the Times Mirror study—despite their occasional satisfaction is seeing the press slapped down, Americans as a whole do not want to see the media muzzled. They may get annoyed by the media's messages, some of which convey information they would just as soon not hear. They may get upset over the media's excesses, some of which are as inexcusable as they are avoidable. They might get frightened by the media's power and their perception of its influence over their lives.

But they believe, on the whole, that the surveillance of the press makes public officials perform their jobs better, rather than preventing them from performing at all. And they believe that the news media help keep democracy alive by providing them with the information they need to evaluate the performance of their public officials.

Their attitude is encouraging. The great French existentialist Albert Camus once wrote that "freedom of the press is perhaps the freedom that has suffered the most from the gradual degradation of the idea of liberty."[18] No one, reviewing the efforts of the Reagan Administration, the radical right, big business, or any of several other special interest groups, can deny that attempts, some more successful than others, are currently being made to degrade the idea of liberty and to restrict the ability of Americans to learn about the activities of and exercise control over those who claim to act in their names. No one can deny that attempts, some more subtle than others, are currently being made to limit the freedom of the press, erode the public's right to know, and keep America uninformed.

No one can deny, either, that the press has come in for its share of criticism, been subjected to its share of attacks, particularly from the Vociferous Critics. These attacks have taken their toll. Some newspapers and magazines, including some major ones, have moved perceptibly to the right. Whether this shift is out of fear, changing philosophy, or the simple desire to maintain access to those currently occupying the White House and running the government is hard to tell. *New York Times* readers and staffers both agree that that newspaper is more politically conservative today than it was a decade ago. Readers and staffers of *Time* magazine say the same thing of that publication. *The New Republic,* once a beacon of Walter Lippmanesque liberalism, has not swung rightward to the point that it can share a political bed with the avowedly conservative *National*

*Review,* but it has moved noticeably to the right in recent years. Many other publications worry about what they see as a rising tide of criticism.

They have reason to worry, for many of the criticisms leveled against the news media are well founded. The press is not perfect. It has made mistakes. It continues to make mistakes and will make more in the future.

Oddly, though, the American public seems to understand this better than some members of the media. For as the Times Mirror study so definitively demonstrates, Americans, by and large, like the press and stand ready to take its side in most, if not all, of its quarrels with a government that would like to restrict it. They are aware that the press has its faults, but they clearly feel that its strong points cancel out at least some of these flaws. They would like the press to improve its performance. But they are clearly willing to live with it until it does.

The American public's response to the Times Mirror survey is reassuring. It shows that Americans, to a greater extent than those who frequently purport to speak for them, understand that the press has its faults. But it also shows that despite these faults, most Americans would rather have even flawed news media than none at all. It does not mean that the press cannot do better or that it should not try. But it does mean that the media have more support than they think they do—and that they can get even more if they heed public opinion and try not to reflect it, but to give the public the information from which it can form its opinion.

# Chapter Thirteen

# Warding Off the Chill

The only thing necessary for the triumph of evil is
for good men to do nothing.

EDMUND BURKE,
letter to William Smith, 1795

Burke's often-used line is appropriate. Evil is not about to triumph, but it could. The nation's newspapers are not about to be shut down. The United States is a long way from the situation that prevails in some Central and South American countries that forces papers to appear with blank spaces where censored stories would have run. The government is not about to take over American television stations and replace newscasters like Dan Rather, Tom Brokaw, and Peter Jennings with federal employees who will offer viewers only the official government line *à la* Radio Moscow. The government is not about to license journalists—and keep them in line by threats of not renewing their licenses. Congress is not about to start the process of repealing the First Amendment.

But this does not mean that there are not people in the United States who would like to do all of these things. Nor does it mean that there are not people in the United States, from the White House on down to the man in the street, who would like to place some fairly severe restrictions on what the news media can do or publish or persuade them to publish or broadcast only what they want the public to read or hear. For the fact is that even if the press is regarded favorably by a majority of Americans, it is under attack by a vocal, influential, and powerful segment of the population, and the object of this war is nothing less than its subjugation to the will and beliefs of this group. And the fact is, too, that unless the press begins to fight back, it could find its freedom, and indeed, its very survival as a key American institution threatened. Jesse Helms has not given up on his attempts to influence what is broadcast on television merely because he and his supporters failed in their attempt to purchase a controlling interest in CBS. The religious right has not abandoned its attempts to pressure the press to reflect what it insists, thus far without proof, to be the values held by a majority of Americans. The Administration has not foresworn its ambitions to weaken the Freedom of Information Act and to limit the ability of the press and through it, the American people, to learn what it and its agencies are doing.

The war against the press, in short, is not over. It is continuing, and it will continue. Presidents, regardless of their political outlooks, will continue to find the press an annoyance at best, an enemy at worst. They will continue, in various ways, to manipulate it for their own ends, and to restrict its ability to criticize or embarrass their administrations. Others will attempt, both subtly and not so subtly, to influence what the media publish or broadcast, and try to persuade the press to see things their way. Many, inspired by recent court rulings and the fear their actions inspire, will continue to file large-damage lawsuits against newspapers, magazines, and television stations whose reports offend them. Some will attempt to exert financial pressure on the press, persuading advertisers to withdraw their business or attempting takeovers.

The press cannot, as the Times Mirror study makes clear, expect much help in this war from its allies. Those who support the press are far less willing to fight than those who oppose it. The press's supporters so far seem unwilling to lend the media more than moral backing. They have thus far shown little stomach for taking to the barricades. The time is approaching, however, when they must.

Right now, though, the press is going to have to fight its own battle and defend itself against those who would restrict its activities and curb its ability to find and report the news. The press must gird itself for a long war, for while its foes are few compared with the U.S. population at large, they are formidable nonetheless.

How, though, can the press defend itself against its enemies? What strategy should it employ to assure not only its survival, but its continued vigor?

The best strategy, it would seem, would be to realize that the best defense is a good offense and to become more aggressive, not less, in its pursuit of news and information. But before the press can go on the offensive, it must put its own journalistic house in order and make sure that its flanks are protected. It can best do this by taking a long, hard look at itself, by recognizing its faults, and by taking some substantive steps to correct them.

One of the press's first actions, then, should be to realize what it is. It is not, to begin with, the government's official opposition, regardless of how it may in recent years have cast itself. In European parliamentary governments, the opposition exists for the sole function of opposing the government. Its job is to keep the government on its toes, to offer alternatives to whatever the government proposes, to serve as a check on its power and even, if one goes by the conduct of opposition parties in Britain, France, and Canada, to harass the government.

Opposition parties have a voter mandate to do what they do. The press, at least in the United States, does not. In fact, under the U.S. Constitution, the press has no mandate at all. The First Amendment does not charge the press with responsibility for learning and publishing stories about what is happening. It does not give the press the right to demand answers, either in its own name or in that of the people, from public officials from the President of the United States on down. It does not legally establish it as the Fourth Estate.

The First Amendment, in fact, does not really say much about the press at all. It does not say that it must be responsible, or fair, or honest. It does not impose upon public officials or private citizens an obligation to respond—honestly or otherwise—when a reporter asks a question or when a television reporter thrusts a microphone into someone's face. It does not require anyone to tell the press anything if they choose not to. All the First Amendment says is that the press must be free, which means that it is free to ask questions and to publish whatever it can learn.

Newsmen, a large number of whom obviously believe that the First Amendment does more, would do well to remember this. They would do well to remember that no one *has* to speak to them. The press may be the means by which the public learns what government is doing. But the press has no more legal right to demand information than any private citizen of the United States, no more than any religious, cultural, or political group.

Reporters would also do well to remember that they are journalists, not modern-day Diogeneses, living in tubs and searching, lantern in hand, for the truth. They would, in a word or two, be well advised to heed the view of journalist Georgie Anne Geyer, who says categorically that "journalism is *not* the 'search for truth.' " Geyer wisely proposes to leave that search to the world's philosophers, theologians, and poets, and assign journalists to a somewhat less abstract task. "Journalism is and must be the search for the little, relative truths that alone keep us sane in the world," she says. "It is the relentless search for what can be known, not for what cannot be known."[1]

Journalism is not the realm of philosophers; journalists are not the high priests of a religion aimed at making men free by making them aware.

"News," as veteran journalist Edwin Newman notes, "is a business, a competitive business. People go into it to make a living. News organizations exist to make profits."[2] Newsmen should heed Newman's blunt words and refrain from thinking of themselves as professional righters of wrongs; journalists are gatherers and disseminators of information.

Journalists might also do well to remember that they are not historians. Journalism can never produce the definitive story on a subject; journalists can never, at least not while reporting for the mass media, write the definitive account of any event. Journalists work under pressure, trying to learn what they can and present it coherently within a time frame shaped by such things as the amount of time it takes to print and distribute a newspaper, or the need to be ready to go on the air when the clocks in New York strike six. Journalism involves learning and telling as much of the story as possible in the time available to do so. It is and will remain a messy, essentially open-ended business. Every journalist must be constantly aware that the story he researches and writes so carefully is incomplete, and can be changed by those events that occur between the time he turns in his copy and the time the paper or magazine for which he works is printed. The best story can be outdated and incomplete less than a day after it is published. Not even television, despite its capacity to show events as they are happening, can get the whole story. It can get only as much of it as the camera can see or as will fit into the ninety seconds allotted to it in the evening news broadcast.

Journalism is not and never will be history. It is the raw material that historians, working at a more leisurely tempo and taking advantage of hindsight and a wider perspective than even the best journalist in the world can bring to his work, will use to write history.

Realizing this, recognizing that their words are not and should not be carved in stone, is something that all journalists need to do. Doing so should help reduce the arrogance that so many journalists so frequently display and give them a better perspective on their work. Recognition of this reality by the public is also important; it will help make it more realistic in its expectations of journalism.

Adjusting their attitudes, though, is only one of the things that journalists should do to help put the media's house in order. Journalists must also alter their behavior. A good place to start this process is with the recognition that the public's right to know is limited, both by law and by common sense. The public does have a right to know what its officials, elected or appointed, federal, state, or local, are doing in its name. It has a right to know why the President is committing Americans to fight a war, what the government is doing to safeguard the lives and property of its citizens abroad, how the government is spending the money it collects from its citizens. The public has a legitimate interest in knowing if the consumer products it buys are unsafe, if the government is allowing industries to bury toxic wastes where they can leach into water supplies; it has good reason for knowing if the politicians who seek its votes are honest and competent.

But there are things that the public has no "right" to know. However curious individual members of the public might be about the subject, they have no right, legal or otherwise, to know about the private lives of public officials and figures unless it can be demonstrated that such private activities somehow impinge upon the performance of public duties. The public does not have a right to know who is sleeping with whom; no individual is obligated, much less required by law, to explain to the press why his marriage failed, or to tell anyone but the Internal Revenue Service how much money he or she makes. The public may want to know such things, and many people, particularly in show business, obviously see no reason why they should not reveal them.

There is no reason why the press should not attempt to satisfy the public's curiosity and provide its readers and viewers with information that entertains, titillates, and excites. But there is no reason for those journalists or news organizations that do so to wrap themselves in the cloak of sanctity and maintain that by so doing they are performing a public service and upholding the public's right to know.

Nor is there any reason for journalists to assume that everything that happens is fair game for their pens or cameras; there are times when a sense of decency should make even the most morbidly curious turn away. One of those times occurred in the aftermath of the bombing of the U.S. Marine barracks in Beirut; there was no need, journalistic or historic, for the American news media, particularly television, to intrude upon the grief of ordinary people reeling from the impact of events they could not control. Walter Jacobson, who anchors the evening news at Chicago's WBBM-TV, was sufficiently upset after his station aired footage of a Marine officer arriving to tell a family that its son had been killed in the explosion to apologize to his viewers. "That film should not have been shown," he said. "It was inappropriate."[3]

Jacobson's apology struck a responsive chord within the broadcast news community, and many television news executives, some of whom had declined to show the footage in the first place, promised to display more sensitivity in the future. Their promise, though, was quickly forgotten when the space shuttle *Challenger* exploded shortly after launching in January 1986. Television and print journalists who had assembled at a

Concord, New Hampshire, school to record the reactions of students as their teacher went into space were quickly and wisely asked to leave. Newspeople were kept away from the woman's family. But this did not prevent the television cameras from lingering overly long on the mother of another *Challenger* crew member as she broke down and wept during a memorial service, and many members of the public resented it. "It's as if they think that we're all performers in a big soap opera," said one woman as she viewed the television coverage of the memorial service. "Couldn't they have the common courtesy to leave people alone once in a while? Does everything have to be public?"[4]

The woman's point is well made. The media might be just a bit more respected if they were a bit less invasive, if they respected people's privacy just a bit more. Journalists might also be a bit more respected if they displayed a bit more manners. Few things annoy people more, it seems, than the spectacle of journalists shouting at the President during news conferences . . . unless it is the spectacle of journalists asking him those questions in tones that convey hostility and disrespect. The reason is obvious. Even people who disagree with a President's politics tend to respect the office he holds. As the only U.S. official elected by all the people, Americans feel, he is entitled to be treated courteously.

The news media might also be a bit better regarded if they remembered to take themselves a little less seriously and hype themselves just a little less. News, after all, is often a readily available commodity; where major news events are concerned, it is harder not to get the news than it is to get it. News may indeed be hard to obtain when a scandal is brewing; then everyone involved tends to go to ground and avoid the media. But on most major stories, the situation is exactly the reverse, and the media are more likely to find themselves inundated by information, little of which is likely to be exclusive; what one television network knows, the others know, too.

So there is generally no need for news outlets, especially television, to act as if they know something that no one else does, or to hype their programs by offering easily obtained information as if it were the legendary pearl of great price. Some more sophisticated news consumers didn't know whether to laugh, cry, or simply shrug their shoulders when, in the wake of the terrorist attacks on airports in Rome and Vienna, NBC's Tom Brokaw heralded his network's coverage of an upcoming statement by the President by saying that it had "learned" that Reagan would impose stiff sanctions upon Libya. Brokaw's statement suggested that NBC had information that no one else had. In fact, government officials had been saying for at least twenty-four hours that that was what the President would do. The morning papers had already carried stories to that effect.

Television stations, in fact, would do well to review their whole approach to the news and try, to the extent that the nature of their medium makes this possible, to draw a clear line between journalism and show business. The network news organizations have already done so; though anyone can find something to criticize in any of them, anyone who spends any amount of time watching the nightly news programs on ABC, CBS, and NBC will have to concede that they are really very well done, that they are clearly reported and edited by people who know the difference between news and entertainment, and they are anchored by people who take the business of informing the public seriously.

But anyone who spends much time watching local television, even in New York, where it tends to be a little better done than it is elsewhere around the country, could easily get the impression that those involved do not really know that a line should be drawn, much less where to draw it. There, on-the-air personnel seem to be assembled like World War II movie bomber crews; each station has its obligatory women, Orientals, blacks, most of whom seem chosen for their ethnic characteristics, well-coiffed appearances, and pleasant voices rather than for any demonstrable understanding of journalism. Some of these people, in fact, are clearly little more than good sight readers, able to read a news story off a typescript or a set of cue cards without understanding anything about what it means. Some behave like comedians *manqué,* making jokes that are inappropriate, tasteless, and, worst of all, unfunny, when they should be concentrating on presenting the facts. Some obviously have so little interest in what they are reading that they cannot seem to take the trouble to learn to pronounce names like Gorbachev or Schevardnadze or words like *apartheid;* one Boston newscaster was apparently, and blissfully, unaware that there is no such thing as the ''Irish Catholic Church.''[5] More than a few seem to have trouble identifying the story on those occasions on which they go out to play journalist; many seem to feel that what the viewers really need to know is where they had to go or what they had to do in order to get the story, not the story itself. Their conduct makes people like Newman cringe. ''What worries me about television news . . . is not bias,'' Newman says. ''Where that does exist, it is a minor problem. What counts is the level of competence, the knowledge, the experience with which the news of the day is approached. Breeziness is not a substitute for those qualities. Hair, real or tacked on, is not a substitute. Smiles don't make up for the absence of judgment. Being told to have a good day, or a good night, or to 'Enjoy,' is less valuable than getting the information you need.''[6]

Newman's complaint about competence does not, however, apply only to electronic journalism. Problems of judgment, competence, and attitude plague all the American news media. Many newspapers, magazines, and broadcasters, in fact American journalism in general, tend to be crisis-oriented. The news media have become expert at mobilizing their man- and womanpower and covering events like airplane hijackings, disasters, and wars. But they demonstrate considerably less interest—and competence—when it comes to following up on these crises or identifying and explaining major trends. Every newspaper, magazine, and television network, for example, has taken at least one major look at the famine gripping Ethiopia and the Sudan and threatening other parts of sub-Saharan Africa. But few have looked at the underlying causes of the famine or examined the worsening population problems that will make famine a continuing presence in Africa for years to come.

American journalism also tends to be adversarial, even when an adversary approach is unnecessary. It tends, in too many cases, to assume the worst, to believe a priori, that the people upon whom it focuses are crooked rather than incompetent. It tends, in a disturbing number of cases, to let careerism or the desire to build circulation or audiences influence its handling of the news. "The greatest danger today is not the ideological predisposition of reporters, as many believed during the Viet Nam War, but rampant careerism," says Geyer. ". . . A lot of the younger journalists have grasped the popular image of journalism in this new age and are in it for the celebrity, the money and the power."[7]

Careerism is undoubtedly dangerous to the future of the U.S. press. But so, Geyer believes, is adversariness. "We in the press are in considerable danger of removing ourselves from society, like some group of self-righteous monks," says she. "And if we remove ourselves from society, as some kind of arbiter or judge, believe me, society will remove itself from us."[8]

Adversariness is not the only attitude, however, that can cost the press unnecessary grief in its relationship with the public. Arrogance can make the media even more enemies. And nowhere does the press display its arrogance more than when it is called upon to correct a mistake. Some publications have long refused to acknowledge errors; the most they have been willing to do is correct their mistakes in subsequent stories. This practice, and the practice on the part of many newspapers of printing corrections in the most obscure of places, has long infuriated the public, many of whose members know that even the Pope is considered infallible only when speaking ex cathedra on matters of religion and wonder why the press must assume that it is even more infallible.

Fortunately, many of the media are becoming more open about acknowledging errors. *The Louisville Courier-Journal* runs its admissions of error on the front page of its local news section under a head reading, "Beg Your Pardon." Its sister paper, the *Louisville Times,* states simply, "We were wrong." Both the *Charlotte Observer,* as well as *The Miami Herald,* regularly mail out questionnaires to people mentioned in certain news stories to ask whether they feel they were treated fairly and accurately. Some papers go out of their way to make good when they make errors. The *Los Angeles Times* learned in April 1983 that it had seriously misrepresented the size of cost overruns on Lockheed Corporation's C-5B military transport aircraft; its corrective story was twice the length of the original, erroneous piece. CBS devotes time at the end of each of its "60 Minutes" broadcasts to letters from viewers, many of whom point out errors in or take strong issue with previous programs.[9] A great many U.S. newspapers have appointed ombudsmen, or "reader representatives," to investigate reader complaints and, if necessary, to correct errors.

Admitting errors and correcting them will go a long way toward winning the support of the American people and help the news media to safeguard their flanks and protect their rear areas. Taking other steps, such as being less invasive and respecting individual privacy, and checking out controversial stories more carefully will also help the press to cement its relations with the American people. And these relations must be cemented, for the media must have the support of the public as they wage their own war against those who would stifle them.

For the media must do battle with its besiegers. They cannot win them over by attempting to appease them.

What, then, should the media do? They should, obviously, continue to do what they do best. They should report the news accurately, fairly, responsibly. And they should realize, as they do so, that their attackers may be no more powerful than they, the media, make them out to be. Its grandiose-sounding name to the contrary notwithstanding, the Reverend Mr. Falwell's erstwhile Moral Majority has never shown that it can, in fact, speak for the majority of Americans. Nor, despite his visibility or the vigor of his attacks, does Senator Jesse Helms have a huge following across the United States. He is, for all his power, essentially a man whose appeal is limited to like-minded conservatives, not the leader of a national movement to rewrite the Constitution and curb the power of the press.

The press should not allow itself to be intimidated by the vociferous right. Nor should it permit itself to be panicked by the rising tide of libel actions. Libel actions are costly to fight; the threat of a libel action should make any editor think twice about any story he plans to publish. But the possibility of a libel suit should not deter any editor worth his blue pencil and green eyeshade from publishing a story he knows to be true. Indeed, defying those who threaten such suits and defending themselves vigorously against such suits as are filed is something the media must do if they are to remain free. Avoiding libel suits by avoiding controversy plays right into the hands of those who seek to silence the press. They do not want to go to court, either; they hope to accomplish their aims without doing so.

They should not be allowed to. The media can protect themselves against libel judgments by increasing the care with which they research, report, and present their stories. Truth, after all, remains an absolute defense against a charge of libel.

But the media can also protect themselves against libel suits by aggressively pursuing those stories that are worth pursuing. Knowing that any libel actions will be resisted vigorously will discourage all but the most determined of plaintiffs from suing. Defendants, after all, are not the only ones who must pay hefty lawyers' fees in court cases.

The media must also fight fiercely against any attempts to limit the public's—and by extension, their own—access to information. There is no reason why the news media cannot lobby against attempts to weaken the Freedom of Information Act, every reason why they should campaign for improvements in the law. Nor is there any reason why the media should hold back when it comes to pressing, at the state and local level, for so-called "sunshine laws," or measures designed to assure that government meetings and records are opened to the public and remain so.

But the most important thing the media must do if they are to remain free and unfettered and capable of bringing the public an uninterrupted flow of information, is recruit the public to their cause. The media must educate and inspire the public to the point that those who support a free press become just as vocal and just as willing to fight for one as those who would restrict or control the news media.

The press need engage in no special pleading to accomplish this. The public's interest and that of the press coincide on this point. For the American public needs a free press. It needs a free press so that it will know what its government is doing for it, to it, with it. It needs a free press so that it can keep track of public business. For, as noted lawyer Harold Cross once said, "Public business is the public's business. The people have the right to know. Freedom of information is their just heritage. Without that, citizens of a democracy have but changed their kings."[10]

Americans may, as their interest in Britain's royal family demonstrates, like kings, at least in the abstract. But none wants to be ruled by monarchs, and few want the freedoms guaranteed them by the Constitution to be eroded. That is why Americans of all political persuasions have a stake in joining to repel the attacks on the press. That is why all Americans must join in the fight. The battle to preserve a free press is nothing less than a campaign to preserve basic American liberties.

Americans can join with those who wish to curb the news media and help impose severe restrictions on the freedom of the print and electronic presses to gather and report the news. But they do so only at the risk of their own freedom as well, for whatever limits the media's ability to inform limits the public's right to know. And without knowledge, without knowing what their public officials are up to, without the information to decide who to put into office and who to keep out, the public is powerless.

The Constitution of the United States states that, in a republic, it is the people who are sovereign, not the government. The people can exercise their sovereignty only as long as they are informed. Without a free press, the American people will be uninformed and worse. Before long, they will not be free.

# Chapter Fourteen
# Fighting Back

It is a newspaper's duty to print the news and raise hell.

The Chicago *Times,* 1861

The above statement, often attributed to many great journalists, including William Allen White of Kansas's Emporia *Gazette,* was written in the days before anyone had even dreamed of, much less heard or seen, the electronic news media. But it applies to them as well. It applies to all the news media, to newspapers and magazines, to wire services, to radio and television.

And it applies today more than ever. For there are forces in the land that would, if they could, restrict the news media's ability not only to raise hell, but simply to report the news. And there are members of the news media—newspapers, magazines, broadcasters—that have been yielding to the pressure exerted by these forces and quietly abdicating some of their responsibilities as journalists and abandoning some of their rights as citizens. To a far greater extent than many of them are willing to admit, editors and publishers and news executives are avoiding the kinds of investigative stories that make headlines while making people angry. Some are turning their editorial pages into mixtures of bland mush, avoiding strong positions for fear of offending someone—readers, advertisers, rivals.

Some newspapers, eager to avoid jeopardizing their access to men in power, from the President on down, have foregone criticism in favor of cheerleading. Others, just as eager to avoid the expense of defending against lawsuits, have stopped running stories critical of anyone, from local politicians to big business. Radio and television broadcasters now bend over backward to assure that their programs meet some new standard of fairness, which increasingly means giving equal airtime to all points of view without making it clear to their listeners or viewers that not all viewpoints are of equal value.

The cause of their conduct is simple. All seek to assure their own survival by not making enemies.

The media's approach is understandable. Everyone may not need what novelist Kurt Vonnegut once called "unlimited amounts of uncritical love." But everyone, including, apparently, the news media, wants at least to be liked.

Unfortunately, this approach is ineffective; it simply won't work. Avoiding controversy and "blanding down" will not make a newspaper more popular; it will merely make it dull. Turning a television program into a carefully worded attempt to please all parties will not make it better; it will merely turn what could be a chance to convey some information into an exercise in ennui that will make viewers reach for their dials to see if they can find a good detective program or perhaps even some wrestling.

The press cannot win friends, much less respect, by trying not to stir up its critics. It can win friends and command respect only by doing what it does best. It can win the admiration of its supporters and the respect, albeit occasionally grudging, of its critics by reporting the news and by raising hell.

For the fact is that the press cannot please everyone. And the reality is that it should not try. How, then, should the press respond to those waging war against it? How should it fight back?

It should fight back, first, by realizing that its attackers are, in most cases, no more powerful than a timid press makes them out to be. It should fight back against its attackers by telling the truth about them, by determining just how large a segment of the population they truly represent and passing this information on to a public that may actually believe, for example, that the Moral Majority *really* represents 51 percent of the population.

The news media should fight back by being more aggressive, not less, in the defense of their rights. They should marshall their talents and resources to defend the Freedom of Information Act against those who would eviscerate it and battle long and hard against any attempts by government to deny the public information about what it is doing in the public's name. The media must never lose sight of the fact that in a democracy public business is, by definition, the public's business.

The media should fight back by being more aggressive, not less, in pursuit of the news. Newspapers, magazines, and broadcasters should increase their investigative reporting, exposing those situations that must be uncovered and allowing an informed public to decide what it will do about them once it knows. The media should be more aggressive, not less, in their questioning of public officials, remembering only that a pointed question can still be asked in a manner that shows respect for the office an individual holds, if not for the individual himself.

The media, finally, should fight back by sticking together. Newspapers, magazines, news services, broadcasters, may, indeed should, compete fiercely to get the news first and present it accurately. But they should form a united front when it comes to defending their rights and, by extension, those of the public. For any successful attack against one member of the media weakens every other. A lawsuit that scares a reporter on a small paper or television station into silence undermines the ability of every other member of the press to pursue his profession and to uncover and report the news.

Most important, the media must realize that, whether the American people like them or not, the nation needs them. We Americans cannot, in fact, survive without a free press.

Freedom of the press, like any other freedom, can be dangerous. A free press can publish unpleasant truths, it can print or air things that people would rather not read or hear, it can hold a mirror to the face of society and let Americans see themselves exactly as they are, showing them the good as well as the bad.

A free press can be a thorn in the side of politicians, an often unwelcome reminder to the public of its failures and flaws. It can be an annoyance. And it can be a guardian of the people's rights and liberties.

But whatever it is, a free press is essential to the survival of a democratic system. For without a free press to keep it informed, the public's other rights and freedoms can be eroded. The press has no power to indict or impeach, no power on its own to right wrongs, no power at all beyond that granted by its audience. It is not the press that is sovereign in a democracy; it is the people, and they can best protect and exercise their sovereignty if they are informed and in possession of the knowledge with which to carry on public debate and make decisions.

The press, the American news media, are far from perfect. No matter how they improve their performance, they will never achieve perfection. Run by humans, the media make mistakes and will continue to do so. But, run by humans, they are, and will continue to be, interested in the things that make human life better. America's news media would do well to remember that, the cries of their critics to the contrary notwithstanding, our country and our people need them. The American people would not merely find it difficult to live without the American press; they would find it impossible. The American press has a responsibility to the public. It must help keep Americans free by telling them the truth. It cannot discharge this duty by hunkering down and waiting until its attackers go away. It is time for the press to fight back.

# Source Notes

## Chapter 1—The Big Chill

1. *Oxford Dictionary of Quotations* (New York: Oxford University Press, 1981).
2. Anthony Lewis, "The Unlovable Press (1)," *The New York Times,* December 27, 1984.
3. "Journalism Under Fire," *Time,* December 12, 1983.
4. Ibid.
5. Ibid.
6. Ibid.
7. Ibid.
8. Personal observation.
9. Personal observation.
10. Personal observation.
11. Thomas Jefferson, letter to Edward Carrington, January 16, 1787.
12. Lewis, loc. cit.
13. *Time,* loc. cit.
14. Ibid.

## Chapter 2—The Necessary Evil

1. Personal communication.
2. Leonard W. Levy, *The Emergence of a Free Press* (New York: Oxford University Press, 1985), p. 4.
3. Ibid. p. 5.
4. *Virginia Bill of Rights.* June 12, 1776.
5. *Oxford Dictionary of Quotations* (New York: Oxford University Press, 1981).
6. *Encyclopedia Brittanica* (Chicago: Encyclopedia Brittanica Publishing Co., 1973), vol. 23, pp. 957–958.
7. Levy, p. 371.
8. Frank Luther Mott, *American Journalism—A History: 1690–1960* (New York: Macmillan, 1962), p. 82.
9. Eve Pell, *The Big Chill* (Boston: Beacon Press, 1984), p. 19.
10. *Pennsylvania Journal,* December 1776.
11. Charles H. Brown, *The Correspondents' War* (New York: Charles Scribner's Sons, 1967), pp. 32–129.
12. *Encyclopedia Brittanica,* vol. 15. p. 973.

## Chapter 3—A New Dimension

1. William L. Shirer, *Twentieth Century Journal—Volume 2: The Nightmare Years 1930–1940* (Boston: Little, Brown & Co., 1984), pp. 271–301.
2. Ibid. p. 309.
3. Ibid. p. 338.
4. J. Fred MacDonald, *Television and the Red Menace: The Video Road to Vietnam* (New York: Praeger. 1985), p. 2.

5. Ibid. p. 26.
6. Ibid. p. 26.
7. Ibid. p. 27.
8. *Broadcasting,* July 11, 1951. p. 44.
9. MacDonald, op. cit., p. 36.
10. "See It Now," CBS Television Network, March 9, 1954.
11. Frank Luther Mott, *American Journalism: A History: 1690–1960* (New York: Macmillan, 1962), p. 859.
12. Personal communication.
13. Greg Schneiders, "The 90-Second Handicap: Why TV Coverage of Legislation Falls Short." *Washington Journalism Review,* June 1985. p. 44.
14. Ibid.
15. "Journalism Under Fire," *Time,* December 12, 1983.
16. Ibid.

## Chapter 4—The Adversary Relationship

1. United Press International, August 5, 1964.
2. MacDonald, op. cit. p. 212.
3. "Face the Nation," August 3, 1964.
4. MacDonald, p. 216.
5. Personal communication.
6. Personal observation.
7. *Variety,* January 5, 1966. p. 101.
8. MacDonald, p. 236.
9. The New Republic, January 14, 1966.
10. MacDonald, p. 237.
11. Ibid., p. 239.
12. Joan Barthey, "Huntley and Brinkley 10 Years Later," *TV Guide,* July 1, 1967. p. 19.
13. MacDonald, p. 242.
14. Ibid. p. 244.
15. Stanley Karnow, *Vietnam: The War Nobody Won* (New York: Foreign Policy Association Headline Series, 1985), p. 19.

## Chapter 5—Watergate and the Court of Public Opinion

1. *Washington Post,* June 18, 1972.
2. Robert Woodward and Carl Bernstein, *All the President's Men* (New York: Simon & Schuster, 1974.), p. 22.
3. Ibid. p. 22.
4. *Washington Post,* June 20, 1972.
5. Woodward and Bernstein, op. cit. p. 44.
6. Ibid. pp. 49–51.
7. Ibid. pp. 69–70.
8. Ibid. p. 72.
9. *Washington Post,* September 17, 1972.
10. Woodward and Bernstein, pp. 82–90.
11. *Los Angeles Times,* October 5, 1972.
12. Woodward and Bernstein, pp. 131–134.
13. Ibid. pp. 115–129.
14. *Washington Post,* October 9, 1972.
15. *Time,* October 19, 1972.
16. Woodward and Bernstein, p. 165.
17. *New York Times,* October 18, 1972.

18. Woodward and Bernstein, pp. 170–181.
19. *New York Times,* October 27, 1972.
20. Woodward and Bernstein, pp. 197–198.
21. Ibid. pp. 201–204.
22. John J. Sirica, *To Set the Record Straight* (New York: Norton, 1979), pp. 63–64.
23. Ibid. p. 68.
24. Ibid. pp. 96–97.
25. Woodward and Bernstein, pp. 273–274.
26. *Los Angeles Times,* March 23, 1973.
27. *Washington Post,* April 19, 1973.
28. *New York Times,* April 19, 1973.
29. Marilyn A. Lashner, *The Chilling Effect in TV News: Intimidation by the Nixon White House* (New York: Praeger, 1984), p. 62.

## Chapter 6—Winners and Sinners

1. Anthony Smith, *Goodbye Gutenberg: The Newspaper Revolution of the 1980s* (New York: Oxford University Press, 1980), p. 179.
2. U.S. military sources, private communication.
3. Tom Wicker, "Not a Pseudo-Event," *New York Times,* July 2, 1985.
4. "Journalism Under Fire," *Time,* December 12, 1983.
5. Ibid.
6. Ibid.
7. Nicholas von Hoffman, "Pack of Fools," *The New Republic,* August 5, 1985.
8. Ibid.
9. *Time,* loc. cit.
10. *The New Republic,* loc. cit.

## Chapter 7—The Media Held Hostage

1. Personal communication.
2. ABC News, June 18, 1985.
3. *Washington Post,* June 19, 1985.
4. Fred Barnes, "Shiite Spin Control," *The New Republic,* July 15, and 22, 1985.
5. CBS News, June 24, 1985.
6. *The New Republic,* loc. cit.
7. Anthony Lewis, "Abroad at Home," *New York Times,* June 20, 1985.
8. Karen de Young, "At Wiesbaden, Waiting in the Wet," *Washington Post,* July 2, 1985.
9. "Terror and TV," *USA Today,* July 2, 1985.
10. Ibid.
11. Ibid.
12. Ibid.
13. Ibid.
14. Ibid.
15. Tom Shales, "America's Ordeal by Television," *Washington Post,* July 2, 1985.
16. Ibid.
17. Mary McGrory, "Made-for-TV Terrorism," *Washington Post,* July 2, 1985.
18. Ibid.
19. Ibid.
20. Stephen Klaidman, "TV's Collusive Role," *New York Times,* June 28, 1985.
21. Ibid.
22. CBS News, July 3, 1985.
23. Morton Dean, "TV's Duty to Cover Terror," *New York Times,* July 12, 1985.

## Chapter 8—A Tilt Toward the Left or a Poll to the Right

1. Tom Wicker, "Press and Patriotism," *New York Times,* March 3, 1985.
2. Albert R. Hunt, "Media Bias is in the Eye of the Beholder," *The Wall Street Journal,* July 23, 1985.
3. S. Robert Lichter and Stanley Rothman, "Media and Business Elites," *Public Opinion,* October/ November, 1981.
   Linda Lichter, S. Robert Lichter and Stanley Rothman, "The Once and Future Journalists," *Washington Journalism Review,* December 1982.
4. Herbert J. Gans, "Are U.S. Journalists Dangerously Liberal?" *Columbia Journalism Review,* November/December, 1985.
5. Ibid.
6. Ibid.
7. Ibid.
8. Ibid.
9. Michael J. Robinson and Margaret A. Sheehan, *Over the Wire and on TV.* (New York: Russell Sage Foundation. 1983), pp. 296–298.
10. Michael J. Robinson, "Jesse Helms Take Stock," *Washington Journalism Review,* April 1985.
11. Jody Powell, *The Other Side of the Story* (New York: William Morrow & Co., Inc., 1984), pp. 110–120.
12. "Viewpoint," ABC-TV, April 17, 1985.
13. Ibid.
14. Associated Press, February 28, 1986.
15. Eleanor Randolph, "White House Said to Curb Media," *Washington Post,* April 29, 1985.
16. Ibid.
17. Stratford P. Sherman, "The CBS Takeover Defense: It's Top-Rated," *Fortune,* May 13, 1985.
18. Bill Abrams and Jeanne Sadler, "CBS Asks FCC to Bar Turner Bid, Cites Issues of Finance and TV-News Content," *The Wall Street Journal,* June 3, 1985.
19. Personal communication.
20. Walter Guzzardi, Jr., "How Much Should Companies Talk?" *Fortune,* March 4, 1985.
21. "Taking AIM Again at Viet Nam," *Time,* July 1, 1985.
22. Anthony Lewis, "If the Press Were Tame," *New York Times,* June 28, 1985.
23. "Rebuttal to 'A Television History,' " *Washington Journalism Review,* June 1985.

## Chapter 9—A Case of Libel

1. *New York Times* v. *Sullivan.*
2. *"The Libel Law at Work,"* Newsweek, February 4, 1985.
3. *New York Times* v. *Sullivan.*
4. *Herbert* v. *Lando.*
5. Michael Massing, "The Libel Chill: How Cold is it Out There?" *Columbia Journalism Review,* May/June 1985.
6. Ibid.
7. Ibid.
8. Kenneth Bredemeir, "Panel Reinstates Libel Decision Against Post," *Washington Post,* April 10, 1985.
9. Walter V. Robinson, "Lakian's Self-Portrait and What Record Shows," *The Boston Globe,* August 18, 1982.
10. Thomas Palmer, "No Libel in 'Gist' of Lakian Story; Parts False, Defamatory Say Jurors," *The Boston Globe,* August 6, 1985.
11. Axel Madsen, *60 Minutes: The Power & the Politics of America's Most Popular TV News Show* (New York: Dodd, Mead & Co., 1984), pp. 194–195.
12. Karen Rothmeyer, "Westmoreland v. CBS," *Columbia Journalism Review,* May/June, 1985.

13. "Text of Statements on the End of Westmoreland's Libel Suit Against CBS," *New York Times,* Feb. 19, 1985.
14. Ibid.
15. Eleanor Randolph, "Four Words Felled Lawsuit Against CBS," *Washington Post,* February 28, 1985.
16. Herbert H. Denton, "Sharon Aims to Teach Time a Lesson," *Washington Post,* January 14, 1985.
17. "Verdict on the Massacre," *Time,* February 21, 1983.
18. *Time,* January 21, 1985.
19. "Absence of Malice," *Newsweek,* February 4, 1985.
20. Ibid.
21. Memo to *Time* Staff, January 29, 1985.
22. Ken Auletta, "A Case of Libel, A Lesson in Journalism," *New York Daily News,* January 13, 1985.
23. Richard M. Clurman, "Fallout From the Sharon Trial: Journalism Loses," *New York Times,* January 30, 1985.
24. Henry R. Kaufman, "Fallout From the Sharon Trial: Sharon Wins?" *New York Times,* January 30, 1985.
25. *Newsweek,* loc. cit.
26. Personal communication.

## Chapter 10—The Perils of Polling

1. Edwin Newman, "A Journalist's Responsibility," *The Responsibilities of Journalism,* ed. Robert Schmuhl. (Notre Dame, Indiana: University of Notre Dame Press, 1984), p. 26.
2. Ibid. p. 26.
3. Ibid. p. 26.

## Chapter 11—Shutting Off the Flow

1. Eve Pell, *The Big Chill* (Boston: Beacon Press, 1984), p. 31.
2. Anthony Marro, "When the Government Tells Lies," *Columbia Journalism Review,* March/April, 1985.
3. Pell, op. cit. p. 31.
4. Marilyn A. Lashner, *The Chilling Effect in TV News: Intimidation by The Nixon White House* (New York: Praeger, 1984), p. 46.
5. Pell, op. cit. p. 32.
6. Donna A. Demac, *Keeping America Uninformed: Government Secrecy in the 1980s* (New York: The Pilgrim Press, 1984.), pp. 28–29.
7. Ibid. p. 79.
8. Ibid. pp. 20–23.
9. *Washington Post,* March 19, 1982.
10. *New York Times,* January 14, 1983.
11. *New York Times,* October 20, 1983.
12. Pell, op. cit. p. 48.
13. Ibid. p. 49.
14. *New York Times,* Feb. 10, 1982.
15. Pell, op. cit. p. 57.
16. Demac, op. cit. p. 77.
17. Pell, op. cit. p. 87.
18. *Time,* November 7, 1983.

## Chapter 12—As Others See Us

1. *Editor and Publisher,* November 30, 1985.
2. Robert F. Erburu, foreword to *The People and The Press* (Los Angeles: Times Mirror, 1986).
3. *The People and the Press,* p. 7.
4. Ibid. p. 4.
5. Ibid. p. 13.
6. Ibid. p. 18.
7. Ibid. p. 19.
8. Ibid. p. 25.
9. Ibid. p. 27.
10. Ibid. p. 28.
11. Ibid. pp. 29–30.
12. Ibid. pp. 47–49.
13. Ibid. p. 50.
14. Ibid. p. 51.
15. Ibid. p. 59.
16. Ibid. p. 59.
17. Jody Powell, *The Other Side of the Story* (New York: William Morrow & Co., 1984), p. 238.
18. Albert Camus, *Resistance, Rebellion and Death* (New York: Vintage Books, 1979), p. 88.

## Chapter 13—Warding Off the Chill

1. Edwin Newman, "A Journalist's Responsibility," *The Responsibilities of Journalism,* ed., op. cit., p. 23.
2. Georgie Anne Geyer, "Journalists: The New Targets, the New Diplomats, the New Intermediary People," *Responsibilities of Journalism,* p. 72.
3. "Journalism Under Fire," *Time,* December 12, 1983.
4. Personal communication.
5. Personal observation.
6. Newman, loc. cit. pp. 37–38.
7. Geyer, loc. cit. p. 76.
8. Ibid. p. 77.
9. *Time,* loc. cit.
10. *The Responsibilities of Journalism,* preface by Robert Schmuhl. p. 45.

# Bibliography

Carl Bernstein and Robert Woodward. *All the President's Men*. New York: Simon & Schuster, 1974.

Charles H. Brown. *The Correspondents' War*. New York: Charles Scribner's Sons, 1967.

Donna A. Demac. *Keeping America Uninformed: Government Secrecy in the 1980s*. New York: The Pilgrim Press, 1984.

Tom Goldstein. *The News at Any Cost*. New York: Simon & Schuster, 1985.

David Halberstam. *The Powers That Be*. New York: Alfred A. Knopf, 1979.

Don Kowet. *A Matter of Honor: General William C. Westmoreland versus CBS*. New York: Macmillan, 1984.

Marilyn A. Lashner. *The Chilling Effect in TV News: Intimidation by the Nixon White House*. New York: Praeger, 1984.

Leonard W. Levy. *The Emergence of a Free Press*. New York: Oxford University Press, 1985.

Axel Madsen. *60 Minutes: The Power and the Politics of America's Most Popular TV News Show*. New York: Dodd, Mead & Co., 1984.

J. Fred MacDonald. *Television and the Red Menace: The Video Road to Vietnam*. New York: Praeger, 1985.

Frank Luther Mott. *American Journalism—A History: 1690–1960*. New York: Macmillan, 1962.

Eve Pell. *The Big Chill*. Boston: Beacon Press, 1984.

Jody Powell. *The Other Side of the Story*. New York: William Morrow & Co., Inc., 1984.

Robert Schmuhl, ed. *The Responsibilities of Journalism*. Notre Dame, Indiana: University of Notre Dame Press, 1984.

William L. Shirer. *20th Century Journey—The Nightmare Years: 1930–1940*. Boston: Little, Brown & Co., 1984.

John J. Sirica. *To Set the Record Straight*. New York: Norton, 1979.

Anthony Smith. *Goodbye Gutenberg: The Newspaper Revolution of the 1980s*. New York: Oxford University Press, 1980.

Tony Schwartz. *Media: The Second God*. New York: Random House, 1981.

Lloyd Tataryn. *The Pundits: Power, Politics & the Press*, Toronto: Deneau, 1985.

# Index

## A

ABC, 42, 91, 108, 159, 200
  personnel of, 4, 49, 52, 53, 60, 107, 111, 113–14, 162, 184
  programs of, 17, 44, 113, 122, 130, 133
Accuracy in Media. *See* AIM
Adams, John, 21
Administrative Procedure Act, 172
Africa, 5
  famine in, 49–50, 201
Agnew, Spiro, 8, 134, 167
Agronsky, Martin, 66
AIDS (acquired immune deficiency syndrome), 55–56
Aiken, George, 64
AIM (Accuracy in Media), 10, 131, 133–34, 145, 165
Alien and Sedition Acts, 21
Allen, Fred, 2
Allen, Ira, 131
"All My Children," 55
"Ambivalents," in study, 189
American Revolution, 26–27
American Society of Newspaper Editors, 176
*American Weekly Mercury,* 25
Anderson, Bonnie, 111
Anderson, Jack, 167, 168
Argentina, 6
Arlen, Michael, 57
Associated Press, 35, 38, 61, 185
*Atlanta Journal & Constitution,* 101
Auletta, Ken, 150, 151

## B

Bagdikian, Ben, 83
Baker, James, 127
Baker, Ray Stannard, 35
Baldwin, Alfred C., 76
Barker, Bernard, 73
Barnes, Fred, 110
Barr, Thomas D., 150
Bay of Pigs, 65

Bechtel Group, 133
Begin, Menachem, 148
Beirut hostage drama. *See* TWA Flight 847
Beirut Marine barracks bombing, 53, 191, 198
Belcher, Richard, 152
Bell, Griffin, 174
Bennett, James Gordon, 30
Berger, Marilyn, 77
Berle, Milton, 42
Bernstein, Carl, 2, 71–80, 84
Berri, Nabih, 108, 111, 114
Bishop, Jim, 96
Bly, Nellie (Elizabeth Cochran), 32
Boston *Evening Post,* 26
*Boston Gazette,* 25, 26
*Boston Globe,* 4, 11, 17–18, 61, 72, 139. *See also Lakian* v. *Boston Globe*
Boston *Morning Post,* 29
Boston *News-Letter,* 24–25
*Boston Post,* 34
Boston *Transcript,* 29
Bradlee, Ben, 54, 73, 78, 84, 98, 152
Brandeis, Louis, 86
Brennan, William, 137
Brinkley, David, 67, 68
Britain, 27, 179, 196. *See also* England; Great Britain.
  royal family of, 203–4
Broder, David, 167
Brokaw, Tom, 17, 162, 184, 194, 199
Brooker, William, 25
Broomfield *Enterprise,* 102
Brower, Brock, 67
Brown, Ben, 143–44
Bryant, William Jennings, 33
Buchanan, Pat, 126
Bulger, William, 10
Bunker, Ellsworth, 58
Bunyan, John, 34
Burch, Dean, 167
Burford, Ann Gorsuch. *See* Gorsuch, Ann.
Burger, Warren, 137, 138

Burke, Edmund, 194
Burnett, Carol, 138
Burt, Dan, 143, 144, 145
Bush, George, 112, 113, 125

C

Cable News Network, 114, 132
California, 94, 102, 160
Cambodia, 63, 65, 67, 99
"Camel News Caravan," 43, 49
Campbell, John, 24–25
Camus, Albert, 192
Canada, 196
Capitol Legal Foundation, 144
*Car Book, The* (National Highway
    Transportation Safety
    Administration), 169
Carswell, Richard, 86
Carter, Billy, 87, 88
Carter, Hodding, III, 121
Carter, Jimmy, 8, 87–88, 92, 93, 106,
    117, 126, 128, 159, 160, 174, 191
    administration of, 166
Casey, William, 175
Cave, Ray, 100, 149
CBS, 38, 42, 43, 72, 108, 110, 111,
    167, 200, 202
    alleged bias of, 126
    and Korean War, 45
    libel action against, 137, 139, 141–45,
        152, 184
    personnel of, 49, 52, 65, 66, 67, 114,
        162
    programs of, 17, 43, 44
    radio news of, 39–40, 45
    takeover attempts and, 122, 131–33,
        184–85, 194–95
    and Vote Profile Analysis, 159
"CBS Evening News," 17, 184
"CBS Morning News," 113
"CBS World News Roundup," 17
Censorship, 18, 187-88
Central America, 18, 50, 167
Chain, John, 10
*Challenger* tragedy, 198-99
Chancellor, John, 3, 4, 114, 184
Chapin, Dwight, 77–78, 79, 80, 82, 83
*Charlotte Observer,* 202

"Checkers Speech," 48
Chicago, 13, 31, 63
Chicago *Daily News,* 61
*Chicago Tribune,* 36, 61
Children, missing, 101–2
*Children in Bondage* (Markham), 35
*Chilling Effect, The* (Lashner), 167
"Christmas in Korea," 45
CIA (Central Intelligence Agency), 169,
    173, 174, 175
Cisneros, Evangelina, 33
Civiletti, Benjamin, 174
Civil rights movement, 12
Civil War, 22
Clark, Marsh, 61
Clawson, Kenneth, 77
Clay, Cassius, 31
Cleveland, Grover, 32
Clurman, Richard, 151
Cody, Edward, 5
Collingwood, Charles, 40
Colson, Charles W., 72, 83
*Columbia Journalism Review,* 124, 139,
    166
Columbia University's Graduate School
    of Journalism, 2, 123
Committee for the Reelection of the
    President. *See* CRP.
*Common Sense,* 26
Congress, 5, 8, 23, 84, 94, 153, 186
    coverage of, 51
    elections for, 162, 163
    and "Fairness Doctrine," 6
    and First Amendment, 20, 21, 194
    and FOIA, 171, 172–74, 176-77
    and World War I, 22
*Congressional Record,* 178
*Connecticut Gazette,* 25
Conservative Political Action Conference,
    9
Constitution (U.S.), 3, 196, 204. *See
    also* First Amendment; Fourteenth
    Amendment; Seventeenth
    Amendment.
Consumer Product Safety Commission,
    176
Conwell, Allyn, 109, 113
Cooke, Janet, 13, 97–98, 99
Corporation for Public Broadcasting, 134

Corry, John, 124
*Cosmopolitan,* 35
Costello, Frank, 44
Coughlin, Father, 41
Crane, Stephen, 33
Crile, George, 143
"Crisis in Korea," 45
Cronkite, Walter, 68
Crosby, William, 20
Cross, Harold, 203
Crowder, David, 139
CRP (Committee for the Reelection of
   the President), 71–76, 78, 82
Cuba, 33, 65, 168
Czolgosz, Leon F., 34

**D**

Daley, Richard, 64
Daly, Michael, 98, 99
d'Amato, Alfonse, 175
Dancy, John, 51
Day, Benjamin, 29–30
Dean, John, 82–83
Dean, Morton, 119
*Deciding What's News* (Gans), 127
Decker, Karl, 33
Declaration of Independence, 26
de Gaulle, Charles, 58
Democratic National Convention protests,
   63
*Denver Post,* 4, 34
Department of Energy, 177, 178
Dewey, Thomas, 36
Diederich, Bernard, 5
Dingell, John, 139
Dolan, Terry, 123
Donahue, Phil, 184
Donaldson, Sam, 53, 114, 130
Doran, Rosann, 102
"Douglas Edwards and the News," 43
Dumont (network), 42
Dunne, John Gregory, 67
Dusek, Ron, 138–39

**E**

*Editor and Publisher,* 4, 182
Ehrlichman, John, 77, 83, 167

Eisenhower, Dwight, 48, 171
Elections, 158–64
Electronic media, 36, 37–56
Elizabeth, Princess, 36
*El Paso Times,* 138–39
El Salvador, 50, 167
   White Paper on, 168–69
"Embittered," in study, 189, 190
"Empathetics," in study, 188–89
Emporia *Gazette,* 205
England, 18–19, 21, 26, 29. *See also*
   Britain; Great Britain.
EPA (Environmental Protection Agency),
   94–95, 177, 178
Erburu, Robert T., 182
Espionage Act, 22
Exit polls, 158, 161, 162, 164

**F**

"Face the Nation," 44, 60
"Fairness Doctrine," 6, 134
Fairness in Media, 122
Falkland Islands, 179
Falwell, Jerry, 6, 10, 165, 202
Faulkner, William, 87
FBI (Federal Bureau of Investigation),
   11, 72, 77, 82, 174, 175, 176
FCC (Federal Communications
   Commission), 6, 124, 132, 167. *See
   also* "Fairness Doctrine"
Federalist Party, 21
*Federal Register,* 178
Federal Trade Commission, 176
Fennell, Molly, 139
Ferraro, Geraldine, 123, 125
"Fireside Chats," 41
First Amendment, 5, 20, 21, 22, 23,
   151, 185, 194, 196
Fo, Dario, 178
FOIA (Freedom of Information Act), 11,
   170, 171–77, 178, 195, 203, 206
Ford, Gerald, 2, 86–87, 159, 174
*Fortune,* 124
Fourteenth Amendment, 23
Fox, Francis, 141
France, 29, 58, 196
Francis, Fred, 50
Frank, Reuven, 54

Frankel, Max, 4
Frankfurter, Felix, 86
Franklin, Benjamin, 25
Franklin, James, 25
Franklin, Marc, 11
Freedom of Information Act. *See* FOIA.
Freedom of speech, 19
Friendly, Fred W., 44, 45, 46
Fritchey, Clayton, 167
Fromson, Peter, 66
*Front Page, The* (play), 2
Fulbright, William, 122

## G

Gallup Organization, 155, 158, 182, 183, 185–91
Gans, Herbert, 124, 125, 127
Garrison, William Lloyd, 31
Gasch, Oliver, 140
Gemayel, Bashir, 147, 148
Gemayel family, 146, 147
George, King of England, 19
George, Phyllis, 113
*Georgia Gazette*, 26
Geyer, Georgie Anne, 196, 201
Gitlow, Benjamin, 23
Glass, Charles, 108
Goldwater, Barry, 60, 122
"Good Morning America," 17, 113
Gorbachev, Mikhail, 153, 200
Gorsuch, Ann, 94–95, 177
Gottehrer, Barry, 10
Gould, Jay, 32
Gould, Milton S., 149
Graham, Katherine, 84
Gray, L. Patrick, 82
Great Britain, 6. *See also* Britain; England.
"Great Debates," 48
Greeley, Horace, 29
Grenada, 3, 4, 5, 178–79, 191–92
Grunwald, Henry, 148n, 149, 150, 153, 179–80

## H

Haig, Alexander, 111, 171
Haldeman, H. R., 76, 77, 78, 79, 80, 83

Halevy, David, 148
Halloran, Richard, 170
Hamilton, Alexander, 27, 28
Hamilton, Andrew, 21
*Harpers*, 96
Harris, Benjamin, 24
Harris, Louis, 155, 156, 158
Hartman, David, 113
Hatch, Orrin, 175, 176
Haynsworth, Charles, 86
Hearst, William Randolph, 2, 33, 34, 95–96
Heatter, Gabriel, 38
Hecht, Ben, 2
Helms, Jesse, 6, 9, 122, 126, 131, 132, 133, 165, 184–85, 194–95, 202
Henry, William, III, 124
*Herbert* v. *Lando*, 137
Hersh, Seymour, 80
Hess, Stephen, 125
Heston, Charlton, 134
*His Girl Friday* (film), 2
Hitler, Adolf, 39, 40
Hogan, Paul, 139
Holmes, Oliver Wendell, 23
Housekeeping Statute, 171–72
House of Representatives, 59, 162, 174, 177
    Energy and Commerce Committee, 139–40
    Foreign Operations and Government Information Subcommittee, 172–73
    Judiciary Committee, 83
Hruska, Roman, 86
Humphrey, Hubert, 60
Hunt, Howard, 71, 72, 74, 76, 81, 82
Huntley, Chet, 67
"Huntley-Brinkley Report, The," 43

## I

Identities Intelligence Protection Act, 169
Information, addiction to, 17–18
Information flow, 165–80
Ingalls, Jeffrey, 115
"Inside Story," 133
Internal Revenue Service, 167, 198
International News Service, 35, 38

Iran, 89–90
Iran hostage crisis, 89, 91–93, 104–5, 109, 112, 114
Iron Curtain countries, 6
Irvine, Reed, 134, 145
Israel, 18, 104, 105, 109, 111, 142, 146–49, 150n
*Izvestia*, 18

## J

Jacobson, Walter, 198
James, King of England, 19
Japan, 43
Jefferson, Thomas, 7, 15, 21–22, 27–28, 167
Jennings, Peter, 4, 49, 162, 184, 194
"Jimmy's World," 97
John M. Olin Foundation, 144
Johnson, Lyndon, 8, 58–59, 60, 63, 64, 66, 67, 96, 128, 167, 172
Johnson Administration, 7–8, 63, 67
Johnston, James, 26
Jones, Christopher, 99
Jordan, Hamilton, 126
Journalism, 196–97
  adversarial, 201
Journalists, opinions of, 2–3
Joyce, Michael, 144
*Jungle, The* (Sinclair), 35
Justice Department, 74, 77, 82, 84, 174

## K

Kahan Commission (Israel), 146, 148, 149
Kaiser Aluminum & Chemical, 133
Kalmbach, Herbert W., 78, 79, 82, 83
Kaltenborn, H. V., 38, 39
*Kansas City Times*, 100
Kaufman, Henry R., 151
Kefauver, Estes, 44
Kennedy, Edward, 72
Kennedy, John F., 7, 48–49, 59, 65, 117, 128
Kent State tragedy, 64
Kerr, Jim, 138–39
Keyworth, Dr. George, 9–10, 122
Khomeini, Ayatollah Ruhollah, 89, 90

Kilpatrick, James, 167
King Broadcasting Company, 68
Kissinger, Henry, 64, 69, 91–92, 109–10, 116, 127, 170
Kladstrup, Don, 111
Klaidman, Stephen, 116
Kleindienst, Richard, 82, 83
Kohut, Andrew, 182
Koppel, Ted, 107, 184
Korean War, 45–46, 57, 59, 63
Kraft, Joseph, 167
Krogh, Egil, 83

## L

*Ladies' Morning Star*, 30
Lakian, John, 139, 140–41
*Lakian* v. *Boston Globe*, 140–41
Lance, Bert, 87–88
Landers, Ann, 184
Laos, 63, 67
Lashner, Marilyn, 167
Lavelle, Rita, 94, 95, 177
Laxalt, Paul, 6, 152
Lebanon, 142, 146. *See also* Beirut Marine barracks bombing; TWA Flight 847.
Leval, Pierre, 142, 145
Lewis, Alfred Henry, 33
Lewis, Anthony, 2, 10, 111, 171
Lewis, Fulton, 38, 39
Libel, 11, 20–21, 135–54, 187, 202–3
*Liberator*, 31
Libya, 88, 199
Lichter, Linda, 123
Lichter, S. Robert, 123
Lichters, the, 124, 125, 129
Liddy, G. Gordon, 73, 74, 79, 81, 82
*Life*, 35, 43, 67
Lincoln, Abraham, 7, 22
Lockheed Corporation, 202
London *Gazette*, 24
*Los Angeles Herald Examiner*, 4, 13
*Los Angeles Times*, 13, 68, 76, 80, 82, 84, 94, 186, 202
*Louisville Courier-Journal*, 202
*Louisville Times*, 202
Lovejoy, Rev. Elijah, 22
Lyon, Matthew, 21

# M

MacArthur, Charles, 2
MacArthur, Douglas, 45
McCarthy, Joseph, 36, 46–48, 122
*McClure's Magazine,* 35
McCord, James, 71, 72, 81, 82
MacDonald, J. Fred, 59
McDonald, Michael, 123–24
McGovern, George, 78
McGregor, Clark, 78, 79
McGrory, Mary, 115–16
Machiavelli, Niccolò, 19
McKinley, William, 7, 34
McNamara, Robert, 60
MacNeil, Robert, 100
Madison, James, 20, 23
Maffet, Charles K., 112
Magazines, 107. *See also*
    Newsmagazines.
Magruder, Jeb Stuart, 76, 79, 81, 82–83
"Main Streeters," in study, 189, 190
Malraux, André, 99
*Man,* 30
*Manchester Evening Herald,* 18
Mardian, Robert, 83
Markham, Edward, 35
Marro, Anthony, 166
Maryland *Gazette,* 25
Mason, George, 19–20
*Massachusetts Spy,* 26
Mather, Cotton, 25
Mather, Increase, 25
Maynard, Robert, 54
Media. *See also* Electronic media;
    Journalism; Press.
  adversariness in, 201
  careerism in, 201
  infallibility of, 201–2
  intimidation of, 202–3, 205–7
  liberal vs. conservative, 121–34
  opinions on, 182–93
  and TWA Flight 847, 106–20
Media stars, identification of, 183–84
Medicaid, 177
Meese, Edwin, III, 117, 166
"Meet the Press," 44, 49
Meiklejohn, Alexander, 137
*Mercantile Journal,* 29

*Mercury,* 27
Metcalf, Donald, 4, 5, 179
Metromedia network, 61
Mexican War, 22, 31, 64
Mexico, illegal immigration from, 101
*Miami Herald,* 202
*Minerva,* 28
Minneapolis *Saturday Press,* 23
Minter, Jim, 101
Mitchell, John, 73, 75, 76, 79, 82, 83
Mobil Oil, 123, 133
Mondale, Walter, 122, 123, 125, 161,
    171
Moorer, Thomas, 145
Moral Majority, 181, 202, 206
Moss, John, 171–72
*Mother Jones,* 96
Mowat, Farley, 178
Muckrakers, 34–35
Murdock, Rupert, 34
Murrow, Edward R., 36, 39, 40, 45, 46–
    47
Muskie, Edmund, 77
Mutual network, 60
*Myth of the Presidency, The* (Reedy), 96

# N

*Nation, The,* 67, 127
National Academy of Sciences, 101
National Center for Missing and
    Exploited Children, 102
National Conservative Foundation, 123
*National Enquirer,* 102, 138
National Highway Transportation Safety
    Administration, 166, 169, 177–78
National Opinion Research Center, 3
*National Review,* 127, 192–93
NBC, 4, 42, 108, 184, 200
  and elections, 159
  and Korean War, 45
  personnel of, 3, 50, 51, 54, 67, 68,
    110, 111, 114, 162, 175, 199
  programs of, 17, 43, 44, 113
"NBC Nightly News," 17, 107
*Near* v. *Minnesota,* 23
*Network* (film), 14
Newell, William, 30
*New England Courant,* 25

New Jersey *Gazette,* 27
"New journalism," 96, 98
Newman, Edwin, 68, 156, 162, 197, 200
*New Republic,* 67, 102, 192
    personnel of, 110
New Right, 144
*Newsday,* 72–73, 84
Newsmagazines, 147
Newspapers, 50, 107
    consolidation of, 12–13
    early, 12, 24–36
    functioning of, 147
    growth of, 28–29
    as monopolies, 6
    reading of, 16–17, 53
    and Watergate, 83
*Newsweek,* 3, 17, 35, 50, 61, 68, 147,
    185, 186
*New York,* 96
*New York American and Journal,* 34
New York *Argus,* 28
New York Associated Press, 31
New York City, 13, 31, 33
New York *Daily News,* 13, 18, 98, 150
*New Yorker, The,* 57, 96–97
New York *Journal,* 33–34
New York *Morning Herald,* 30
New York *Morning Journal,* 32
New York *Morning Post,* 29
*New York Post,* 13, 34, 56
New York *Sun,* 29 30
*New York Times, The,* 2, 3, 4, 6, 10, 13,
    16, 17, 50, 56, 61, 65, 68, 94, 99,
    116, 123, 145, 170, 175, 184, 186,
    190, 192
    and Pentagon Papers, 63, 187
    personnel of, 93, 111, 124, 171
    scandal at, 98–99
    and Watergate, 72, 73, 78–81, 83, 84
*New York Times* v. *Sullivan,* 136–37, 153
New York *Transcript,* 30
*New York Weekly Journal,* 20, 25
New York *World,* 32–33, 34
Ngo Dinh Diem, 58
Nguyen Cao Ky, 65
Nguyen Van Thieu, 65
Nixon, Richard, 8, 60, 63, 64, 65, 69,
    86, 167
    and "Great Debates," 48–49

and Watergate, 2, 70, 72, 73, 77, 80,
    83, 84, 173, 174
Nixon Administration, 8, 63, 67, 68, 69,
    167, 170
Northern Ireland, 98
Novak, Robert, 122
NSD 84 (National Security Directive 84),
    169–71
Nuclear Regulatory Commission, 177

## O

Oakland *Tribune,* 54
O'Brien, Larry, 70
*Observer, The,* 22
Odle, Robert, 76
Office of Management and Budget, 178
O'Neill, Michael, 18
"Open Hearing," 44

## P

Paine, Thomas, 1, 26–27
Palestine refugees massacre, 142, 146–47
Paley, William, 39
Parkinson, Kenneth, 83
Patterson, Eugene, 11
Pauley, Jane, 113
PBS (Public Broadcasting System), 123,
    133, 134
Pennsylvania Declaration of Rights, 19
*Pennsylvania Freeman,* 31
*Pennsylvania Gazette,* 25
*Pennsylvania Journal,* 26
*Pennsylvania Magazine,* 26
*Pennsylvanian,* 30
Penny papers, 28–29
Pentagon, 66, 104
Pentagon Papers, 63, 187
Philadelphia, 31
*Philadelphia Inquirer,* 152
Philbin, Philip, 159n
Phillips, David Graham, 35
Pike, Douglas, 134
*Pilgrim's Progress* (Bunyan), 34
Polls, 155–64
Porter, Herbert, 79, 81, 83
Powell, Jody, 191–92
*Pravda,* 18

*Present State of New English Affairs,*
    *The,* 24
Press. *See also* First Amendment; Media.
    distrust of, 6–14
    freedom of, 18–23, 27–28, 31, 187,
        207
    growth of, 23–24
    as liberal elite, 93, 95
    opinions on, 182–93
    weakening, 14–15
"Press Conference," 44
*Prince, The* (Machiavelli), 19
Privacy Act, 174
*Progressive,* 188
*Publick Occurrences Both Foreign and*
    *Domestick,* 24
Publitzer, Albert, 32
Pulitzer, Joseph, 2, 31–33
Pyle, Ernie, 36

### R

Radio, 17, 36, 37–42, 44, 45, 68
Radio-Television News Directors
    Association, 166
*Ramparts,* 96
Rather, Dan, 17, 49, 52, 118, 131, 162,
    167, 184, 194
Reagan, Ronald, 7, 8, 11, 106, 116,
        152, 153, 186, 189, 199
    election of, 159–61
    and EPA, 94
    and Grenada, 191
    and information flow, 166–68, 169,
        170, 171, 177
    and media bias, 6, 93, 95, 122, 123,
        125–26, 131
Reagan Administration, 3, 4, 11, 111,
        112, 117, 118, 130, 192
    and information flow, 165–69, 170,
        171, 174–77, 178–79
Reedy, George, 96
"Reflexives," in study, 188
Reston, James, 2, 167
Ribicoff, Abraham, 64
Rickover, Hyman, 87
Robertson, Pat, 6
Robinson, Michael J., 123, 125–26, 182
Robinson, Walter, 140, 141

Romanov, Nicholas, 64
Roosevelt, Franklin Delano (FDR), 7, 41
Roosevelt, Theodore, 34
Roper Poll, 129
Rostow, Eugene, 171
Rothman, Stanley, 122–25, 129
Rusher, William, 121, 122, 126, 127,
    129
Russert, Tim, 110
Ruth, Babe, 36

### S

*Sacramento Bee,* 152
Sadat, Anwar, 52
Safer, Morley, 66
San Francisco, 31, 33
San Francisco *Examiner,* 152
Santayana, George, 64
Sauter, Van Gordon, 142, 143
Scaife, Richard Mellon, 144
Schenck, Charles, 23
Schlafly, Phyllis, 122, 127
Schlesinger, Arthur, Jr., 122
Schmertz, Herbert, 123
Schneiders, Greg, 51
Schoenbrun, David, 65
Schorr, Daniel, 167
Schwartz, Tony, 37, 54
Sedam, J. Glenn, 76
Sedition Act, 22
"See It Now," 46
Segretti, Donald, 77–78, 79–80, 82, 83
Seligman, Dan, 124
Senate, 35, 59, 162, 174, 176
    censures McCarthy, 47–48
    Crime Investigating Committee, 44
Sevareid, Eric, 67
Seventeenth Amendment, 35
Shah of Iran, 89–91
Shakespeare, William, 8, 30
Shales, Tom, 108, 115
Sharon, Ariel, 139, 141, 142, 146–51,
    152
*Sharon* v. *Time,* 142, 145–51
Shaw, Bernard, 114–15
Shevardnadze, Eduard, 200
Shirer, William L., 39, 40
Shumway, Van, 73, 75

Silbert, Earl, 80–81, 82
Sinclair, Upton, 35
Sirica, John J., 80–81, 82
"60 Minutes," 17, 202
Sloan, Hugh, 75–76, 78–79, 81
Smith, Anthony, 90
Smith, Howard K., 60
Smith, William French, 174–75
Sofaer, Abraham, 142, 146, 149, 150
Sons of Liberty, 27
Sophocles, 11
South America, 18
*South Carolina Gazette,* 25–26, 27
Southeast Asia, 7. *See also* Vietnam
    War.
Southwick, Solomon, 27
Soviet Union, 18, 168
Spanish-American War, 2, 22, 33–34,
    64, 95–96
Sparrow, Herbert G., 145
Speakes, Larry, 9, 166, 178–79
Stahl, Lesley, 114
Stamp Act, 26
Stans, Maurice, 73, 79, 83
"Star Wars," 122
State Department, 104, 168
Steffens, Lincoln, 35
Stern, Carl, 175, 176
Stethem, Robert, 105, 113, 115
Stevenson, Adlai, 46, 122
St. Louis *Dispatch,* 32
St. Louis *Post,* 32
Stokes, Rose, 22
Storer Broadcasting, 61
Story, Francis, 29
*St. Petersburg Times,* 11
Strachan, Gordon, 78, 83
Strauss, Robert, 127
Sullivan, Ed, 42
"Sunshine laws," 203
Supreme Court (U.S.), 6, 23, 86, 173
    and libel, 11, 136–38, 153
Sussman, Barry, 73
Swayze, John Cameron, 43
Sylvester, Arthur, 66

## T

*Tampa Tribune,* 138, 139

Tarbell, Ida, 35
Tavoulareas, Peter, 139, 140
Tavoulareas, William, 139–40, 152
TBS (Turner Broadcasting System Inc.),
    132
Teach, Edward (Blackbeard), 25
Teenage suicides, 101
Television, 6, 12, 17, 36, 38, 197
    appraisal of, 117–18
    coverage of, 49–52
    documentaries on, 44
    and "Great Debates," 48–49
    growth of, 42–44
    influence of, 55–56
    and Korean War, 45
    local, 13, 52, 200
    and McCarthy, 46–47
    network, 13, 52, 159–62, 200
    and newsmen, 53–54
    panel discussions on, 44
    and TWA Flight 847, 106–20
    and Vietnam War, 62, 66–67
    and war, 60
    and Watergate, 83–84
Terrorism, 118–19
Testrake, John, 106, 108, 109, 115
Thatcher, Margaret, 52
Thomas, Isaiah, 26
Three Mile Island, 52
*Time,* 3, 4, 17, 35, 43, 50, 61, 68, 152,
    185, 186, 192
    personnel of, 5, 100, 124, 153, 179
    and *Sharon* v. *Time,* 139, 141, 142,
        146–51
    and Watergate, 77–81, 84
Times Mirror study, 182–93, 195
Timothy, Peter, 27
"Today," 17, 113
"Town Meeting of the Air," 44
*Toxic Substances Dilemma, The,* 178
Trout, Robert, 40
*True American,* 31
Truman, Harry, 36, 45, 59, 171
Tuckner, Howard, 68
Turner, Ted, 132, 133
*TV Guide,* 67, 143
TWA Flight 847, 104–20
"20/20," 17, 133
Tyler, Patrick, 139

## U

"Uncounted Enemy, The," 141–42, 144
United Press, 35, 38
United Press-Fox Movietone, 43
United Press International, 61, 131, 185
United States, 7, 43. *See also* American
    Revolution; Beirut Marine barracks
    bombing; Iran hostage crisis;
    Spanish-American War; TWA Flight
    847; Vietnam War.
  and Grenada, 3, 4, 5, 178–79, 191–92
  and Shah of Iran, 89–90
United Technologies, 123
University of Missouri, 2
U.S. Army Signal Corps, 45
*USA Today,* 143–44
U.S. Immigration and Naturalization
    Service, 168
*U.S. News and World Report,* 17
U.S. President, office of, 199

## V

Vanocur, Sander, 113–14
*Variety,* 42–43, 65
Velde, Harold, 46
Verne, Jules, 32
Videotape, 43
"Vietnam: A Television History," 133
"Viet Nam Perspective," 67
Vietnam War, 2, 8, 12, 57–69, 85, 134,
    142–45, 167
"Viewpoint," 122, 130
Virginia Bill of Rights, 19–20
"Vociferous," in study, 189–92
*Voie Royale, La (Royal Road, The)*
    (Malraux), 99
Voltaire, 170
von Hoffman, Nicholas, 102
Vonnegut, Kurt, 206

## W

WAGA-TV, 152
Waldron, Rev. Clarence, 22
Wallace, Chris, 114
Wallace, Mike, 67, 142–43, 184
*Wall Street Journal, The,* 16, 17, 102,
    123, 133, 152–53, 190

Walters, Barbara, 52, 184
Warren, Earl, 86
Washington, George, 27, 171
*Washington Journalism Review,* 51, 123
*Washington Post, The,* 16, 50, 56, 61,
    68, 94, 144, 146, 167, 186
  and information flow, 169–70
  and libel suit, 139–40, 152
  personnel of, 5, 54, 108, 115
  scandal at, 13, 97–98
  and Watergate, 2, 70–80, 81, 82, 84
Watergate, 2, 70–84, 173, 174
Watt, James, 130
WBBM-TV, 198
Webster, Noah, 28
Webster, William, 175
Welch, Joseph, 47
Wells, H. G., 48
Westmoreland, William, 139, 141–45,
    184
*Westmoreland* v. *CBS,* 142–45
Weyler, Valeriano, 33
*What Everyone Should Know about the
    Quality of Drinking Water,* 178
White, David Manning, 159n
White, Kevin, 141
White, William Allen, 205
White House Correspondents'
    Association, 130
*Wichita Eagle-Beacon,* 101
Wicker, Tom, 93, 167
Wieghart, James, 176
Will, George F., 116, 184
Wilson, Woodrow, 7
Winchell, Walter, 38–39
Winship, Thomas, 11, 85
Woodward, Robert, 2, 71–80, 84
World War I, 22
World War II, 35–36, 39–40, 57, 63

## Y

Yankelovitch, Skelly and Wright, 155,
    156, 158
"Yellow journalism," 33–34, 95–96

## Z

Zenger, John Peter, 1, 20, 25